With all good wishes to
Dr + Mrs John Bickley

S.S. Hinshaw

March 11, 1960

The Teacher Who Changed an Industry

The beloved professor at ease at Dayton, Ohio, 1959 (*Tamaska*).

THE TEACHER WHO CHANGED AN INDUSTRY

A BIOGRAPHY OF DR. SOLOMON S. HUEBNER OF THE UNIVERSITY OF PENNSYLVANIA

by Mildred F. Stone, C.L.U.

RICHARD D. IRWIN, INC.
1960 · HOMEWOOD, ILLINOIS

First Printing, February, 1960

Library of Congress Catalog Card Number: 60–8390

PRINTED IN THE UNITED STATES OF AMERICA

With this book the author pays tribute to Vassar College on the occasion of its centennial

The Author's Foreword

MORE than thirty years ago a young Vassar graduate attended her first life insurance sales meeting and heard a dynamic college professor speak about new concepts in life insurance selling. How little did she dream of what the coming years would hold in gigantic development of the life insurance industry, in the revolutionary effects of the professor's vision of professionally trained life insurance salesmen, and of her own close contact with that exciting era of history.

I was that college girl new to the life insurance business, and Dr. Solomon S. Huebner was the college professor. As Dr. Huebner had had the vision for the life insurance business, so he emerged as the leader in the great crusade, crystallizing the ideals of the industry. Each year at the C.L.U. conferment exercises when he presented the charge to the successful graduates, he stood as the symbol for the new profession. Each year a growing group of men and women, as new C.L.U.'s, repeated after him the solemn words:

> In all my relations with clients I agree to observe the following rule of professional conduct: I shall, in the light of all the circumstances surrounding my client, which I shall make every conscientious effort to ascertain and understand, give him that service which, had I been in the same circumstances, I would have applied to myself.

Following such a ceremony in 1958, it suddenly came to me that *somebody* should write Dr. Huebner's biography. Soon I decided to do it myself if he were agreeable, and would help. How quickly the focus changed from Dr. Huebner in life insurance to Dr. Huebner in the whole field of finance and insurance. His great variety of activities in connection with the New York Stock Exchange and in government service had been largely unknown to me, and I had not appreciated his leadership in the insurance world beyond my own life insurance limits.

It was thrilling to develop the picture. The whole insurance industry today honors Dr. Huebner. Students during a half century at the University of Pennsylvania recognize what his teaching has meant for them. Leaders in business education throughout the United States and in many countries abroad acknowledge his influence.

The Mutual Benefit Life Insurance Company, glad for the opportunity to honor Dr. Huebner, has made it possible for me to write this book. Its purpose is to bring enjoyment and inspiration to many friends and former students as well as to others who may never have the privilege of knowing Dr. Huebner personally. It also will contribute to work among international students in America and to the S. S. Huebner Foundation for Insurance Education to which royalties are being assigned.

The book aims to present Solomon Huebner, the man, with his personal interests and characteristics, as well as Dr. Huebner, the educator and public servant. In addition it includes the essence of Dr. Huebner's teaching in relation to security and produce exchange markets, the creative functions of life insurance and the human life value concept, professional standards in business, life conservation, and personal family finance.

Writing this story of a remarkable man has been a great privilege. A large part of the material included came from many days of personal interviews with Dr. Huebner. Insofar as possible his own vivid phraseology has been used in telling the story. Conversations and other unidentified personal material are reported practically verbatim from him, and from Mrs. Huebner and other members of his family who also were most generous in answering questions.

Many interviews with associates of Dr. Huebner yielded

much helpful information which the men preferred generally to have used without individual identification. These people, whom I thank most sincerely, included Dr. Harry J. Loman, Dr. Ralph H. Blanchard, Dr. C. M. Kahler, Mr. Maxwell L. Hoffman, Mr. Julian S. Myrick, Mr. Joseph H. Reese, Dr. Joseph H. Willits, Dr. Alfred H. Williams, Dr. C. Canby Balderston, Dr. T. Grier Miller, Dr. Willis J. Winn, Dr. Davis W. Gregg, Mr. Herbert C. Graebner, and Dr. Dan M. McGill. Dr. Roy F. Nichols and Dr. Leonidas Dodson were most helpful in providing material relating to the University of Pennsylvania.

I am deeply grateful to the Mutual Benefit Life and to its president, Mr. H. Bruce Palmer, for his personal interest in the project. Special assistance, which is gladly acknowledged, was given by Dr. Davis W. Gregg, who from the beginning encouraged me in the undertaking and who gave me most helpful creative criticism and suggestions as I worked on the manuscript. Readers will surely join me in thanking Mr. Howard D. Shaw who took many of the contemporary photographs included in the book. I want also to express publicly to Miss Claire Marra, my secretary, my appreciation for her capable and cheerful cooperation in the tedious labors of typing and retyping copy; and to Mrs. June D. Proulx my gratitude for valuable work in connection with Dr. Huebner's bibliography. Words fail me to thank both Dr. and Mrs. Huebner and their family who gave me every possible help with materials, suggestions, and careful checking of the manuscript.

MILDRED FAIRBANKS STONE

Newark, New Jersey
January, 1960

Dedicated to

my brothers

whom I have proudly encouraged

along professional paths in life insurance

DAVID G. STONE, F.S.A.

FRANKLIN A. STONE, JR., C.L.U., C.P.C.U.

Table of Contents

CHAPTER ONE

A Man for His Time

His mother always said that a two-hundred-acre farm was not big enough for him. He did his full share of the chores, and then had energy besides to go fishing or rabbit hunting in the woods, to climb the windmill or to walk the ridgepole of the barn. She never knew where she would find him.

When he grew to manhood he became a teacher, but one university campus and academic limits of study were too narrow a field. He traveled the world in his teaching and chose an expanding industry for his service.

As there is no power like that of an idea for which the time has come, so there is no story like that of a man who steps upon life's stage prepared to meet the need of the hour. Solomon Huebner was such a man for the great business and science of risk and risk bearing in the twentieth century.

In his veins ran the blood of pioneers, men and women who crossed the seas and the prairies to establish homes in the bountiful farmlands of Wisconsin. He could say with the Psalmist: "Yea, I have a goodly heritage," for his parents led him to a profound belief in God and commitment to the highest standards of personal integrity. They also taught him to work, and inspired him with confidence in the value and power of education.

The little boy listened eagerly to the stories of Indians who had made the arrowheads turned up by the plough in the field. The lad attentively heard his father discuss experiments in plant breeding and soil conservation. The college student eagerly opened his mind to new ideas about the course of history and the science of wealth. Always he wanted to learn. Always he wanted to relate what he learned to practical matters and the problems of people. He was no theorist. He wanted facts set out simply and in order so that he and others might understand them and make them useful.

Solomon Huebner grew up on a farm, but he could not stay there. The pull of the cities, which, at the turn of the century, was beginning to change the course of American life, drew him too. When the time came for him to choose the field for his work as a teacher it was a New York daily newspaper which gave him a flash of inspiration and guidance. The paper was full of news of the stock market and insurance affairs, but universities were not teaching those subjects along economic lines. The young man who believed that knowledge and understanding affected performance saw a need and an opportunity for service. There was generated within him a great desire to teach what young Americans would find it increasingly useful to know.

And so he became a teacher at the University of Pennsylvania, pioneering the first collegiate-level courses in the world in insurance from the economic point of view and in organized commodity and security exchange markets. Of necessity he became an author also, for in his early university days there was no study literature on these subjects. His first published volume was a collection of lectures which he edited after they had been presented to his classes at the University of Pennsylvania by men who were actually working in the leading forms of insurance. Within a decade he wrote four major textbooks—each a pioneer in its field: *Property Insurance*, *Life Insurance*, *Marine Insurance*, and *The Stock Market*. Each became a classic.

As student and teacher of maritime affairs, before World War I he was called to government work in a Congressional steamship investigation which led to the United States Shipping Act of 1916 and the formation of the United States Shipping Board. This was the first of many government assignments where he served as "expert to the committee" in official investigations or on advisory boards of various kinds. In these tasks he was still a teacher. Facts developed through the Congressional inquiries were organized and presented for the understanding of legislators. The power of education was demonstrated in the decisions reached.

Very early as a university professor Dr. Huebner began to take lecture engagements speaking to businessmen and the general public on subjects in his chosen field. Before 1929 he was greatly in demand as a speaker on the stock market. He gave no tips on how to make a fortune, but discussed the services of the stock market from the economic point of view. His exposition of the insurance functions of the organized commodity and security exchange markets gave workers in those fields a new understanding of their place in the business community. He helped men to think better of themselves and of their work.

More and more he was drawn to activity in the field of insurance, and particularly in the area of life insurance. There the time was indeed ripe for what he had to offer. As Dr. Huebner was beginning his teaching the life insurance business had just come through the searing exposures and scathing blasts of criticism of the Armstrong Investigation in New York State. The status of the life insurance salesman was at the lowest possible point. Yet the institution of life insurance had come into being to render a unique service—to meet a human need that could be met in no other way. Though companies and men had failed, the service must survive. Now purged, it could go on to new eras of benefit to families and business. Dr. Huebner, the teacher, saw what education could do for the public who needed life insurance, and for the men and women by whom its service was made available. He had confidence that people would use life insurance to a degree previously unknown when they recognized it as a tool to accomplish their purposes for family and business security. He was sure that a proud future awaited life insurance company sales representatives who would commit themselves to professional standards of service and through education prepare to help the buyers of life insurance use the instruments which the companies could provide.

It was a time when all business and industry was beginning to turn to the schoolroom for assistance. Business literature was developing in many fields, as Dr. Huebner was pioneering with his writings. The idea of specialized education for careers in business was being increasingly accepted. Work was getting under way in scientific time and motion studies in industry. If a professor with a stopwatch could help a bricklayer, it was easier to see how a student of economics would be useful to insurance men.

In the twentieth century business expansion created new risks which demanded insurance. New industries, new services, new financial conditions all nourished the need for new kinds of insurance protection, and for limits of coverage broader than past generations could have imagined. In life insurance, for instance, the salesman must do much more than read a rate for a thousand dollars of death benefit. He must be able to understand the problems of life and of business and to give the life insurance solution, even though it involved concepts of hundreds of thousands or millions of dollars.

Both buyers and sellers of life insurance needed to learn the possibilities of the expanding industry. Dr. Huebner was ready to teach. He was prepared to present far more than just the facts of life insurance operations. He had crystallized a new understanding of the essential foundation of life insurance. It gave to the industry a track to run on in expansion, to the buyer a basis for appraising his own use of the service, and to the salesman a creative concept for his underwriting. Dr. Huebner called this philosophy the human life value concept. It revolutionized thinking about life insurance ownership.

The idea is simply that a human life has an economic value that is made up of all the talents, skills, and experience of any individual. As property values can be appraised and capitalized, and protected against risk of loss, so can life values. That concept is the true economic basis of life insurance.

Inspired by this idea, and keenly aware of the needs of life insurance buyers and sellers, Dr. Huebner became a crusader for a double program of education.

As head of the Insurance Department of the University of Pennsylvania he worked through the regular channels of University courses. He taught evening school and University extension classes. He lectured to the general public, to professional groups from lawyers to veterinarians, to women's clubs, and everywhere to life insurance salesmen. His impression on the public was widespread, but difficult to measure.

With the life insurance men results were more tangible. His vision and vigorous promotion brought into being, in 1927, the American College of Life Underwriters. Its purpose is to establish certification of professionally qualified life insurance salesmen. There are now more than 7,900 Chartered Life Underwriters (using the designation C.L.U.) who have passed the five professional, collegiate-level examinations of the College and given evidence of satisfactory experience and ethical conduct in life underwriting. On the same pattern Dr. Huebner was a leader in developing the American Institute for Property and Liability Underwriters, organized in 1942. There are now over 2,500 Chartered Property and Casualty Underwriters who have earned the designation C.P.C.U.

These programs of education have raised the standards of insurance service to the American public. They have also created opportunities for thousands of men and women to find a profitable and satisfying vocation on a professional level. These people are happy in a calling which challenges their capacities and which merits social approbation.

Collegiate-level education must be provided through teachers with collegiate-level training. Here, too, Dr. Huebner has played a key role. He was himself a pioneer teacher of insurance at Columbia University as well as at the Wharton School. He trained other teachers at the University of Pennsylvania. Personally, and through the American College of Life Underwriters, he inspired the introduction of insurance courses in many other universities and colleges, both in this country and abroad.

In 1940 the life insurance business established the S. S. Huebner Foundation for Insurance Education to honor this teacher who had made such an immeasurable contribution to the industry. The Foundation program is administered at the University of Pennsylvania and has already helped some fifty men to acquire their doctorates and prepare for insurance teaching. Moreover, the Foundation has published eighteen different books which have been sold to the number of about 50,000 copies around the world.

Because of the many Oriental students at the Wharton School, Dr. Huebner's teaching has had a particularly important influence in Japan, and formerly also in China. His personal contacts with the Far East have been established not only through campus activities but also through two extensive lecture trips. The first was in 1927 when he continued around the world and lectured also in Germany before his return home. The last was at age seventy-six when he and Mrs. Huebner flew 40,000 miles, visiting universities and insurance organizations in Japan, the Philippines, Australia, and New Zealand with the sponsorship of the State Department of the United States.

While in Japan on this trip he was awarded the Third Order of the Sacred Treasure by the Emperor of Japan. This was a most unusual honor for a foreigner, and reflected the appreciation of the Japanese for his contribution to the insurance industry in their country.

In 1953, the autumn after he retired from teaching at the University of Pennsylvania, the National Board of Fire Underwriters sent Dr. and Mrs. Huebner on a goodwill trip to South America. They visited Brazil, Uruguay, Argentina, Chile, Peru, Colombia, and Ecuador in a little more than two months. Dr. Huebner lectured at universities and before insurance groups of various kinds, and they were lavishly entertained by gracious South American hosts.

As he tallies his score at the end of 1959, Dr. Huebner estimates that he has talked to over a million people in classes or lectures averaging better than one such session a day for fifty-three years. These engagements have been in every state of the Union except Nevada, and on five continents. This record is evidence of tremendous physical stamina.

Dr. Huebner has indeed been blessed with his generally vigorous good health and what his doctor calls his "farm reserve." But he has had two major health problems. The first was a devastating infection caused by tick bites in Yucatan, Mexico, in 1933. This resulted in crippling arthritis which disabled him completely for months and which has left him with permanent calcification of the spine. His ribs and back are rigid, which makes many normal movements difficult or impossible. But this has never interfered with his crusades for education.

The second health trouble, which would have conquered a man weaker in body and spirit, was a cancerous jaw, discovered in 1954. This was presumably the result of years of heavy smoking. Skillful medical treatment, in whose painful processes Dr. Huebner cooperated completely, have apparently

Dr. Huebner, professor emeritus, in his new office at the American College. Notice books and papers readily available for work and the talc specimen on the desk as a paperweight.

given a cure. During this ordeal also, Dr. Huebner pressed forward with all his educational programs. Few men have faced such difficulties with such courage and determination.

While building his programs and his organizations, Dr. Huebner has also built himself. He early determined that his life would be centered at the University of Pennsylvania, and many temptations did not deflect him from that purpose. His convictions about the essential value of insurance, and especially life insurance, have strengthened and deepened during the years. He believes in the principles of risk sharing and has an evangelistic zeal in imparting his ideas to others. He has confidence in the power of education, that if people know and understand they will act wisely. He seeks not to impose his judgment on others but to present facts and open men's eyes to truth so that they will voluntarily make sound judgments.

Through the years he has acquired habits and tastes which have become celebrated among his students and friends. The clenched fist and vigorous gestures during personal conversations as well as in the course of lectures are always remembered. The red necktie is a Huebner trademark. The rocking chair is part of the Huebner picture as often in his government office or at a hotel interview as at his University desk or in the study at home.

There is mutual pride in the Huebner family. Three daughters and a son regard him with deep affection and a little awe. He speaks with enthusiasm of their varied achievements. Mrs. Huebner is always his helpmeet, his companion in work and play. Though he has spent much time away from home, yet he feels that his wife and family are an integral part of his existence.

Solomon Huebner has been a teacher for a lifetime. He has had to be a fighter, often losing a battle, but never the war. His purposes have been unswerving and unselfish. He has not spared himself or his associates in pressing toward goals he believes important. He has been kind, honest, self-disciplined. He loves good company, good food, and good hard work. Travel is his delight.

He has accomplished more than seems possible for one mortal man, but through it all he has been supremely human. To some he is Sunny Sol; to others, The Father of Insurance Education or Mr. C.L.U. To thousands of men and women in the United States and around the world, who have listened to him in the academic classroom, on the lecture platform, and from behind the banquet or luncheon table, he is *the beloved professor*. It is his story which the following chapters unfold, the record of the teacher who changed an industry.

CHAPTER TWO

Badger State Boy

WHEN Frederick August and Wilhelmina Dicke Huebner looked into the face of their first-born son on March 6, 1882, they surely hoped that he would take his good place in the world. But their brightest dreams were not more rosy than the reality of the past seventy-five years. A scholar and a teacher they could have envisioned. But their son's part in giving important technical service to his nation during two world wars, in transforming a great business, and in influencing a major field of university training throughout America and abroad, would certainly have been beyond their view.

Godly folk, they named the baby Solomon, remembering the young king of Bible times who pleased the Lord by choosing to ask for wisdom above all gifts. They too set a high value on things of the mind and spirit. Love of freedom, desire for opportunity, ambition to achieve, and willingness to work hard—these characteristics were the colors repeated often in the pattern of family tradition.

Historically, the Huebner family tree is broken short. It begins abruptly in the stormy days of the Franco-Germanic wars, when armies were marching and countermarching across Alsace-Lorraine. In an abandoned house German soldiers found a baby boy—nicely dressed but with no shred of identification. Perhaps the baby smiled, perhaps he just appealed to the father-heart of a childless German soldier named Huebner, going home to the village of Memel in East Prussia. Whatever the cause, that young man took the child to his wife. They named him Ludwig and raised him lovingly as their son. Little today is known of him except that he received a good education, grew to manhood, married, and had a son named Frederick Wilhelm. That Frederick Huebner was educated on the collegiate level and became a forester by profession in a land which respected its forests and practiced scientific forestry. All over Europe there are woodlands where forest crops have been carefully planned for generations. The same acreage has produced continuously the timber for fuel and other commercial uses.

Frederick Wilhelm Huebner was also a shoemaker, for at that time every man was required to have a trade as well as a profession. He must know how to work with his hands for his family and his neighbors.

The early nineteenth century was a period of oppression and unrest in many European countries. The Hungarian leader was Louis Kossuth. He was a journalist who urged freedom of the press and abolition of all feudal privileges. His writings and his influence spread throughout Europe and had a large part in the political upheavals of the 1840's. Somehow freedom-loving Frederick Huebner came to know Kossuth. Subsequently his own espousal of democratic doctrines made him a marked man. He was arrested, imprisoned, and condemned to die. Then one night before the death sentence could be carried out, the prison door was opened and Frederick escaped. Under shadow of darkness he headed for the seacoast and an unknown fate. For all he knew pursuers might reach him after any turn of the road. But he arrived safely at Königsberg on the Baltic Sea and there found a sailing ship bound for New York. He said to himself, "If the captain is one of us I am safe, otherwise the dogs will find their prey." Fortunately the captain was sympathetic to the cause, smuggled Frederick aboard and hid him until they were safely on the wide Atlantic. In New York he was welcomed by many Germans who had left the oppressions of the Fatherland for the land of freedom and opportunity. Like so many of these emigrants Frederick Huebner carried with him talents, skills and character which greatly enriched the country of his adoption. Leaving New York, he pressed on to the western part of the old Northwest Territory. Since 1836 that had been Wisconsin Territory and had included Wisconsin, Minnesota, Iowa, and part of the Dakotas. He arrived just as Wisconsin was being separated as a state, and it was admitted to the Union in 1848.

Many Germans had settled north of Milwaukee along the western shores of Lake Michigan in Wisconsin. There Frederick Huebner purchased, at fifty cents an acre, a thousand acres near the lake port of Manitowoc. That is the area where Father Marquette landed, coming down from Canada in the early seventeenth century in his great trip of exploration of the Mississippi Valley. The people of Two Rivers still expect someday to find the keel of his boat buried in the mud of their harbor. In this wilderness country Frederick Huebner in 1847 had his choice of acreage which generally was richly wooded with white pine. Being a forester he knew that healthy trees meant good soil. Guided by the best trees, he picked his sections. Timbering gave him his start although dealing in real estate developed to be his main source of livelihood. His wife followed him safely from Germany. That ocean voyage, according to family tradition, took seventy days, as long as the famous passage of *The Mayflower* two hundred years earlier. Thus the Huebner family of America was begun.

Frederick Huebner had bought some of his property from a man of Lawrence County, New York, whom he met en route to the West. The balance was purchased from the United States Government, but it was in the country of the Winnebago Indians whose rights he also recognized. Like William Penn long before in Pennsylvania, he respected the Indians and had peaceful relations with them. He said the land was theirs first and he would not fight them for it. One of the provisions in a treaty which, according to family tradition, he helped make with the Indians was symbolic. It was agreed that when a white man and an Indian shot at the same deer and there was doubt as to who hit it first, always the Indian should have the right to the deer.

Although Frederick was condemned as a political revolutionist in Germany, he was still a conservatist and a religious man. When he arrived in Wisconsin he sought church fellowship. At first he met with a little group of Baptists who welcomed him gladly. For some time he worshipped with them and supported their work. When asked to join the church he refused because there were some features of their beliefs which he could not accept. The ensuing debates crystallized their differences and he left them with the observation, "If you are right in the strictness of your tenets, in heaven you won't be able to hear your own echo; there will be so few of you." Frederick became a Methodist, setting the course for future generations of Huebners.

While Frederick was still clearing his acres in the Wisconsin wilderness some time in 1851 or 1852, he was visited by Kossuth. The name of Kossuth Township next to Manitowoc Township reflects not only hero worship but the fact that the famous leader walked the forest trails in person. He talked long with Frederick about conditions in Europe and prospects in America. His advice to his young friend was "Stay here," but he returned to Europe, though he lived and died in exile from his beloved Hungary.

In 1850 Frederick August Huebner was born, the first white child whose birth was recorded in Manitowoc. His first words were in German, though he learned English too, and also some of the language of the Indians. His father's friendship for the Indians and respect for them was expressed in a plan which he fostered of exchange visits between Indian and white families. For a week at a time little Frederick August would go live with the Indians and an Indian boy would live with the Huebners. Frederick August learned to know the trees and plants of the forest. He grew skillful in trapping and hunting the woodland animals, and fishing the streams. He watched the Indian women grind corn, work the deerskins for clothes, do their weaving and make pottery.

The home which the little Indian lad visited was less different from his own bark house than from Wisconsin homes today. Meals were cooked over an open fire, in a black iron pot hanging from the fireplace crane, or in a three-legged skillet pushed over the coals. Venison and fresh fish were staples in their diet and corn meal cakes were baked for nearly every meal. But the white family also had meat, fresh and smoked, from their own hogs, eggs from their own chickens and yeast-raised bread and biscuits. The day's activities were largely timed by the sun. Parents and children got up early and went to bed soon after sundown. But they had candles of their own making and lamps which burned precious coal oil so that the evening meal could be lighted sometimes by more than the fire blazing on the hearth. The father could read his German Bible or study the treasured German works on forestry which he had in several fat volumes.

The little Indian visitor knew respect for the women in his own tribe. The Winnebagos were a high type socially though a primitive people. There was a sort of system of matriarchal inheritance among them. They were honest and never lied. He must have been interested, however, in the German home to recognize the respect paid to the mother, to overhear, though he could not understand, the frequent discussions between the parents on matters of history and philosophy. He probably felt his share of the maternal discipline too, for a grandson later said of this mother, "She was a devout Lutheran, strong-minded on matters of politics and religion, a real Trojan in family affairs. She was strong and healthy, outliving her husband by many years. When she died at age 92, the clock just stopped."

Frederick August's keen mind was stimulated early but he had little formal schooling. He learned his three R's from his parents and in occasional two-week school periods when an itinerant Methodist minister held classes in homes in the neighborhood. That schoolmaster was dedicated to the children and beholden to nobody. He came when he could, earning his livelihood by making chairs of rye straw and willow baskets from the trees in the swamps. That pedagogue has long since gone. New times have organized teachers and pupils, regimented them according to calendars and curricula, housed them in schools which are marvels of engineering and efficient planning. But Frederick's son says that the schoolmaster's willows still grow in the lowlands of what was the old Huebner farm a century ago.

Though farms were isolated, young Frederick August came to know pretty dark-haired Wilhelmina Dicke who was a seamstress for the best families in the neighboring town of Manitowoc. He had to walk or ride horseback seven or eight miles to cultivate her friendship, but it became increasingly precious to him. About 1874 they were married.

Wilhelmina's family had come to America from the Hamburg area in Germany and settled in Bremen, Ohio. The Dickes are still very numerous in that region and throughout Ohio, but Wilhelmina's father was a happy, adventurous fellow, and pressed his way further west, with his wife and three small children. Wilhelmina had been born in Bremen and she was then two years old when they moved to Sheboygan Falls, Wisconsin. There her father worked as a cooper, a maker of casks and barrels. The country was still new. What people could not make for themselves with simple tools, they had to get from back East. Wilhelmina's father wanted some sort of machinery for his cooperage works and went back to Ohio to buy it. There he died of pneumonia. Mrs. Dicke was thus left with a small son and two little girls, alone and far from her relatives. She was a purposeful and capable woman who resolved to stay and raise her family in the country their father had chosen for them. She was physically strong. Also she believed herself, and seemed to be, immune from the dread diseases of the day. Small pox and diphtheria were the scourge of every community. The horror of yellow fever came often. Cholera, traveling up the Mississippi River from New Orleans, had been known to wipe out a third of a town's population in a week. Mrs. Dicke made a living for her family by nursing, with some little help from her people in Ohio and with the co-operation of the children themselves. Wilhelmina and her sister both learned to sew as little girls and became accomplished dressmakers. This was a skill in much demand even in frontier towns, in the days before mass production had developed in the needle trades.

Frederick August's father approved his pretty and capable daughter-in-law. His son had proved himself as a farmer. So he gave the young couple two hundred acres of land and his blessing for their new life together. The early years brought prosperity on the farm but shadows and heartache in the home. One little daughter was born, but while she was still a baby Frederick August had black smallpox. At first it was not diagnosed. They did not isolate the sick man and the little girl played beside his bed. She also got the disease and died, though he recovered.

Another daughter was born. While still in infancy she developed typhoid fever and died. The ignorance of the so-called "doctors" in the little rural towns of that time was truly heartbreaking.

And so through the winter of 1881–82 Frederick August

Left, Solly Huebner, about two years old.

Above, Solly Huebner, about age six.

Left, Grandmother Dicke.

and Wilhelmina looked forward with hopes and fears to a new baby. Frederick's springtime flowers which he loved so well were beginning to bloom on the southern window sill—fragrant hyacinths and white calla lilies, scarlet and purple fuchsias with their drooping bells—when Wilhelmina had her third baby. Of course she stayed at home for the birth, in the familiar rooms, with sounds from the kitchen and the barn, and the comforting presence of her husband and capable mother.

The baby Solomon Huebner came to a home full of love. Parents, and nearby, two grandmothers, made him the apple of their eye. Many friends rejoiced with Frederick August and Wilhelmina in the son who was doubly precious because of the little sisters whom he had never seen. Two years later another son was born, Grover Gerhard, and the family was complete. This boy's second name was for a favorite brother-in-law. Grover was for Grover Cleveland, first elected to the presidency in 1884. That self-made man with his honesty and fearless energy in political affairs had caught the imagination of the idealistic Huebners. "The veto governor" of New York State appealed to them, and they shared the national excitement as they waited several days to hear the outcome of the closely contested presidential election. When their newspaper finally brought them the word, they were delighted.

Frederick August was a prosperous farmer. He had built a roomy wooden farmhouse with a cupola, topped with a lightning rod, and all painted dark brown. The house was flanked by big barns and outbuildings arranged to form a sheltered barnyard for the animals in winter. Unlike many farmers Father Huebner took time for flowers, for he had a way with them. His flowers and plants came from all over the world. Their bright blossoms in the flower beds around the house made an island of color in the midst of the green of his magnificent orchard and his golden fields. Other farmers in their wagons,

Huebner family farm showing father Huebner, little brother Grover, and Solly.

farm wives or ladies from town admired the sight as they traveled the dusty road past the high ornamental Huebner gate.

Over this place of sunshine the shadow of death had come twice. Accident again brought near-tragedy to little Solomon. The house was heated by iron stoves, which of course became furiously hot. When the boy was two or three years old, running heedlessly, he fell with both hands against the firebox. They were hideously burned. The relatives were summoned. Doctors came. The child was in shock. For days healing seemed impossible and the doctors declared that amputation of the hands was the only way to save the boy's life. But valiant Grandmother Dicke said no. She could not see a farm boy without hands. She was determined to bring healing to this beloved grandson. So she who had defied smallpox and cholera now defied infection and dehydration. With tenderest care and raw potato poultices she nursed the seared flesh. The baby must have felt her courage and comfort. Gradually healing came. The hands were saved, even without permanent scars.

A sick child often becomes spoiled, but there was always discipline in the Huebner household. Little Solomon had punishment when he needed it, which was probably often enough. He was active and curious, the sort who can think of more things to do than a busy mother can anticipate and forbid. When he got into trouble as a very small boy he had a refuge of comfort—a little double rocking horse. To that he would run, climb over the side, stuff his petticoats down over his striped stockings and rock and rock until he fell asleep.

As soon as Solomon, called Solly by his family, grew old enough, he joined his father in chores. A big farm always had more work than could be finished. Little boys could help by feeding the chickens, finding the eggs, bringing in kindling, dropping seed potatoes, and doing many other necessary light tasks. In the summer farm families got up at four o'clock. The boys went for the cows which had been in the fields all night,

Frederick August Huebner in his potato fields with the hired man and little Grover.

often a quarter of a mile away, and drove them back to the barn for milking. By the time Solly was twelve he could help with the ploughing, driving a straight furrow with two horses. A couple of years later he was doing the full work of a farm-hand, pitching as much as ten tons of hay a day. Hayloaders and other laborsaving machinery were still unknown on the Huebner farm.

Those summer days which began with sunrise were strenuous indeed. After the milking the men had breakfast. What break-fasts they were and what appetites they had to satisfy! There were heaps of fried bacon and thick slices of ham, dozens of eggs cooked sunny side up, fresh johnny bread and all the cof-fee they could drink. Then out to work in the fields, with a mid-morning break for hearty sandwiches of cold pork and smoked herring on homemade bread. That kept them until high noon when they had a real meal again. There was lots of farm food and plenty of help in the kitchen to roast the meats, pre-pare the home-grown potatoes, beets, carrots, beans, peas, and many other vegetables; and serve up the fresh-baked pies, or doughnuts warm from the deep fat. Such a meal stoked the engines for the afternoon's work, but more fuel was necessary after a few hours and again sandwiches helped them carry through until supper. That was dinner all over again. Often with these meals the workers enjoyed what they called raspberry vinegar, a homemade nonalcoholic drink, which after all the years today is remembered as "oh, so good."

Farm families were almost self-sufficient in those days. They bought coffee and salt and sugar, though they need not have gone to the store for the last. For they tapped their maple trees, collected the sap and boiled it down in great iron kettles. After much boiling they had clear rich maple syrup. Cooking still more, they got sugar which could be cooled into cakes and stored for later use. Each farm had a smokehouse where, with choicest hickory and beech from the wood lot, they smoked hams, bacon, sausages, and fish. Solly often drove wagon loads of wheat or rye to the mill to be ground into the flour for his family's homemade bread.

They picked all the berries of the changing seasons—strawberries, blackberries, raspberries, and cranberries. The orchards yielded cherries, plums, pears, and apples of many varieties and in great abundance. The womenfolk stored the cellars with all kinds of canned stuffs, preserves, jellies and pickles galore. In the fall the woods gave them rich harvests of nuts, especially hazel, beech, and hickory.

For all his hard physical labor, Father Huebner was, however, not an ignorant farmer. He was intelligent, a thinker and ever curious about the processes of agriculture. He had a microscope and studied the secrets of botany. He developed new strains of potatoes and in later years became a large grower of seed potatoes for the seedsmen of the Northwest. He was a conservationist who worked to maintain the fertility of his soil. Much of his acreage was planted to peas, for the climate of the

Frederick August Huebner with his prize potatoes.

Wilhemina Dicke Huebner.

area is particularly favorable to that crop. Manitowoc is still a great pea-growing center. In those days most farmers, after the pea crop was harvested, cleared the land and ploughed it in preparation for the following spring. Father Huebner believed that was poor practice. Instead he planted winter rye, dragging it in immediately after the pea crop, and with wonderful results. He also followed a ten-year cycle of crop rotation with very heavy fertilizing with barnyard manure and some imported guano. He hauled bedding straw to stables in town in return for manure later, which all winter he had spread on his fields, producing extraordinary fertility and bumper crops. He once grew a beet that weighed forty-seven pounds, and one of his potato plants had three huge potatoes averaging over three pounds apiece. He often got six hundred bushels of potatoes to the acre. He became known as a farmer with theories that worked and sometimes was invited to lecture to the students in agriculture at the University of Wisconsin at Madison.

For twenty years Father Huebner, who never really went to school himself, served on the school board of Two Rivers Township, much of the time as chairman. He welcomed that responsibility at first so that he might help choose the teachers for his own sons. He continued because of his great belief in the value of a good education. Children in those days walked to school. Solly and Grover had a mile to go to the country grade school and four or five miles to the Two Rivers high school. In winter with temperatures down to 20 or 30 degrees below zero and winds blowing, they wore hooded caps which covered all their faces but the eyes, home-knitted mittens and socks, and many layers of wool between. Their father was strict about their school attendance, for the sessions were short in that farm country where boys were needed to work. He would not tolerate tardiness and the Huebner boys were never late to school. Their father spurred their ambition for education. He was always holding before them the excitement of learning, the satisfactions of using their minds, until they were like two dogs pulling on the leash eager to get all that books and teachers could open to them. He taught them constantly too in his own daily associations with them. He told of his father's life in Germany and his reasons for coming to America. He recalled his childhood experiences with the Indians, and pointed out to Solly the variations in the Indian arrowheads which turned up so often as they ploughed the fields. There was a strange little hill on the Huebner farm which apparently had once had religious significance to the Indians, drawing them constantly back to the place where they left traces of their coming and going. Father Huebner encouraged his son to collect and compare the different kinds of arrowheads, and to those early flints the boy-grown-to-man today ascribes his lifelong interest in geology and the collecting of mineral specimens. One day after a storm had interrupted their ploughing, Solly and his father returned to their field to find a strange new furrow cut deep through the grass. Where it ended they saw something had buried itself in the ground and was still hot. Father Huebner explained that a meteor had hit, that the universe is full of them and millions large and small hit the earth every day, usually without anyone's knowing.

For natural reasons Wisconsin is a good birthplace for geologists. In prehistoric times the great glaciers moved down over Wisconsin and melted back. They gouged out the lakes and rivers. They lifted great masses of gravel in the north and dropped them in the south. The resulting gravel pits on Wisconsin farms were like money in the bank to the farmers who sold the raw material for roads at ten cents a load. For a boy like Solly the pits were a fascinating place to dig for strange rocks and the spectacular fool's gold.

Father Huebner loved animals. He had a theory that they should not be tied up. The horses ran free in the fields and were never tied in their stalls. The cows were not tied in the barn and even in winter whenever possible were brought free into the barnyard to eat their feed spread on the snow. Father Huebner raised race horses and Solly loved to ride. As a youth he enjoyed especially a beautiful little white Morgan mare and they had many good times in the woods and fields together. One day the horse stepped into a hornet's nest with terrifying results. Stung many times, she went wild with pain and fright. She bucked and broke from all control. Solly held on as long as he could, but finally was thrown. He could have been killed. He did hurt both wrists badly, and the long weeks when his hands were bandaged and helpless made him remember with gratitude his Grandmother Dicke.

All the farm boys then went fishing, and started at a very early age, going alone to the river when only six or seven years old. There were yellow perch, bullheads and pickerel. There is a family story of the biggest fish Solly caught as a very little fellow. It was a wall-eyed pike, too big for him to carry. So he left the hook in its mouth and dragged it home. When they arrived, he was worn out, and so was the fish, literally. Solly felt greatly abused when his mother refused to make any efforts at salvage and cook him a fish dinner. Suckers were a fish which they caught with nets in the early spring when ice was still in the water. These were smoked and used all year. The fishermen got soaking wet and their clothes even froze to their bodies, but nobody caught cold in those days.

As he grew older Solomon greatly enjoyed going with the commercial French Canadian fisherman from Two Rivers out onto Lake Michigan. They went in big open rowboats, locally called mackinaws, with three or four men at the oars. They would take a boy who promised to stand whatever came without complaint. If a storm broke they gave him oilskins, but still he often got cold and wet. When the lake roughened up with great waves like the ocean, they tied the boy fast so that he could not fall overboard even if so seasick he might like to. These youthful experiences on rough water made later for Solomon's comfort in his far travels. The English Channel never bothered him. He sailed happily in the choppy waters between Messina and Sicily while others were greatly distressed.

Solomon and Grover often went hunting. As ten-year-old boys they had their shotguns. They would go out to the woods alone to get their rabbits, and somehow their mother never worried. Later they grew skillful also with deer and other game. Once duck hunting in a boat Solomon fell overboard and nearly drowned, an experience which, strangely, prevented his ever wanting to learn to swim.

Solomon loved the woods. As a man he often recalls the coolness and stillness of late summer in the white pine forests. The straight trees rose eighty or one hundred feet tall. Sunlight slanted through their branches as through cathedral windows, down on a carpet of brown pine needles and dark shining wintergreen with its bright red berries. There alone, with a squirrel frisking about or a blue jay calling, he knew pure enjoyment.

His love of the woods intensified for him the terror of the forest fires. Often set by lightning as well as by human carelessness, they raged in the dry woods of late summer and fall. When they were near there was the frightening danger to house and barns.

Father Huebner had fire insurance, but he never owned life insurance. The strict Lutherans and Methodists of that time and place did not believe in it. Basically that was because they felt it would be flying in the face of Providence and demonstrating lack of faith in God's care for them. They believed in supporting their prayers for the safety of their homesteads, however, and when fires threatened repeatedly Solomon was called upon to do his part, stationed on the roof with a bucket to quench a burning brand or spark before it could do damage.

Sometimes he would sit there all night, listening to the unforgettable roar of the devouring flames, watching the eruption of sparks as some great tree crashed. Even when the fire itself was not close, if it was bad the wind would bring the ashes, sifting them down sometimes as much as a quarter or half inch thick over the whole landscape, a pall of death, speaking of beautiful trees that were gone, animals painfully killed and a ravaged countryside. Forever after Solomon feared and dreaded fire.

In spite of the hazards of nature and hard work, Solomon had a happy childhood. For him and all the Huebners life was full. Their great interest beside the farm was the church. There was respect for Sunday as the day of worship and of rest from unnecessary work. The family went four miles to church, sometimes walking to spare the horses. They also attended Wednesday evening prayer meeting whenever possible. The boys went to Saturday catechism class and learned a long list of Bible verses by heart each week. Far from New England, they lived a Puritanical life, with no card playing or dancing or even music, which suggested the dance hall.

A social center of the Germanic and Scandanavian people who made up the great part of the population of the towns young Huebner knew was the turnverein or gymnastic hall. There the people met for calisthenics, folk dancing, and programs of intellectual interest. There several times during the winter would be held a Farmers' Institute. For several hours in the early evening speakers would present material of interest, or would-be interest, to the assembled farmers. Father Huebner urged Solomon to seek opportunities to speak. As the son said later, "Father had the idea that one should learn the gift of gab, and I learned." He prepared a series of talks on the early history of Manitowoc County. Of course he had the resources of family tradition, and a local newspaper editor also helped supply material. He did not become a headliner throughout the state, but he told his stories to a respectable number of audiences who heard him through. It is interesting to reconstruct from fragments of fact a picture of the sturdy young speaker on a winter night. He stood before his audience at one end of a barn-like room. The place was weakly lighted

Two Rivers, Wisconsin high school graduating class, 1898. Valedictorian Huebner at the extreme left of back row.

by oil lamps in brackets against the walls. It was heated—overheated for some—by wood stoves. The room smelled of tobacco smoke and oil, of wet leather and wool, of horses and hard-working humanity. He looked out bravely over the rows of expectant listeners on their hard wooden chairs. The men saw a slender boy about fifteen years old with a shock of brown hair parted a little to the right of the middle, bright blue-gray eyes and a ruddy complexion. The high-buttoned jacket of his suit was of dark rough wool. The matching trousers were narrow and a bit "high-water," by today's standards. The suit was his year's only new one, and his shirt was made by his mother, who for many years made all the family clothes, except the men's suits. As he began to talk the audience sensed a young fellow who wanted to get his story across. Though no orator by the standards of the time, he was a vigorous and straightforward speaker. He told the story of their common heritage vividly. With a gesture he dramatized the cutting of the forest. He thumped the table beside him as he spoke of the ideals which drew the pioneers westward. There in embryo was the teacher.

Perhaps the crowd heckled him a little in spite of their sympathetic interest. It was a rough audience and the Farmers' Institute men liked their jokes. One night a professor from the University of Wisconsin came over to talk about farm animals. An old Norwegian on the front row got up and asked: "Professor, why is it that in a flock of white sheep once in a while you get a black one? What makes the sheep black?" The professor began an answer, starting with the Bible story of Jacob's speckled and spotted cattle. The old Norwegian interrupted; he'd read that story too, but it was no answer. What made the sheep black? The professor hedged a bit and finally said he really didn't know. Whereupon, to the delight of the audience, the old farmer said: "It's their wool which makes black sheep black."

Solomon's early teachers in the country school were often men. Two of them especially helped him to lay a sound foundation for his education. They were competent scholars and went on to college teaching, the one at the University of Wisconsin and the other at Washington University in Missouri. In high school Solomon's teachers found him responsive and hard working. They encouraged him to do the regular four-year course in three years, and he was the class valedictorian at graduation.

As the time for decision about college drew near, there was much discussion in the Huebner home. Their German Evangelical minister urged that Solomon go to a Methodist college. A Unitarian preacher, whom the Huebners had come to know and respect, strongly recommended Beloit College, then a Unitarian school. Just then Professor Balthasar Meyer came from the University of Wisconsin to give adult education courses in the Two Rivers neighborhood. Many parents attended, including the Huebners, and they took that opportunity to ask advice about Solomon. Professor Meyer assured them that it would be a great mistake to send him to a denominational college. He had the ability to make the most of opportunities at a big university and should go down to Madison. Father Huebner was persuaded and made the decision, but it was not unwelcome to his son.

CHAPTER THREE

Student Days

SOLOMON HUEBNER could have been ready for college at fifteen, but the rule of the University of Wisconsin was that no freshmen younger than sixteen were admitted. Therefore he continued schoolwork to graduate with the class of 1898 and his continued help was welcome on the farm, so the year of waiting was well spent. In the fall of 1898 he boarded the train for the 120-mile trip to Madison via Milwaukee. Interestingly enough, a student from Manitowoc today could not travel that way, because the automobile has ended that railroad passenger service. Solomon had been on a train often enough before and that in itself was no adventure. During his boyhood, distances too far for the horses were traveled by local train, and his parents had taken him to Chicago for the World's Fair in 1893. But as he watched the landscape flash by at twenty-five miles an hour he must have felt himself projected into a new life. He did not feel the hard seats or notice the soot from the engine which begrimed the coach and its passengers. The dirty windows did not dim his vision of the rich tables of learning for which his father had whetted his appetite, and which were almost within reach.

When Solomon arrived at Madison he found a turmoil of growth in the school on the high shores of Lake Mendota. Although the university was about fifty years old, it had developed slowly until about 1887. Then with a change in leadership the student body expanded to four or five times its previous size. The number of campus buildings had about doubled in the decade and the new construction included separate facilities for the law and engineering schools as well as a whole cluster of buildings for the agricultural campus, and an armory and a gymnasium. Dormitories for men were lacking, since there was not enough money for everything. There was a Ladies Hall for women, for the university had long been co-ed, and the president had recently announced that any question as to the desirability of that had been "swept away by the energetic hand of experience."

So Solomon took his place with some two thousand students drawn mostly from the farms and middle-class homes of the State. He searched out a rented room in a private home, for he wanted no noisy boarding house to disturb his work, and he registered in the College of Letters and Science. He was quickly attracted to Professor Richard T. Ely in the newly organized School of Economics, Political Science and History. Economics was a new field for Huebner but he felt right away that "it was the pond I wanted to swim in." Under Professor Ely's leadership he studied eagerly the classic principles of production, distribution, exchange, and consumption. He did not then give a thought to the complete absence in economic textbooks of reference to the whole great field of insurance. In his early years also he studied English, much history, advanced mathematics, and a required course in Anglo-Saxon, which he hated and which he almost failed. Another required course was "forensics" or public speaking, and that was an unforgettable experience. His teacher had acted with Otis Skinner, and knew how to coach. He gave each student a famous oration to memorize and to learn to deliver. Huebner's was James G. Blaine's oration at the funeral of President Garfield. At first his delivery was wooden and lifeless. But his teacher exhorted him: "You

Above, University of Wisconsin debating society about 1901. Solomon Huebner at the left end of the back row.

Left, Solomon Huebner, B.L., University of Wisconsin, 1902.

must watch the casket brought in. You must see Blaine looking down into the face of his dead friend. You must feel the tragedy of it all and make your listeners feel it too." With repeated practice and repeated coaching Solomon began to come to life. Finally one day something clicked, he knew he had caught the passion of Blaine's delivery. When he next performed for the professor the teacher was satisfied, "Boy, you've *learned*," he said. For all the rest of his life, vigor and conviction became characteristics of his speaking. The qualities of showmanship which helped make him a popular and effective teacher surely were stirred to life by that Madison professor.

In his sophomore year Huebner became interested in college debating. Its challenge and competition stirred him. Each battle of logic and wit he enjoyed greatly. It became his chief extracurricular activity through the balance of his five years at Madison.

For a couple of years he also worked his way in part, though that was not necessary, as his father was well-to-do and willing to provide the needed funds. However, at the time Solomon wanted to do it to satisfy some theories of his own. The job was to do some very minor writing and to clip items from many sources and paste up the pages for a review for municipal officials which was edited by one of the university professors.

The experience crystallized a conviction that a university student should "tend to his business," and devote his college years solely to study and college activities if that is at all possible. That decision was strengthened by Professor Ely who urged him to highest endeavor in his studies and held before him the goal of a doctor's degree.

University athletics never appealed to Solomon. Vigorous physical exercise was no treat to the farm boy and he left those activities at Madison completely to others. Moreover, during all his college vacations he returned home and worked on the farm, so the strictly student life at the university was a welcome change.

The debating was not only a great delight to Huebner, but he credited it with winning him the coveted Phi Beta Kappa key. Only fourteen students were elected from his senior class to that highest honorary fraternity. Eligibility was determined first by excellence in scholarship. Then a man must also show leadership, he must *do* something in addition to his studies.

Solomon's enthusiastic and constant activity in debating sealed his double qualification.

The Wisconsin years were an education for Solomon in the contact with great minds as well as through the information which he assimilated. Frederick J. Turner,* later author of *The Rise of the New West*, and Charles Haskins, another professor of history, enlarged his understanding of the past which had always interested him because of its part in the present and the future. Benjamin Snow, a physicist, and Paul Reinsch, who later became United States ambassador to China, were men whose influence was lifelong. They spurred his interest in science, in economics, and in all the developing problems of our civilization. They made him appreciate lectures as a vital part of university instruction. They convinced him that a dynamic teacher can transmit learning and stimulate research even for large groups.

From Dr. Ely he also gained inspiration about the broad responsibilities of a teacher. Huebner said in after years that he spent as much time as a professor in personal counseling with his students individually as in the classroom, and he got that idea from Professor Ely in his own college days.

The turn of the century at Wisconsin was a time when academic freedom was being vigorously debated and defended. Dr. Ely had been charged with radical socialistic ideas, in fact he was even brought to formal trial, though he was completely cleared. The university president made a statement then which

---

* When Dr. Huebner first knew Professor Turner, he had just recently (1893) presented his epochal paper, *The Significance of the Frontier in American History*. He developed the thesis that successively from the seventeenth century, in each era of American history, the frontier took from the European colonist his old way of life and thought, and changed him into an American. The following much-quoted words of Professor Turner give a vivid picture of the times of which he wrote: "Stand at Cumberland Gap and watch the procession of civilization, marching single file—the buffalo following the trail to the salt springs, the Indian, the fur-trader and hunter, the cattle-raiser, the pioneer farmer—and the frontier has passed by. Stand at South Pass in the Rockies a century later and see the same procession with wider intervals between."

became a beacon light in higher education and was regarded as part of the Wisconsin Magna Charta. Cast in bronze the following words appear on the wall of the entrance hall of the university's main building:

> WHATEVER MAY BE THE LIMITATIONS WHICH TRAMMEL INQUIRY ELSEWHERE, WE BELIEVE THAT THE GREAT STATE UNIVERSITY OF WISCONSIN SHOULD EVER ENCOURAGE THAT CONTINUAL AND FEARLESS SIFTING AND WINNOWING BY WHICH ALONE THE TRUTH CAN BE FOUND.

This atmosphere of free inquiry and independent thinking also had its influence on young Huebner. It helped set before him the ideal that a college professor can help affect the future as well as understand the past.

Huebner's boarding place at Madison was next door to the professor of astronomy. Often the student and the teacher walked up the hill to the campus in the morning or down at night. Solomon had always been interested in the stars and took advantage of these opportunities to learn more of the science. The professor also loaned him books on astronomy which he read eagerly. He began to grasp the staggering concept of light-years. As he became acquainted with the immensity and age of the universe he was overwhelmed by the idea of a firmament without beginning or end. As his finite mind struggled with infinity he began, as many of the young men of his day did, to move away from the religious ideas of his boyhood. He says that he has an abiding faith in God the Creator, and it is greatly strengthened by his knowledge of astronomy. He classes himself now as a Unitarian. The strong moral precepts of his godly upbringing have born their fruit all his life in his standards of honor and truth, integrity, and self-reliance. He recognizes the power of religious and moral ideas in human conduct and often expresses the wish that the principles about work laid down in the Scriptures were given more prominence by contemporary religious leaders.

Huebner's own experience at the University of Wisconsin always influenced his judgment on the question of a large university versus a small college. He believes there is something about a university, where a student mingles with thousands of others and is of necessity largely unsupervised, which enlarges his view and his capacity. The experience of mixing with others with diverse opinions and background always has seemed to him one of the great aspects of education. He has emphasized it strongly to his own children.

At his commencement exercises Solomon was one of seven speakers from his class of 325. As a young man he had many heroes. He was inspired by the men he met in the flesh and by those in the pages of history. One of the great figures of the nineteenth century was Cecil Rhodes. That son of a country English vicar as a boy seeking health went to South Africa. There he found a fabulous fortune in diamonds, became the outstanding political leader of the country and gave himself to passionate work for world peace through his vision of the unity of English-speaking peoples. He died in March 1902 and Huebner chose him as the subject of his commencement address.

Huebner's interest in Rhodes seems almost prophetic, for the latter often said that his life had been supremely influenced by an idea which he found in Aristotle that the greatest happiness in life is to be derived from conscious pursuit of a great purpose.

The graduation ceremony was held in the university gymnasium, but the speaking program was presented in the afternoon following luncheon. Father Huebner came to hear his son speak and to rejoice in his new Bachelor of Letters degree. Then they went back to the farm where Solomon worked during the summer. He returned to Madison for graduate study in the fall, majoring in economics. Working under Balthasar Meyer, who later was for many years a member of the Interstate Commerce

Commission, he volunteered to take as a research subject "The Distribution of Stock Holdings in American Railways." To his surprise and disappointment he discovered no literature on the subject. He went to Professor Meyer and attempted to beg off from the assignment. The professor told him, "Don't let lack of material stop you. That is a challenge to an original mind. Go back and find the facts for yourself." That resulted in an enormous exchange of letters with railroad officials all over the country. The young student found these men co-operative and ready to give information even in that day when publicity in the affairs of great corporations was far less common than now. A few of their letters were typed, but generally they were still handwritten in beautiful script by a clerk and signed by the officer. Often long sections of the law were also so copied out for him. He organized and presented his findings so effectively that his teacher was most complimentary. That paper was published in the *Annals of the American Academy of Political and Social Science*, the first of his many subsequent appearances in those learned pages.

He received his M.L. degree from Wisconsin in 1903 and was ready to drive on toward the Ph.D. goal set before him by Professor Ely, who urged him to become a teacher. Wanting to ease the burden of support for his father, Solomon applied for fellowships offered for advanced study. He wanted most the Harrison Fellowship in Economics at the University of Pennsylvania in Philadelphia. This was the highest fellowship of the university and competition for it was keen. Not daring to hope too much, Solomon likewise applied for admission to the University of Berlin, for advanced study, also in economics. Then he went off to Europe to see the world before he settled down to his most serious studying. He had $400 from his father, and his bicycle, the same "wheel" that he had ridden to high school from his Manitowoc Township home to Two Rivers. It was a heavy old English machine, powerful, with thick, single-tube rubber tires. It had taken him safely summer and winter, for his father had invented a leather covering for the tires which enabled him to go through snow without slipping.

From New York he sailed on July 4 aboard the old *Furnesia*, ten days to Glasgow. On the ship he met a young student named Cummings from Western Reserve University in Ohio. He was "a capital fellow." He also had a bicycle and was planning a cycling trip through Europe. So he and Huebner decided to join forces, and it proved a most congenial arrangement. The boat stopped for a day or two at Londonderry in the north of Ireland, and they were able to make a short expedition into the country, which they found very beautiful. The memory of the pale blue peat smoke and the black-garbed Catholic sisters on the streets forever after was associated with that brief visit. Off the ship at last in Glasgow they quickly realized they were in a strange land. One after another they had three little experiences which symbolized how many new things they had to learn. They stopped for a glass of beer at a Scotch tavern. All they could get was unknown English ale. As they drank, they soon realized how much more potent it was than anything they had known at home, and marked it down to be avoided. Then Solomon decided to weigh himself on a sidewalk scale. He looked at the registered weight and was sure the machine was broken. They came to another and he tried again with similar results. Somebody finally enlightened them that in Britain weight is in "stones" not in pounds. They saw for sale large yellow fruits rather like oranges, and bought a couple. The fruit, however, was disappointing: it defied peeling and was bitterly sour. The two college boys from midwest America had for the first time met a grapefruit. These were then imported to Britain from the colonies in the West Indies. From Glasgow they went to Edinburgh and through the Scottish Highlands, then they cycled happily south through the

English lake country. They had rain, rain, and more rain, but when the sun did shine they knew why that lovely land bred poets. Huebner bought a cyclist's rain cape which covered him and his bicycle like a tent and made the traveling comfortable in spite of the weather. The roads were good too. Also he had joined the English cycling tourists' club which provided a list of inexpensive inns and taverns where they found clean beds and good food all along the way.

In the Midlands of England the Americans' ears heard a speech which they completely failed to comprehend, and though they thought that they spoke the King's English the people there could not always understand them either. However, they greatly enjoyed all the sights and the sense of a civilization so much older than they had known at home. The castles particularly fascinated Solomon and he told often of an ancient grapevine planted in the days of Queen Elizabeth I and grown to the size of a huge tree, bearing tons of grapes each year. In England, and later on the continent, the young men easily rode a hundred miles a day, pedaling along the highways or the country lanes with horses and pedestrians usually the only competition.

Leaving England Huebner and his friend Cummings crossed from Ipswich to Amsterdam where Solomon wanted to see the diamond industry. They were surprised to find the Hollanders in the city as energetic and devoted to business as any Americans. In the country one evening they came to a Dutch inn where they decided to spend the night and take an early morning start. The host was a friendly soul. He sat with them as they ate their supper, serving them generously the hearty soup, sausage and cheeses and home-baked bread. The boys talked. They all sang together. In a mixture of German and English and some words of Dutch, with their pipes and their beer, they had a fine evening together. At bedtime the proprietor showed them to a Dutch-clean room under the gables with a most comfortable bed. The boys enjoyed all this good treatment but began to wonder a little about how much it was going to cost. They decided to let the morning solve that problem and took a good night's rest. Their host awakened them early, as requested, again served them a fine meal, and, to crown the experience, refused to charge them a cent for all the entertainment. Nearly half a century later a businessman went up to a famous visiting professor lecturing in Columbus, Ohio, and asked, "Does the name Cummings mean anything to you?" After a moment the visitor recognized him. "Yes, indeed, on a bicycle through Europe in 1903." Then Cummings asked: "Think quickly. What was the most memorable experience of all that wonderful summer?" Without hesitation the professor knew he was remembering the genial host of the Dutch inn, who had treated two American college boys so royally and felt amply repaid by the pleasure of their company.

Through Belgium and France, with days never long enough in Paris, the companions traveled on to Switzerland. There they had to quit their bicycles. Going down hill was fine, but even their youthful strength was not equal to the long hauls up the mountains. Huebner wanted to sell his bicycle, or even give it away, but that the Swiss customs officials would not allow. He had to crate and ship it home, an expense which he always remembered with annoyance.

The boys went over the Alps into Italy, traveling now by train and coach. On their students' budgets they continued the course of the Grand Tour of Rome and all Italy which wealthy families then considered a necessary climax for a young man's education. They stayed a week at Naples before going to Sicily from whence they planned to take a boat to Greece.

But cholera was raging in Greece and visitors were strongly advised to keep away. So back Solomon went to Naples and the hotel where they had recently stayed. The hotel-keeper welcomed him with excitement. What a blessing he had returned!

A most important letter was waiting that the American Express Company had been forwarding all over Europe. He had not known what to do with it and now it could be delivered.

The letter brought word that Solomon Huebner had been awarded the Harrison Fellowship in Economics at the University of Pennsylvania, and requested immediate acceptance. Immediate! And the letter was a month old. Huebner cabled to Philadelphia, hoping he was still in time. He took the first available boat, the *Nord Amerika* from Naples, an old tub which was condemned the next year and which was carrying two thousand Italian immigrants to New York. All the way across the Atlantic memories of the European holiday were mixed with hopes and fears for the future. Would he be too late for the fellowship in Philadelphia? If the door were closed at the University of Pennsylvania, and he had now left Berlin behind, what would he do?

Momentous in consequences as the breath of wind which deflects a raindrop on the mountain crest, so that it runs down the steep western slope to the Pacific, rather than down the eastern valley that leads at last to the Atlantic, so was the professors' decision that held the Harrison Fellowship for Solomon Huebner. He arrived in Philadelphia on October 8, 1903, and found that the door was still open. So he entered upon a life of service and creative leadership that was to make his name known around the world.

CHAPTER FOUR

The Wharton School

WHEN Solomon Huebner entered the University of Pennsylvania in 1903, he came to an honored and historic institution. It traced its origin in colonial days to godly and benevolent citizens who were inspired by the great evangelist, George Whitefield. They laid the foundations of what would become the University in plans for a "charity school" and the actual construction of a large building for public worship, especially for free preaching by Whitefield and others. After a few years Benjamin Franklin became a moving spirit in developing collegiate instruction upon this foundation, and in his *Autobiography* he referred to himself as one of the founders of the University. The Wharton School came into being the year before the birth of the man destined to have "Mr. Wharton School" as one of his many nicknames. The School was established with a $100,000 endowment from Joseph Wharton, a very wealthy Eastern ironmaster. The original announcement presented as its aim:

> The design of the instruction in this School (founded by Joseph Wharton, Esq. in 1881) is to give a thorough general and professional training to young men who are looking forward to business pursuits, and to fit them for the understanding of those scientific and economical problems which they may expect to meet in business life, beside imparting to them that discipline in business habits and that moral training which are the foundations of genuine success.

The Wharton School's double ideal of technical training for business and the development of a general cultural background was quite revolutionary in the great old traditional university. Yet it was personified in the founder. He was a captain of industry in an expanding era of the Nation's history. Without formal college education or technical training he became widely read and a leader in the field of chemistry, especially in the producing of zinc and other nonferrous metals. He not only was interested in Wharton, but helped found Swarthmore College and was always a strong friend to a liberal arts education.

It was natural that Huebner should have looked to Wharton. That was the first collegiate school of business in the United States, or in fact in the world. Similar programs at the University of Chicago and the University of California were still young, having been started in 1898. Wharton had attracted men of vision and practicality, many of them from the Middle West. They came to Pennsylvania largely free from bonds of tradition and created a climate for experimentation and individual development which was to give Huebner his own opportunity for unusual growth. He in turn added his strengths to theirs in developing a School within the University which perhaps was as surprising to that staid alma mater as was the ugly duckling to its old mother hen.

Outstanding among the Middle Westerners whom Huebner found at Wharton was Edmund J. James, an economist, who had become a member of the faculty in 1883 and made a lasting impression on the character of the School. The University's official history reports of him:

> Professor James, a graduate of the University of Illinois, came directly from taking his doctor's degree in political science in Germany. He was full of enthusiasm for the introduction of a new group of interests into the University and into the staid civic life of Philadelphia. For thirteen years he was the leading force in the new school, and fathered or supported many outside projects ger-

> mane to the general educational objects of the University, though not directly under its control. University Extension, the American Academy of Political and Social Science, with its widely circulated publication, the *Annals*, and other old and new organizations either owed their inception to him or long felt his directing hand.

Another Middle Westerner who molded Wharton in the early years was Simon Nelson Patten. He also was an economist, with high reputation in this country and abroad. He had warmth of personality and academic talents which combined to give him great influence in developing the new program. Again, a quotation suggests the stimulating associations which Huebner found in his new life at Wharton:

> Dr. Patten was an economist of much originality and distinction, a natural-born teacher and intellectual leader, especially attracting advanced students. He was the constant center of wholesome economic and social dispute, and raised a whole generation of disciples who became men of influence.

Dr. Emory R. Johnson and Dr. John Bach McMaster, who will be mentioned later, were two other men from the Mississippi Valley who did brilliant pioneering work at Wharton. It was into this group of men that Huebner from Wisconsin entered bringing his own practical and pioneering abilities.

In Huebner's first years at Wharton the founder was still returning periodically to visit and address the students. They listened respectfully to his exhortations that every person should save money whether he be rich or poor. They joked at his penny tie which seemed to them incongruous with his millionaire's pocketbook, and exchanged questioning looks when he ate his chicken in his fingers, gnawing eagerly to get every shred of meat from the bones.

Mr. Wharton had strong convictions on the subject of thrift and individual financial independence. As an objective of his school he stated in making the endowment that he wanted every graduate drilled in the idea "of the deep comfort and healthfulness of pecuniary independence whether the scale of affairs be small or great" and he repeated this philosophy often. His statement was later written in large letters and framed for the wall of Dr. Huebner's office. It hung there for many years, and the professor often pointed to it as full justification for insurance courses in the curriculum of the Wharton School.

As Harrison Fellow, Huebner outlined a course of study for his doctorate. His focus, of course, was economics. His courses included advanced economic theory, political science, history, accounting, sociology, and transportation. His preceptor was Dr. Emory R. Johnson, a man who had been born and raised in Wisconsin, and whose wife had taught school in Manitowoc. He had come to the University of Pennsylvania some years before to the Economics Department and was a professor of transportation. Although he did not know Solomon, undoubtedly he had read with unusual interest the study of stockholdings in the railroads which had been submitted with Huebner's application for the Harrison Fellowship. Possibly he had had some influence in holding the fellowship open when Solomon could not make an "immediate acceptance." At any rate, the men became fast friends and Dr. Johnson was a great help to him throughout his formative years. During his first year at Penn, young Huebner assisted Dr. Johnson in research in colonial commerce.

The graduate school in those days was small. The faculty encouraged friendly contacts among the students who had no dormitory life or many campus activities to draw them together. Early in the fall of 1903 at a faculty reception one evening several second-year students were invited to meet the new first-year people. A slender fair-haired girl from Queen's University in Kingston, Ontario, a graduate student in history, stood with friends at one side of the crowded room. They were spotting the newcomers and sharing their information about them. "There's a man who must be very clever," one said. "See his Phi Beta Kappa key." And the young Canadian asked, "What is Phi Beta Kappa?" for that honorary fraternity was not then in Canada. She did not know the significance of the key, with its honored American history, but she looked with interest and admiration at the young man who wore it. He was of medium height and stocky. His heavy hair was brushed long from a slightly right-center part. His blue-gray eyes flashed as he clenched his fists to emphasize a point in his discussion. Ethel Mudie met Solomon Huebner that night.

They met often again as fellow students in the seminar of John Bach McMaster. Both had been attracted to that course because of McMaster's fascinating *History of the People of the United States*. The people and events of American history came alive in those pages. The *History of the University of Pennsylvania* says of Professor McMaster and his writings:

> Educated as an engineer, member of the United States government survey unit in the far west just after the close of the Civil War, he was more impressed with the empire-building going on at that time in that region than in the political events of the past. He determined therefore at this early date to write a history to be occupied with the domestic and peaceful interests of the American people . . . It was a new kind of history . . . drawing its materials from contemporary sources previous historians had seldom thought of using. The first volume, which appeared in 1883, had an immediate success, and American history being an evident need of the Wharton School, he was promptly invited to leave Princeton and his mathematics and to come to Pennsylvania as Professor of American History . . . Here he remained for the rest of his teaching and writing life, his success in the latter, it may be said, being greater than in the former.

Huebner found that Professor McMaster let his students run the class sessions to suit themselves. He assigned subjects for their research and then expected them to share the results of their study with each other while he pursued his own interests in the Jacksonian period, reading the *Congressional Record*, and generally lost to their existence. It was an unusual opportunity for students to converse on matters of personal interest. Who could blame those who made the most of the situation? Huebner often said later, "The course was a great disappointment, but I got one good thing from that class."

In those early Pennsylvania days Solomon adopted a middle name. He had been annoyed by the assumption by registrars, passport authorities, and many private citizens that everybody ought to have a middle initial. He grew tired of explaining that he was simply "Solomon Huebner." So he talked it over with his family and selected "Stephen." That means "peace" and his father liked it. Thus he soon became Steve to his friends or Sol, and the childish Solly gradually was forgotten.

About this time, too, he began his addiction to red neckties. There wasn't a bet or a dare or a vow. He just liked red neckties. As the blue and green and brown wore out, they were replaced with red, bright red for many years, later tempered to a maroon and garnet when a red badge on a professor might suggest calls to the F.B.I.

As a student in Philadelphia Huebner lived in a rooming house on 36th Street north of Lancaster Avenue. His first day in the city when he found that the Harrison Fellowship was still his, he set out to locate a place to stay. He stopped a young man on the street and inquired if he knew of lodgings for a student. The answer was, "Come along. I live just around the corner and I think they have room for another." This proved to be the home of a Captain McIntyre who had been in the Battle of Gettysburg. Living there, Huebner from Wisconsin, where the German settlers had been strongly interested in the thoughts and events of the Civil War and had given one ninth of the State's population to serve in the Union Army, filled in many pages of his United States history. He enjoyed his daily contacts with the other students too. His first friend who had brought him to the place was secretary to Congressman George Edmonds, and later proved very helpful when Huebner worked with Mr. Edmonds for many years in his special service for the Government. Another young housemate was Herman Newman, a Hicksite Quaker. Together they went to the Friends' Meeting where the spirit often moved Newman mightily to speak, and Huebner never. Newman later became the editor of the national magazine, *The American Friend*. He was a man who practiced what he preached, a godly fellow and a fine gentleman. Huebner never knew him to "get mad" or to say a mean or unkind remark. In the same house, too, was a young woman who taught at the nearby Friends' school. She eventually married Mr. Newman. Huebner attended the wedding, which was his first experience of a Quaker wedding where the parties marry themselves by exchanging vows without any officiating cleric.

About this time Dr. Huebner became a Mason, and a member of the Stephen Girard Lodge in Philadelphia. The Masons were popular in Wisconsin during his youth, and he had long rather envied friends and relatives at home who had been initiated. So this ambition was satisfied soon after he attained his majority and could qualify. He eventually became a thirty-second degree Mason in the Scottish Rite. He was a member of a York Rite chapter also but never took his commandry because of University conflicts. In addition he is a Shriner and was a charter member of the Acacia Fraternity at the University of Pennsylvania, a Masonic college fraternity.

After a year of concentrated study, Solomon Stephen Huebner had completed his work for the degree of Doctor of Philosophy by the University of Pennsylvania, but he had not yet fulfilled the two-year residence requirement. Therefore he had to wait until 1905 to be awarded his diploma. Then at twenty-three he was one of the youngest men in University history to receive his Ph.D. His thesis was on marine insurance in the United States, and was largely historical. He had hoped to be the first Ph.D. in Dr. Johnson's Department of Transportation, but some technicalities stood in the way and he received his Doctor of Philosophy "in economics in economics," instead of "in economics in transportation."

Dr. Huebner in 1905.

With his Ph.D. work accomplished, what should the young student do in the year of waiting for his degree? He felt he would like to enter immediately upon a teaching career. Professor Ely at Wisconsin had assured him he would be a successful teacher. His parents would be pleased. One wonders if he asked Ethel's opinion. She was returning to Canada to be associated with her father in his law office.

He had plenty of teaching opportunities. The best job possibly was in the Philadelphia public Central High School. That offered $2,500 a year. But a teacher there would be "cooped up." He had an offer also from the Philippines. The most exotic opening was in the Imperial University of Japan. Penn then had more students from the Orient than any other American university. Dr. Huebner made life-long friends among them. The Imperial University would pay traveling expenses and $3,000 a year in gold, but the taker would be obligated to stay for three years.

Huebner had come to love the University of Pennsylvania. He felt that he would really like to stay there. He had great admiration and liking for Dr. Emory Johnson. Dr. Johnson was a great teacher and able in the practical application of his knowledge of economics. He had written many books on his subject, he had served as special consultant to the Government and later would do the gigantic task of calculating the schedule of tolls for the Panama Canal. For Huebner, teaching economics at the Wharton School under Dr. Johnson was an attractive possibility.

With all these roads branching before him, the need for decision subconsciously pressing, Mr. Huebner sat one night reading the *New York Journal of Commerce.* That paper was always fascinating. There he saw translated into flesh and blood, products and profits, the principles from textbook and classroom. He methodically ploughed right through the paper. He scanned page after page reporting events and prices of the stock market and of the produce market. Suddenly he said to himself: "That subject's not in the Wharton School!" He turned the next page, and another and another. They were devoted to news of insurance. Almost like a revelation Mr. Huebner realized that that subject also was not taught at Wharton. The oldest and biggest collegiate business school in the country was giving no training at all in two fields of business which filled a major part of the nation's outstanding business newspaper. In his mind he canvassed other colleges with which he was familiar. He could think of none which had courses to meet the need which had suddenly become clear to him. His quick imagination jumped ahead. Great possibilities opened up. He went to bed cocksure that he now knew the road he wanted to take.

In the morning Mr. Huebner went to Dr. Johnson and recounted the previous night's experience, ready to defend his new idea. Dr. Johnson listened attentively to his favorite student. Almost immediately he answered: "That's a very good suggestion. It's strange we never thought of it before. Let's go see Professor Patten."

Dr. Simon N. Patten was head of the Wharton School. He listened thoughtfully, and again without hesitation said: "I don't see why we shouldn't do it. We'll go see Mr. Harrison."

Mr. C. C. Harrison was provost of the University and a multimillion-dollar sugar refiner in Philadelphia. In his business he was a czar and even in University affairs he seemed to have had little patience with committees. He saw committees galore that talked a lot and did not "commit," and felt he accomplished more without them. When Dr. Patten and Dr. Johnson laid Huebner's story before him, Mr. Harrison expressed surprise that the proposed subjects were not already in Wharton. "They should be," he said. "I'll approve that right now. Who will be the teacher?"

That was Mr. Huebner's opening and he did not miss it. He applied for the job. "Did you ever teach? Do you think you can?" To these questions he answered quickly "No" and "Yes" and added that everything had to have a beginning—a new teacher for new courses might work out well.

Dr. Patten argued weakly that Huebner was too young; he

would have students older than he was. But he withdrew the objection with Huebner's promise to grow a moustache which would make him look older. When the question of pay came up Dr. Johnson whispered to Huebner to take it for nothing if need be, certain that he could prove himself. But the University was too fair for that and promised a first-year salary of $500. The official confirmation of this historic appointment was signed by the Secretary of the University Trustees and read:

> Dear Sir:–
>
> I have the honour of informing you that at a meeting of the Board of Trustees, held October 4th, 1904, you were duly appointed ASSISTANT IN COMMERCE with a salary at the rate of $500. per annum, payable monthly.
>
> Respectfully yours,

The designation "assistant in commerce" was slightly a misnomer, for Huebner was a teacher from the beginning, giving classes in transportation as well as in insurance and in the security and commodity exchange markets. He was included in Dr. Johnson's Department of Transportation. The Wharton School then occupied Logan Hall which had been vacated by the University Medical School as obsolete. The number of students in Wharton was about 225, less than the size of the faculty today.

Thus in the fall of 1904 Solomon S. Huebner began to teach the first organized courses in the world on the stock exchange and insurance from the economic point of view. The actuarial phases of life insurance had entered some universities through the doorway of mathematics. Life insurance law had also found its way into college classrooms by way of policy contracts. But the product of life insurance, its uses and its place in human affairs were scarcely known in academic circles. Very infrequently some professor would have a special lecture on the stock exchange or some insurance topic, but there literally were no organized courses in these subjects prior to those at the Wharton School. The only half-useful textbook, from Dr. Huebner's point of view, was *Elements of Life Insurance* by Miles M. Dawson, an eminent actuary. Naturally enough, the material was heavily mathematical and the whole text lacking in any real economic interpretation.

Necessarily Huebner had to plan and outline his courses for himself. There was no literature for the classes to use. As he collected materials from the newspapers and current journals, as he thought about the principles and experiences involved, his enthusiasm grew. He interviewed people. He observed what was actually happening in these two great fields of finance.

At first his insurance classes were small, and always elective until 1928. Dr. Huebner never taught from what he calls a "high-hat standpoint." In life insurance, for instance, he began by discussing what life insurance is for, what it can do. He got his students excited about services of which they had only the vaguest concept. When they asked, "How can these things be?" Dr. Huebner told them to wait a while. When they really appreciated the importance of life insurance to families and business, it would then be time to learn about the machinery. He habitually introduced simple and vivid ideas in his lectures. For instance, one student never forgot his comment about a funeral which he had recently attended. The minister was presenting an elaborate eulogy of the deceased, but Dr. Huebner said *he* was wondering about the amount of life insurance left to his widow and their little children.

One plan Huebner followed that first year was to bring to his classes lecturers who were men actually working in various phases of insurance. They presented carefully prepared papers which together were planned by Huebner "to give a brief and thorough treatment of the importance and nature of the leading forms of insurance, and the principles and methods upon which the insurance business is based and conducted." These papers subsequently were edited by Dr. Huebner and published by the American Academy of Social and Political Science under the title of *Insurance*. This volume became a valuable textbook at Wharton, and later at other schools. It was published in 1905 —his first major work in print, and the first of many publications he would do for the Academy.

The whole field of life insurance was getting great publicity just at that time because of the growing abuses and scandals among many companies which culminated late in 1905 in the Armstrong Investigation in New York State. That was a very comprehensive legislative investigation of life insurance operations in the state under Senator Armstrong with Charles Evans Hughes as counsel for the committee. Writers in the weekly journals made the most of the lurid details of exploitation of policyholders, misuse of funds, legislative lobbying and flagrant nepotism. Newspaper reporters sought out the young professor for help in understanding the situation. He said years later that the Investigation and the corrective legislation that grew out of it were one of the best things ever to happen to life insurance. It put the business on the curve upwards, in his opinion. He agreed with Theodore Roosevelt who said: "The men with the muckrakes are often indispensable to the well-being of society, but only if they know when to stop raking the muck."

Incidentally, this was only one of many points on which he agreed with the famous president whom he had admired first as the Rough Riding Colonel in the Spanish-American War. They were alike in their crusading spirit and vigorous campaigning for causes they espoused. Some people felt that Dr. Huebner even grew to look like Teddy—the same square figure, stiff brush of hair, thick glasses, drooping moustache, and aggressive jaw.

In 1906 Dr. Huebner was appointed assistant professor. In that year also he began his evening school work with the University. A little later extension work took him "over the mountains" to Wilkes-Barre and Scranton, Harrisburg and Reading. The teaching of adults in the evening and extension classes always was a great satisfaction. He liked the response of minds which were seeking education, often at great sacrifice,

Dr. Grover G. Huebner in the 1930's.

in marked contrast to many of the day students who were having learning thrust upon them at parental expense. Dr. Huebner's effective teaching was rewarded by full professorship in 1908. That four-year march to the highest teaching rank in the University of Pennsylvania is probably the fastest climb on record. His official title was Professor of Insurance and Commerce, which continued throughout his active career. When he came to handle only insurance courses he protested that the "and Commerce" should be dropped, but the University thought the change unimportant. For Dr. Huebner that was one of the frustrating demonstrations of academic rigidity.

In 1908 also his brother Grover, who had followed him to Wisconsin and then to Penn for a Ph.D. there in economics in transportation, became a member of the Wharton School faculty. For forty years they pursued their academic careers in the same setting, enjoying their associations both as brothers and as fellow members of the University staff. The younger man was a sound scholar and the author of many valuable textbooks. He was a conscientious teacher, but quiet and reserved, dispositionally very different from his brother. The University students recognized the contrast and came to refer to the gregarious, effervescent man as Smiling Sol or Sunny Sol. The latter nickname achieved a questionable celebrity when a Wharton student put his business training into practice as a manufacturer of a bright yellow cleaning fluid. Seeking a name for his product he thought of his former professor, and the name Sunny Sol went on his bottles.

CHAPTER FIVE

Dr. Huebner at Home

Dr. Huebner not only had a boyhood training of respect for family relationships and assumed obligations, but also upon his attaining the age of 21 his parents had followed the old Wisconsin custom of having a serious discussion with him about the governing principles of manhood. He remembered especially two precepts from each one. His father emphasized particularly the importance of carrying through on a bargain even if it were not a good one. "Don't try to crawl out of it," he said. Also he warned his son about the evils of borrowing money. Possibly that advice was inspired by the college debts, but young Huebner had convictions himself about that kind of loan. He preached that the wisdom of borrowing depended upon what use a man planned to make of the money.

His mother reminded him that money was not the biggest thing in life and urged him to weigh his values. Her most earnest advice, however, was about marriage, which she believed was a person's most important step and one to be viewed very seriously. She particularly recommended taking time in courtship knowing that the affections of youth are often surprisingly fickle.

Ethel Mudie had been back in Philadelphia for two years teaching at a private school for girls. With renewed association Dr. Huebner knew that he could safely trust the attraction developed by their earlier congenial companionship.

With full professorial rank at the University, though with $2,500 of debts from his college days, Dr. Huebner felt he could assume the responsibilities of matrimony. True to his principles he protected the home-to-be with a substantial life insurance policy. After the close of school in June 1908 he traveled to Ottawa, Canada. Ethel Elizabeth Mudie's father had died and she and her mother were temporarily in that Canadian capital. The wedding was on June 24, with the bride in a dress of white satin and lace. It was a simple home service and the husband of one of Ethel's good friends, who was minister of a local church, performed the ceremony.

Ethel's heritage was Scotch and English. Her great-grandfather was a Huguenot who had fled to Scotland from religious persecution in France and her grandfather married a daughter of the MacLeod clan in the Highlands of Scotland. They must have been poor, she thinks, for they emigrated to Canada where her father became the only survivor of their eight children. He was sent as a boy to the Fort Edward Institute at Fort Edward, New York, and took his B.A. degree at Queens College in Kingston, Ontario. He was a lawyer and was appointed the Master in Chancery in the County of Frontenac with the responsibility of settling civil cases by arbitration out of court, at great savings of time and money for the citizens involved. Ethel's mother was Canadian-born of English parents. They believed in education, and as has been mentioned, Ethel took her degree at her father's alma mater, then become Queen's University, and did postgraduate work in history and literature at the University of Pennsylvania where she took her M.A. degree.

The Huebner family could not make the long trip to Ottawa for the wedding, so visiting in Manitowoc was a part of the honeymoon. The newlyweds first took a little trip through Canada and had a short stay at Mackinac Island where the surreys with the fringe on top were then not interesting antiques. They little thought how often Dr. Huebner would return there as the

Ethel Elizabeth Mudie at the time of her marriage to Dr. Huebner.

honored guest of insurance conventions. The next stage of the journey was made by boat to Milwaukee across Lake Michigan, and then by train they went to Manitowoc and all the waiting relatives.

Toward the end of the summer Dr. and Mrs. Huebner returned to Philadelphia and their first home, which was a pleasant rented house on Buckingham Place. Into that home the next year came a little auburn-haired baby, Margaret. Unlike many babies of her generation, she was born in a hospital. Her

The Huebner family in 1916: Dr. and Mrs. Huebner with Margaret, John, and Queenie.

brother John who came two years later was born in Kingston, Ontario, during the summer holidays. The family's choicest story of young Dr. Huebner as a parent is of his being left alone one afternoon with Margaret. She inherited his "bounce," and as he was holding her in his arms, rocking in his favorite chair, she suddenly braced herself against him and plunged over his shoulder. His hand followed her quickly and grabbed her petticoats. He could hold on, but she was a heavy child and in that awkward position he could not lift her. History does not report whether he yelled, but she did and rescuing mother came running.

For five years then the Huebners were only four—a family expensive enough for a young professor's salary. Dr. Huebner with boundless energy and intense interest in his work never turned down an opportunity for extra jobs in his field. He constantly taught evening as well as daytime classes. He edited three more volumes for the American Academy of Political and Social Science, all dealing with organized security and produce markets. In 1911 his first book was published, *Property Insurance.* This was a pioneer in the field. It became a standard text and went through many editions, being used by educational institutions throughout the country and abroad. *Life Insurance* was published in 1915. This textbook presented first the nature and services of life insurance and followed with its science—the pattern of teaching which Dr. Huebner had developed so successfully in his classes.

In speaking of his evening classes Dr. Huebner always recalls how hungry he was when he got home. He would raid the icebox and greatly enjoy his late suppers. He has always been a hearty eater. He still loves bacon and eggs, and apple, pumpkin, and mince pies are his favorite desserts. Those eating habits probably are rooted in his early farm days. He admits that he does not generally follow Benjamin Franklin's advice and leave the dinner table still hungry, but he keeps a reasonable weight around 170. In his adult years he never got into a routine of heavy exercise, at least in sports or the gymnasium. However, he often was told that in his teaching he used more energy than a ditchdigger.

For the family of growing children needing a nurse and a cook the Buckingham Place house was too small. Walking with Dr. Huebner and the babies one Sunday afternoon to Dickens Park in West Philadelphia, Mrs. Huebner admired a house at 516 South 44th Street. It was comfortably big with an open lawn. She commented that it was the kind of home she would like. Dr. Huebner told her simply, "If that's what you really want, I'll see what I can do." The house was owned by his friend and colleague, Dr. Emory R. Johnson, whose wife was ill so that they were living elsewhere. For a few years the Huebners rented the house, and then when it had become really home, they purchased the property. There two more daughters were born, Ethel Elizabeth (Queenie) and Esther Ann. The childhood memories of all the children center around this house, called by them "516."

The atmosphere of that home was largely determined by Mrs. Huebner. Something of its warmth and security for all it sheltered can be imagined from a note written her by a Scotch nurse who lived with them for many years. Long after Annie MacIninch married and left she wrote an anniversary letter in grateful remembrance ". . . years ago today as a lonely person I landed in Philadelphia and was taken into your home."

Mrs. Huebner believed that the home was the source of a child's basic education and moral training. She quoted Benjamin Franklin's philosophy that to empty your purse into your head is your best investment. Education is something that will not rust and which nobody can steal. Thus it is not surprising that the family eventually amassed eleven earned degrees, one honorary degree and two diplomas in special fields (Queenie in occupational therapy and Esther Ann in horticulture). Discipline was firm. Nobody was ever able to play one parent off against the other. If a child went to Dr. Huebner about some controversial matter he always asked first: "What did your mother say?" And she followed the same course.

Of necessity the children did not see too much of their father. During their childhood he followed a prodigious schedule of work. The university classes were basic, including a full teaching load during the day and two hours a night on Mondays and Tuesdays. From 1915 through 1919 he taught also in New York for Columbia University. Under the School of Business there were a class in insurance for graduate students and life insurance lectures for life insurance salesmen. The latter classes ran to 150 students and were held in the handsome Chamber of Commerce room in the Woolworth Building on lower Broadway, then the tallest building in the world and the mecca of all tourists. After a few years the University decided that these classes should be held at the uptown campus and Dr. Huebner discontinued his work. He was succeeded at Columbia by one of his Wharton graduate students in insurance, Dr. Ralph H. Blanchard. Dr. Blanchard had also been a teacher in the Insurance Department of the Wharton School. During these years Dr. Huebner also had interesting activities connected with the New York Stock Exchange. In addition he was often commuting to Washington doing special work for the government and giving much time and thought to the development of a professional program of education for life insurance salesmen. These activities are described separately in Chapters 7, 8, and 9.

Dr. Huebner always worked twelve to fourteen hours a day. He did most of his writing at night, whether at home or on the train and in hotel rooms. In Philadelphia he usually had breakfast about seven o'clock, before the children, and was on his way to classes early. One year Esther Ann felt honored because for a couple of days a week it was he who walked with her to kindergarten, seeing her safely to the door on his way to the University. The family had an early dinner together so that Dr. Huebner could get back to his evening classes or into his study where he would work until midnight or later. Often when the writing was going well he would hardly go to bed at all. In those years he did all his writing by hand with pen or pencil, generally on large-size ruled yellow paper. He sat in his rocking chair using a dressmaker's lap board for a desk. He said the motion of the chair helped him to think and its mobility made it easy to pick up notes from all the papers piled about him on tables, chairs and the floor. His book *The Stock Market* was published in 1922, and two volumes which he edited for the American Academy of Political and Social Science appeared: *Modern Insurance Problems* in 1917 and *Modern Insurance Tendencies* in 1927.

The children understood this schedule and respected it. They had deep affection and great admiration for their father even though they did not feel very close to him. One daughter said, "When you asked Father a question, he always answered it too well." He could not get away from professorial habits even at home. Another aspect of his family behavior is reflected in a remark by one of his little girls which the family continued to quote with amused understanding: "The trouble with Father is that he has his mind on higher things."

The strength of his character, his integrity, his high sense of responsibility and service made strong impressions on his family. Even when he was physically absent from home his presence was there. "We always felt Father's spirit," one daughter later commented. As honors began to come to him, as citations were given pointing out his achievements and personal characteristics, those things influenced the ideals of his family for themselves. One of his children said: "Knowing what Father has made of his life, I couldn't be satisfied with an ordinary commercial job. I have caught from him a compulsion for service."

Dr. Huebner was by no means insulated from family affairs. He tried always to be home by Saturday night, and when the children were little, shared their summer holidays. In the early days of their marriage the Huebners spent the summers in Canada. Later when Dr. Huebner was working for the government the family went to Cape May in South Jersey and he commuted as his activities allowed. Much was the important writing he did on the weekend Pullmans. His powers of concentration enabled him to accomplish mountains of work while other men dozed or read the newspaper.

Incidentally, he believes that generally people waste an inordinate amount of time in newspaper reading. When he is at home in Philadelphia he eagerly welcomes the morning and evening newspapers. He turns to the stock market and weather reports, and scans the headlines to keep abreast of the news of the world. He has, however, made it a habit not to spend more than ten minutes on a paper.

In the summers when Dr. Huebner taught at Columbia the family took a cottage on the North Jersey shore. He then had a daily commutation trip including a delightful sail from lower Manhattan to Sandy Hook which somewhat compensated for the noisy and noisesome subway ride at one end and a dirty little shore railroad run at the other. When the children were old enough for camp, Mrs. Huebner often traveled with her husband as he covered the country for life insurance appointments and on business for the American College of Life Underwriters.

Dr. and Mrs. Huebner believe strongly in camp experience for young people. Results in their own family pleased them. For a boy among three sisters it was a good change. For all, it gave an opportunity for adjustments to many kinds of people in daily living and for development in self-reliance apart from the shelter of the home.

Dr. Huebner co-operated in the children's interest in goldfish and polliwogs, although he was considerably astonished one day to come home and find live frogs on the piano. The polliwogs had grown up during his absence and had escaped the confines of their bowl. Of course even goldfish were a problem in time of family holiday. There is a favorite story about Father's struggles in taking a five-gallon aquarium *with water and fish* on the commuters' train to Chestnut Hill where kind friends were going to care for them during the summer.

A pair of cobalt parakeets also penetrated his consciousness. Before the days when parakeets were popular household pets, these lovebirds had been sold to Esther Ann. They never lived up to their name as long as they were with the Huebners. They began to screech and scold when Dr. Huebner sat down to breakfast. The ringing of the telephone bell set them off to making a frightful racket. Finally they were presented to the Philadelphia zoo where there were no specimens of their color. There they promptly retreated from each other. One demonstrated his previously advertised disposition billing and cooing with a bird of yellow plumage. The other chose a pea-green mate, and kept as far as possible from his bright blue brother.

Of course for some years there was a dog, Van Bibber, a Basset hound of friendly disposition. Dr. Huebner received him kindly and petted him often until it was discovered that the annoying redness developing on his hands came from allergy to dog hair. From that time man and beast admired each other from a distance.

University and family affairs merged in the entertaining of foreign students. Dr. Huebner had always been drawn to the Oriental students who came to Penn in great numbers. Each year he had a party for the Japanese and for the Chinese separately. The menu was generally the same for both groups—chicken à la king, quantities of boiled rice and salted almonds. These American dishes seemed like home to the guests too and were supplemented by other less familiar items which the visiting students were beginning to enjoy. After a few years individual students were entertained also, those who were sons or relatives of previous students who followed fathers and cousins into Dr. Huebner's classes and to his hospitable home. These students always came to America with some little gift for the beloved professor and his gracious wife, and many of these momentos are still on display about the house.

The worshipful attitude of these students who streamed through their home rather puzzled the children. Why should the young men place their father on such a pedestal when they knew he was so human? They had seen him go into quite a childish tantrum over a lost vest, which he himself had hung on the wrong hook in the clothes closet. They had carried the message to his study, "Father, dinner is ready," and had been answered, "Yes, I shall be there shortly"; and they had heard him storm out twenty minutes later, demanding to know why the meal was delayed, then switching to an irritated, "Why didn't somebody tell me?" They knew their father was frustrated by inanimate machinery so that he never did learn to drive an automobile, which seemed to be well within the capacities of their friends' fathers, or even mothers. In later years they saw his petulant annoyance with the dial telephone and his complete inadequacy to the tuning of TV.

As the children grew older and appreciated their father's vision in connection with his work, recognized how far ahead of his times he was in many ways, that picture was thrown into relief by what they knew at home. They remembered how their mother hated the deadly weapon of the old-fashioned razor which their father insisted on using long after everybody else had safety razors. They recalled how he stuck to the messy old shaving stick, rejecting the convenient tube of shaving cream.

Christmas has always been a festive season with the Huebners. The German tradition of feasting and carols, of the evergreens and the bright Christmas tree means much to Dr. Huebner. In early days even the tradition of real candles was followed. It was beautiful to recall the old legend of Martin Luther's picturing the stars from the Christmas sky in candles burning on the tree, but for Dr. Huebner with his deep-lying fear of fire, the pleasure was clouded. He had always a large bucket of water handy and constantly warned the children to be careful. Christmas became merrier for everybody when electric lights appeared on their tree. Each year still Dr. Huebner helps with the trimming. The Star of Bethlehem shines at the top and all the variegated balls and strings of tinsel are like those he has known from childhood. He rejoices then in the gathering of the family and enjoys children and grandchildren.

In his big family he likes to be scrupulously fair, and gives to all as he gives to one. Such a pattern does not always permit much individuality in gifts. But for Mrs. Huebner it is different. Years ago he asked her what she wanted for Christmas. Thinking quickly she remembered his study, its walls lined with shelves which were comfortably filled with books and then stuffed to untidy overflowing with old proofs and manuscripts. "All I want for Christmas," she said, "is for you to clean out your study book shelves and throw away all that stuff you don't need." He looked at her sadly without comment. A few days later he said he would give her the requested present if she would help him do it. So they sorted, piled and discarded. Three barrels of hand-written manuscripts went out in the trash, and it was Merry Christmas for the housekeeper. Mrs. Huebner's understanding of her husband and her great pride in him, as well as his deep love for her and dependence upon her, mark them as a couple to be envied. Through all the years they both must have felt her part in his great achievements.

CHAPTER SIX

The Father of Life Insurance Education

ONE morning Dr. Emory R. Johnson came into the office and said, "I think the time has come to fire you." At Dr. Huebner's startled look of inquiry he quickly added, "Don't worry. I want you to have your own department and I think now is the time for that change." This meant that Dr. Johnson voluntarily curtailed his own jurisdiction to give another man the chance for growth. The insurance courses and the courses on the security and commodity exchange markets were taken from Dr. Johnson's Transportation Department to make the new division. There was logic as well as reasons of personality for including the market courses, for organized commodity exchange markets as well as the stock exchange market make possible a practical spreading of risk through hedging and in other ways. Dr. Huebner's teaching on the insurance service of such markets is presented in Chapter 7.

Dr. Huebner became head of the Insurance Department in 1913. He had played a vigorous part in strengthening the Wharton School within the University. In his early days many of the trustees and faculty were not in sympathy with Wharton's practical programs. They wished still to emphasize the School of Arts, and extended bare toleration to the innovations of commerce. In spite of this cool climate, by 1915 Dr. Huebner had developed a teaching staff of four men in addition to himself.

How that group had grown by 1940 was described by Dr. David McCahan at a great meeting honoring Dr. Huebner.

> Dr. Huebner has gathered about him a staff of twelve experienced full time teachers who have acquired an understanding of their subject which can come only with research, continued study and maturity. Five of his associates in Pennsylvania's Insurance Department are full professors, one is an associate professor, four are assistant professors and two are instructors. Except the two instructors, all have taught at the University of Pennsylvania for at least fifteen years. Many contributions to insurance literature have been made by these associates and numerous are the constructive services which they have rendered in a great variety of responsible private and public positions. Within the Wharton School itself, one is now serving as Director of the Graduate Course in Business Administration, and another as Director of the Institute of Local and State Government.

With good reason even in the early days Dr. Huebner was being called "The Father of Life Insurance Education." He always liked strong men around him. Frequently he picked his teachers from among his own students. He built his department with the best men he could get and he attracted many who were, like himself, outstanding in ability and deep integrity. He never hesitated to take those who might be greater scholars than he. He gave added responsibility and promotions based upon performance rather than on seniority alone. He offered a challenge to young men with ability. None of his associates felt they need be "yes men." In fact department meetings were often marked by radical differences of opinion. Nobody ever doubted Dr. Huebner's personal honor or his fairness. He was straightforward and fine in all his dealings. One associate said: "His staff felt completely free to express independent judgment. They talked back. They rolled him over. But he welcomed it and loved it."

As in all strong characters, his personal idiosyncrasies easily were exaggerated by high-spirited young men who sometimes in private would mimic his performance in class or in staff meetings. They might make a little sport of his great earnestness, but everybody liked and respected him. One of his early associates said: "He wanted so badly to accomplish his objectives, that you felt toward him rather like toward a little boy. You hoped he would not be disappointed."

Some of the students delighted to repeat verbal incongruities, spoken in the heat of excitement or urgency. Such things as the man who "worked tooth and nail to the nth degree," "editorial liberalities," the character who was "a nonentity par excellence" became a legend. One day a number of his students in the big lecture room did not take their seats according to the chart. They roared with laughter and quoted far and wide Dr. Huebner's attempt to correct the situation, beginning with, "Some of you seem to be sitting in empty seats."

Wharton School Insurance Department staff, 1936. *Front row, left to right,* C. A. Kline, E. L. McKenna, S. S. Huebner, R. Kip, G. W. Hoffman. *Back row,* D. McCahan, C. M. Kahler, H. J. Loman, G. A. Amrhein, S. B. Sweeney, and C. K. Knight.

World War I began for the United States in April 1917. There was no great immediate effect on the University though some students responded to patriotic speeches and enlisted. The next month, however, the country began to be disturbed about farm labor requirements and students were urged to volunteer for that work. At Pennsylvania, if a student were in good standing, he was allowed to leave for the farms in May and still have credit for the full term's work. By fall of 1917 the draft was cutting in heavily so that classes were noticeably reduced in numbers although the University's general pattern of operation was still fairly intact. By spring of 1918 throughout the country the exodus of college students to the services was so serious that the government created the Student Army Training Corps. That blanketed the students into the Army to allow them to finish their academic year's work with certain elements of military training added to the academic program.

At Pennsylvania, as elsewhere, they attended classes in uniform and quipped that their designation of S.A.T.C. meant "Safe At The Colleges." A University observer said that the plan gave the young men "enough military training to destroy the curriculum, but not enough to produce good soldiers."

Of course young professors as well as students enlisted or were drafted. Dr. Huebner with a wife and children was not in early danger of the draft. As others left he carried an increasingly heavy load of academic work with large classes. He also worked under a Navy program, lecturing on insurance for five hours on Friday each week to the members of the Navy Pay Corps School at Princeton, where four hundred ensigns were in training. When the Armstice came the question was raised about the future of these young officers. That Princeton program was partly under the direction of Lieutenant Commander Frederic A. Savage, who in private life was general agent in Baltimore for the New England Mutual Life Insurance Company. Commander Savage realized what a problem there was in the more than forty billion dollars of term life insurance protection on the lives of servicemen under the Goverment War Risk Life Insurance policies. He went to Dr. Huebner with the suggestion that these service policyholders needed help. They were everywhere being discharged in ignorance of the value of their convertible policies. He proposed that Dr. Huebner give his ensigns a thorough life insurance training. Then they could be sent all over the country to Navy bases to sell the servicemen the idea of keeping their government life insurance policies. Dr. Huebner said he was too busy and added: "You've got three of my men in the Navy now." That was not an objection, but an answer to Commander Savage. He said: "If you will start a school for the ensigns at the University of Pennsylvania, I'll get your men back to teach it. I've authority to requisition men from anywhere in the world."

Dr. Harry J. Loman was nearby. The Navy brought him back to campus immediately and the school was organized. The other two men, Dr. Charles K. Knight and Dr. Robert Riegel, had to be located and transferred from overseas so they did not return until the special classes were practically over, but the assignment was a great help in bringing them back in time for the fall term. For these Navy groups, Dr. Huebner did the lectures and Loman, Knight, and Riegel* took the quiz classes.

The Navy boys liked Dr. Huebner as much as his civilian students did. They grew accustomed to a professor who pounded his fists and waved his arms, and who moved actively from

---

* Dr. Loman had started teaching for Dr. Huebner in 1917 before he had his degree. Dr. Huebner had identified him as outstanding in a class of graduate students. He called him to his office and invited him to join his teaching staff. Loman reminded him that he was still an undergraduate and technically unacceptable to the University. Dr. Huebner, for the moment frustrated, rocked back and forth and chewed his moustache. Suddenly light came to face, "I have it. You don't need a degree for evening school. You can start there and I need you." Dr. Loman has been dean of the American Institute for Property and Liability Underwriters since 1942. Dr. Knight was a member of the Wharton School faculty until his retirement in 1958. Dr. Riegel is Professor of Statistics at the University of Buffalo.

desk to blackboard and back again. In lecture sessions they heard him easily in the back rows of the big lecture room, as did other people down the hall or through several walls of adjacent classrooms.

In all his teaching career Dr. Huebner had a strong personal attraction for the young men. They liked his happy disposition, his enthusiasm, his evident enjoyment of life and ideas. He had the wonderful gift of stimulating young minds and of influencing others, which is the test of a great teacher. Many times he was voted the most popular professor on campus.

Dr. Huebner's former students, asked about their impressions of him, are quick to respond: "He was a man greatly beloved," "He was terrific in class," "He always kept you awake and made you think," "I came to Penn so that I could study under him, and lots of other fellows did too."

One student made an observation that was most complimentary in its essence but seemed at first hearing a bit startling. He said: "Dr. Huebner was not interested in reading books. He wrote them. He didn't quote to us in class the opinions of dead authorities, but reported some experience of yesterday or an item from the morning paper to support his point."

In his life insurance teaching Dr. Huebner felt the importance not only of getting away from the mathematical side of the business, but also in making his approach from the angle of life, not of death. He saw that the students who came to Wharton were interested in the profit motive. He had to relate life insurance to money making and separate it from funereal associations. So he expounded the advantages of life insurance for the man who pays the premiums. He helped the young men to understand the investment features of life insurance, to see how it promotes thrift, to realize that a man who protects his family has a freer mind for business matters. Especially did he demonstrate that freedom to venture in many commercial enterprises depended upon the possibility of sharing the risk of loss. The place of property insurance in underwriting great enterprises had been long understood, but he made clear in a new way how life insurance fitted the picture too. When a new manufacturing process depended upon the know-how of one scientist to guide through the development period, there was a place for life insurance. When young partners were risking every cent they could pull together to make and distribute a new product, the man with contacts for the foreign market, for instance, might be the key to their success. There life insurance could carry the risk which the young men could not dare assume. Seeing life insurance in such a setting brought it into the circle of students' major interests.

Dr. Huebner himself grew in his appreciation of these truths as, in daily contact with his faculty associates at the Wharton School, he saw the influence of individual men in the growth of America. The other professors reported to him news from the world of commerce and industry. It was the time when great personalities were laying the foundations for fortunes and when many a business was still the lengthened shadow of one man. It was exciting to see how life insurance could release such men from the inhibiting effects of the fear of the future. The courage of confidence affected their dynamic leadership, helping to keep them out ahead, breaking new ground, bringing changes in marketing, manufacturing and in all the way of life in America. This picture of the service of life insurance Dr. Huebner transmitted to his classes. No wonder his department was popular.

Dr. Huebner was not an easy teacher. Students took his work because they wanted the experience not because his courses ever were known as a snap. When a boy played around and wasted his time, Dr. Huebner pulled no punches in taking him to task. Particularly if he felt the student's parents were sacrificing for his education, he recalled him vigorously to his duty and opportunity. He was strict in his personal relationships. If a student was late to an appointment, he refused to see him at all, believing that promptness is a basic business virtue. From his own school days when his father insisted on punctuality, he has been meticulous in keeping personal and business appointments. His family often chide him about always being early for appointments. They say it is the only way he ever wastes time.

Dr. Huebner's personal popularity naturally "attracted the customers" to his classes and to the Wharton School. Because of his dynamic leadership on campus and travels all over the country, the Wharton School was getting the reputation of being an *insurance* school rather than a *business* school, and by 1922 Wharton was by far the largest school of the University. It was natural that some faculty members with less forceful personalities and smaller energy looked with a jaundiced eye upon the relative dominance of insurance in the University picture. Some criticized Dr. Huebner's scholastic attainments. One associate, who felt very confident of his own superior intellectual equipment, was said to have remarked, "Wouldn't it be wonderful if one man could have my brains and Sol's energy!"

One long-time friend said: "It is true that as a precise, careful research scholar Sol is open to criticism. But he has that rare and subtle talent called creativity. A typical scholar could not possibly have created as he has both in the University and in his outside affairs."

Commenting about the conflicting emotions Dr. Huebner aroused among the faculty, one University colleague said: "You will find appraisals varying all the way between a messiah and a charlatan, and of course he was neither."

Dr. Huebner's enthusiasm for all areas of insurance led to specialization in University courses that was debated heatedly by other members of the faculty. Somebody charged, "Any curriculum is a good curriculum to Sol if it has enough insur-

Dr. and Mrs. Huebner in 1927.

ance in it." Educationally, many other members of the faculty believed that undergraduates should not be allowed the specialization which he offered. They urged the School to recognize that men need other things beside insurance. A quotation from the official history of the Wharton School written for its fiftieth anniversary may well express what many were thinking:

> The men in the Wharton School are being educated for their life work; but no man's life is limited to his vocation. "Man does not live by bread alone." The satisfactions of life come mainly from mental and spiritual growth, from the pleasures afforded by literature, history, science and art, from unselfish labors on behalf of others, from being of service to one's community and one's country. The man is not educated and is not trained for the life a business man should lead, or that a professional man or any other man should follow, unless his education has aroused his interest in the garnered fruits of civilization. The educated man is the man who has both a vocation and an avocation, a fad, a zeal for something other than the accumulation of wealth.

It is true that real education is a matter of balance, but for great achievement balance often must be disturbed. Dr. Huebner's ability to win the interest and enthusiasm of many students resulted in a focus of creativity at the Wharton School that had far-reaching influence for the University and for all the fields of insurance. The students kept coming and class registration overcame academic theory. By the time Dr. Huebner retired, the list of available undergraduate courses in the department had grown to ten. These included basic courses in insurance, life insurance and the security and commodity exchange markets with their insurance functions. Then there were more specialized courses in the various types of property insurance, in loss prevention, in the services of life underwriting, in social insurance; and two senior seminar integrating courses.

The enthusiasm of his students led to Dr. Huebner's first trip to the Orient. The alumni of the University of Pennsylvania in Japan urged him to come there for a tour of Japanese universities. Invitations were received also from China and other countries where former students recalled with affection the professor who had meant so much to them in Philadelphia. Dr. Huebner sailed for Japan from San Francisco early in June 1927, with Mrs. Huebner accompanying him for the summer while the children were in camp.

In effect the trip was an exchange professorship involving a semester's leave with pay from the University and he considered it as an honor and an award. His own itinerary was planned to take him still west from Asia to the University of Berlin.

On the ship from San Francisco was a retired Roman Catholic priest, traveling on an annuity. Discussion revealed that he had been a teacher for the Church and years before in Martinique had used with his students Dr. Huebner's *Life Insurance*. From him Dr. Huebner learned of the Church's realistic attitude toward economic problems of family life and was pleased to discover that his writings were being widely used in Catholic schools.

By way of the Hawaiian Islands the voyage was continued safely to Japan. It was a time of unrest there. Upon Dr. Huebner's arrival he found that the whole economic faculty of one university was under arrest, having displeased the government by some of their teachings. At another college the students were on strike against the dean. In spite of such difficulties Dr. Huebner lectured at thirteen leading Japanese universities and addressed all kinds of insurance groups and organizations throughout the islands. He traveled by train then, of course, and was given free transportation by the government, which owned the railroads. He developed great admiration for the Japanese perfection in organization. In thousands of miles of travel on their narrow gauge railroads he was never late for connections or appointments. He said, "Everything clicked." Punctuality was a national standard. If one should be as little as two minutes late for an appointment, the polite thing was to go home, write an apology and seek another date. Dr. Huebner visited the lower schools of Japan as well as the universities. He admired the discipline of the children. As he and his guide stepped into a classroom not a child turned a head. Only after the teacher had explained the visitors and given permission did they look at the interesting stranger. Dr. Huebner always remembered too the unusual art work of these children, which showed great skill and originality. He was told that the children never were allowed to copy. Each was to express what he himself saw whether he was drawing his honorable father or the cherry tree in the garden.

The military were in considerable evidence in Japanese cities in 1927. Dr. Huebner had no great admiration for them with their sword rattling and airs of importance. However, in general Dr. and Mrs. Huebner both fell in love with Japan, drawn to the country as they had been drawn to the Japanese students at home. They were fascinated by the architecture and by the Shinto shrines and Buddhist temples, and enjoyed the treasures of Japanese art. Everywhere the friends showed them the most cherished possessions and the most lovely and interesting sights of each locality.

The occasions of Dr. Huebner's lectures at that time were usually very formal. In the daytime he wore striped trousers and a cutaway; at night, formal evening clothes with white tie. There were many social events and the banquets with their elaborate toasts and greetings, music and entertainment were held in the geisha houses. Shoes must be removed upon entry there, and Dr. Huebner always was careful to have no holes in his socks.

The speaking schedule included a series of lectures at some universities (as many as twelve talks at one), and single addresses at others. The audiences were men from all fields of insurance, which is divided there into life, nonlife (i.e., casualty) and fire and marine. Dr. Huebner talked sometimes about American finance in general and security markets. Most of all, he spoke on principles of insurance. He discussed often, too, his concept of the human life value, and the Chartered Life Underwriter movement which was developing in the United States (see Chapters 9 and 10) and found his audiences keenly interested. In fact he learned that some C.L.U. textbooks had already been translated into Japanese. The audiences in Japan as well as in China and Korea later were eager to hear about corporate bonding. That kind of insurance was little known because the Oriental family system had always made the family head responsible for any defalcation of a member. With the development of modern business and changing social standards, the assumption of such responsibility was bringing intolerable risk to the family. New generations were seeking new methods of meeting the need for such protection in business affairs.

Dr. Huebner usually lectured with the aid of an interpreter. The translation was not verbatim, sentence by sentence. He would speak for ten or fifteen minutes. Then a Japanese professor of insurance, who had been one of his students at the Wharton School, would repeat his ideas in Japanese. Thus an hour's lecture would take about two hours. This process was used in spite of a rather wide knowledge of English on the part of the lecture audiences. In fact Dr. Huebner felt that a larger proportion of people knew English then than he found thirty years later.

From Japan the Huebners had planned to go to China. Officials in the American embassy protested that China was too unsettled and danger was great. Dr. Huebner insisted that he had all kinds of engagements with insurance people, businessmen and even Rotary Clubs, and he intended to fulfill his commitments. The embassy warned that he would go only at his own risk and in trouble could not claim the protection of the American Flag.

Dr. and Mrs. Huebner thought of all their friends in China. The chief officer of the Bank of China in nearly every big city was a Wharton School graduate. The head of the Chinese railway system had often, as a student, been in their home. They decided to go, and got along beautifully. The universities were closed for the summer but meetings for lectures were arranged with groups of teachers, students, and insurance underwriters. They went to Shanghai and Hong Kong. They traveled on a Japanese freight and passenger steamer up the coast and into the Pei River to beautiful Tientsin and to Peking. Dr. Huebner after thirty years recalls Peking as one of the tremendous experiences of their lives. The beauties and wonders of that city which had been the capital of the Chinese Empire for five hundred years were opened to them by former students who vied with each other in giving pleasure and honor to their beloved professor. The Huebners marveled at China's Great Wall and at pagodas and temples. They delighted in the Forbidden City within its walls of purplish glazed brick topped with yellow tiles, its red-columned imperial buildings upon their white marble terraces under the bright blue sky, and gardens everywhere.

They went on to Manchuria by rail. The manager of Chinese railways provided a private car for them with a cook and a guard of four soldiers. At every stop they were saluted by friends and the admiring populace. At Mukden the Huebners especially enjoyed a museum whose Japanese curator showed them the beauties of the past and spoke eloquently of Japan's great plans for future developments.

They continued to Korea which was then Japanese controlled. There they found that a Korean, who was a former Wharton School student, was head of the international press, and he helped give them another very pleasant time.

Dr. Huebner lectured at Seoul at a hotel which he remembered as one of the most beautiful he ever enjoyed. It had been built by a German architect who combined European comfort with the verandas and gardens of the East. It was a jewel in a well-ordered city where the gentle Korean people went about their business dressed in immaculate white and strange high-crowned, flat-brimmed hats.

At the end of the summer Mrs. Huebner returned to Philadelphia, by way of Vancouver and the Canadian Rockies, to supervise the children in school and college. Dr. Huebner continued to the Philippines, Ceylon, the Malay Peninsula, India, and Egypt. He gave a few addresses at scattered points along the way, although there were then no student friends in Ceylon or India. On this part of the trip he met again the priest whom he had liked on the Pacific crossing. They talked insurance and theology and all subjects akin or diverse. They crossed the Lybian Desert together in a rattletrap old car with no spare tires. When Dr. Huebner questioned what they would do if the terrific heat caused a blowout, the Moslem driver shrugged his shoulders and committed their destiny to Allah. The tire did blow. As the Moslem struggled to repair it Dr. Huebner commented, "Allah was not with you," and the man became very angry. This impressed upon him that no man's religion is to be made sport of, for to him it is sacred.

All through the East the demands of the beggars and the spirit of *caveat emptor* disturbed him. He saw tourists fleeced by smooth-talking traders and mentally compared their business standards with those of his good friend John Wanamaker who had died only a few years before in Philadelphia having established new ideals in merchandising. How much of American progress was based upon mutual trust and good faith?

In Italy Dr. Huebner saw again with pleasure the sights he had enjoyed in 1903. He found that much progress had been made in the excavation of Pompeii and walked in wonder through its ancient streets. He left the greater part of his luggage at Naples and went on to Venice and Austria, at last reaching Berlin where he lectured at the University of Berlin to a large group of the faculty and many invited guests including high government officials. It was his first visit to the land of his fathers. He enjoyed the Black Forest, which reminded him of his forester grandfather, and the old university cities, with their associations with German scientists and philosophers.

Back at Naples he found his bags safely aboard ship, but in that day of Mussolini's power he discovered that they had all been carefully searched. The ship touched at Genoa and Marseilles, then a last stop at Gibralter before setting course across the Atlantic and home after seven months of memorable experience in giving and receiving.

The crossing was rough, as bad as the captain had ever seen, and they arrived in New York in a fog that kept them lying in the harbor from morning until late afternoon. Mrs. Huebner was at the dock to meet him and finally they were on their way home to Philadelphia and the children. The family was very used to Father's comings and goings, but this was for all a special homecoming.

At the University the faculty of the Insurance Department had a welcome-home gift for him—a new rocking chair for his office. It was a sturdy, high-backed "mission" style wooden chair, well cushioned for comfort, and it has served him ever since. He uses it at his desk in the American College headquarters today.

It was good to get back to his classes at the University, daytime and evening, and to meet his extension students again. He plunged back into C.L.U. affairs and resumed government service. He picked up again his activities as member of several committees in nonlife insurance organizations where he served as a life insurance specialist: the Committee on Insurance and Pensions for the American Association of University Professors; the Insurance Advisory Committee for the United States Chamber of Commerce; and the Committee on Insurance and Fire Prevention for the Philadelphia Chamber of Commerce. In 1928 he became a member of the Committee of Insurance Advisors for the General Federation of Women's Clubs with its nearly three million membership in twenty thousand clubs. He edited another volume for the American Academy of Political and Social Science, *Organized Commodity Exchanges.*

In 1930 a great honor came to him in election to membership in the American Philosophical Society. That had been founded in colonial times by Benjamin Franklin and today is a scholars' organization. Dr. Huebner learned of his election through the newspapers as he was returning from Washington where he had been serving one of the Congressional committees. About a dozen Americans and half as many others from abroad are admitted to the Society each year and share in a program of learned papers.

During all this time Dr. Huebner was having a formative

part in Wharton School affairs beyond even his contacts with students in his own department. The official history of the School reported concerning that period:

The Wharton School Insurance Department faculty about 1931. ***Front row, left to right,*** **C. K. Knight, David McCahan, S. S. Huebner, H. J. Loman.** ***Second row,*** **C. M. Kahler, J. F. Jeremiah, G. W. Hoffman, S. B. Sweeney, C. A. Kulp.** ***Third row,*** **G. L. Amrhein, Henry Everding, C. A. Kline, E. L. McKenna, D. A. Locke.**

Without doubt the majority of the students graduating from the Wharton School would testify that the most valuable course taken or work done during their four years of study has been in "senior research." At the end of the junior year each student is called upon to select a subject which he is to investigate during his senior year and upon which he is to write a thesis. A satisfactory senior thesis is required as a condition of graduation. The investigation and the preparation of the thesis are under the supervision and guidance of members of the faculty. The purposes of the requirement are to train the student in methods of investigation, to cause him to think things out for himself, to give him exercise in the appraisal of data, the arrangement of material and the writing of good English. The investigation usually brings the student into contact with business men and oranizations—in insurance, merchandising, manufacturing, banking or in other kinds of business—and often these contacts aid the students, upon graduation, to start their life work under favorable conditions. The requirement of the senior investigation and thesis made a distinct addition to the value of the educational work of the School. The faculty members in charge of senior research in the several departments constitute the "Committee on Senior Research Work" that, under the able chairmanship of Professor S. S. Huebner has set the standards to be attained and has adopted and carried out the regulations governing the manner and methods of supervising senior research.

The two-year Graduate Course in Business Administration had been started in 1922. Although it was not strictly a part of the Wharton School the teachers were members of the Wharton faculty. It was organized especially to meet the needs of graduates of colleges and universities that did not have collegiate schools of business, and it attracted men from all over the world. Insurance courses were offered, of course. By 1931 there were more than a hundred students in the Graduate Course and the enrollment of the Wharton School was about two thousand.

The Wharton School was fifty years old in 1931. As part of the anniversary celebration honorary doctoral degrees were awarded to five men who had contributed greatly to the institution's growth and development. One of these had, in fact, become the personification of the Wharton School to a national industry. His citation, read as follows:

> SOLOMON STEPHEN HUEBNER—Son of the University of Wisconsin and of this University. For over a quarter of a century you have followed the calling of the teacher with high seriousness of purpose and with outstanding success, winning the admiration and affection of your students and of your colleagues in the faculty through the soundness of your scholarship and through rare gifts of personality. Your influence upon the lives of large numbers of American youth cannot be measured, as you have contributed generously and unsparingly to the development of the Wharton School. As an eminent authority in your chosen field, you have written books that have gained wide recognition, and your services as consultant have frequently been sought by branches of our National Government. In your consideration of business you have ever emphasized its more human aspects, and by your work you have had extraordinary effect upon the economic fundamentals which underlie the great business of insurance.
>
> In recognition of what you have accomplished for mankind in one of the important economic fields and in recognition of what you have done in the service of the University by holding before your students high standards of personal integrity and of social responsibility, we have invited you to be present today in order that public honor may be given you. Mr. President, I have the honor to present Solomon Stephen Huebner for the degree of Doctor of Science.

CHAPTER SEVEN

The Professor in the Market Place

FROM the beginning Dr. Huebner was fascinated by the stock market. He saw its hazards and risks, of course, but he looked beyond the surface manifestations and found, as he says, that "the real soul of the industry is insurance." With the growth of his knowledge of both fields came increasing conviction about this interpretation which is so surprising to the uninitiated.

Dr. Huebner's constant desire to make practical use of what he learned naturally led him to personal experiment in stock ownership. His first transaction was in 1906. He had saved a thousand dollars and decided to buy a block of Pennsylvania Railroad stock. In those days it was possible to operate on a 10 per cent margin and he made his purchase in that way. He was on the eve of departure for a holiday fishing trip in the West where he would be beyond the reach of his broker. The man told him frankly that if the market went down they would sell him out. Dr. Huebner agreed and left for northern Wisconsin. Some weeks later when he came back from the woods to his old home in Manitowoc, the first thing he did was to get a newspaper and check the quotations. He saw that his stock was far higher than when he had bought. But had it gone down first? Had he been sold out? Eventually he found that he still owned his shares and had made 100 per cent on his margin deposit.

As soon as he returned to Philadelphia he sold and took his profit.

The broker apparently had mixed feelings about this experience and took the opportunity to give some strong advice. He said, "Young man, you were lucky. Don't put this good result down to your intelligence. It is nice to have a thousand dollars on top of your first thousand, but now put it away somewhere and don't try to do it again. If you tried again, you might win again. Then you would be bound to keep it up, but you'd get your solar plexus some day. This kind of thing gets to be a fever and you don't want to catch it."

In telling this story Dr. Huebner added: "I always relished that fellow. He did a lot for me. I learned more from him than from anybody else in the stock market." He emphasized to Dr. Huebner that his employees were strictly forbidden to express opinions or to offer advice. He wanted to be sure that nobody ever blamed his staff for what happened to them in their speculations. The broker also told Dr. Huebner that as he watched the people in his board room, in those days of buying on a 10 or 15 per cent margin, he saw a turnover about once every three years. Even people who might be lucky at first eventually washed out in about that time.

Impressed by such experience Dr. Huebner has always taught strongly against buying stock on margin except for a purpose, such as for a man who wants to get a controlling interest in a corporation and needs to use credit. He says that you risk losing two ways when you buy on margin. You risk your money—which is obvious. You also risk your calling; you risk personal disintegration. His observations make him believe that anxiety in watching the market, obsession with the level of prices, and deflection of attention from a person's main job are too big a price to pay for what may seem like a possible profit. Of course current law has changed the picture, but for many years marginal buying was a real problem.

The chief question now is the risk in outright stock ownership. Dr. Huebner feels that the great mass of the population has no conception of what they are getting in a stock certificate. In a period when the average man turns to the stock market page in the newspaper before he looks at the funnies, Dr. Huebner is disturbed. He says to himself, "Now stocks are being shifted from those who know more to those who know less." He always emphasizes that stock ownership involves no promise of any money value currently or in the future. The certificate gives the owner only the right to participate, as in marriage, for better or for worse. A stockholder may vote (generally) and he must take what comes.

Dr. Huebner strongly disapproves of plans for stock ownership by employees. The transit employees of Philadelphia were encouraged to buy stock in the company with no understanding of the risks that were involved. The result was resentment when values went down, and a feeling that somehow the company had stolen their savings. Similar experiences have disillusioned employees in many other places in the past generation.

Dr. Huebner believes that nobody should be encouraged to buy stock if he cannot afford the possibility of loss of capital. Without question, in his mind, really adequate life insurance provision and home ownership come first for a man with a family. He regards stock ownership as a patriotic duty. Capital is made available for great creative purposes through the willingness of investors to take certain risks. In the long run this is an advantage to the whole community. In regard to selecting a stock to buy, he comments that a principle to remember is that the stock market reflects the average of judgments about what is coming. Therefore it is, as he says, "always ahead"—a discounter of future market events. In buying stocks, he advises, if you want to play safe, act the opposite of what you read, what you see, and what you hear, and therefore of what you think. Such independence of decision is uncommon, to say the least.

An equity contract which cannot be a promise, Dr. Huebner believes definitely should be separated from a life insurance contract which is completely a promise. Equity investments for a life company portfolio are another matter. He has never been opposed to a reasonable proportion, like 5 to 10 per cent only of the portfolio, of well-chosen stocks as corporate holdings for policyholders.

Dr. Huebner presented his first course in "Organized Security and Produce Exchange Markets" at the Wharton School in his first year of teaching, 1904. It was popular from the beginning, for he emphasized the human side of exchange activities—what services were being given to buyers and sellers and the whole business community—rather than the operational procedures. He constantly exposed himself to practical financiers and other teachers. By 1911 he had edited three comprehensive volumes on these subjects for the American Academy of Political and Social Science: *Bonds and the Bond Market*, *Stocks and the Stock Market*, and *American Produce Exchange Markets*. He was given the freedom of the floor of the New York Stock Exchange when that was still rare and a great honor. He often served as expert witness for the New York Stock Exchange in government hearings testifying about the facts and economic services of speculation, short selling, and similar matters. He introduced an element of sobriety and science in what were often highly emotional and prejudiced proceedings.

Dr. Huebner for a short time taught his Wharton School course on the security and commodity exchanges also in New York City. The course was presented under the auspices of New York University and the classes were held at the Stock Exchange. A number of members of the Exchange were in the class. They knew a great deal more than he did, of course, about practical things. But they wanted to have the advantage of the organized academic study of their business and especially to learn his concept of the insurance services which underlay their buying and selling.

A complete review of Dr. Huebner's ideas is not desirable here, but a few suggestions will be significant. Insurance is the spread of risk, or the elimination of risk. Dr. Huebner explained that the exchanges of our country and of the world normally constitute a continuous market. The price of a security on an exchange represents a composite judgment of experts as to its value. Thus the stock market spreads the risk of error in an individual judgment and provides an average, with discounting also of the future. The eyes of the experts on the exchanges are always on the future and the prices at which they are willing to trade are based upon their judgments of coming events.

The continuous market of the exchanges, both security and produce, makes quick sales possible. This enables an arbitrager to buy low on one market and sell high on another, reducing the risk of loss which delay would cause.

Speed in the process of trading on the organized exchanges makes possible short selling. Though the public often criticized this practice, Dr. Huebner explained it, too, as economically beneficial. It is selling what you do not have—a security or produce—at such a price that you can anticipate completing the transaction at a profit. In a falling market, the need of buying on the part of those who have sold "short" helps create a continuous demand which supports the price and reduces the possibility of extreme losses.

The exchange practices of "puts," "calls," and "straddles," and the use of "stop-loss" orders, are all basically insurance, setting the limits of losses on the transactions involved.

Hedging is technically an operation of simultaneous buying and selling, but it is essentially insurance. In fact, when Dr.

Huebner went to Japan in 1927, he found the Japanese exchanges using the expressions "insurance sales" and "insurance purchases" to convey the meaning of hedging. Frequently, dealers, processors, and manufacturers enter into contracts for future delivery of a product in necessary ignorance of the future price of their raw materials. Through the process of hedging on a produce exchange they can do this safely, in effect thus insuring their trade profits. Concerning this, Dr. Huebner wrote:

> The speculative market is used to eliminate speculation in business, the gamble of speculative price fluctuations being thrown upon those whose business it is to assume such risks. . . .
>
> Leading produce exchanges, such as the Chicago Board of Trade and the New York Cotton Exchange, render in this respect a function as legitimate and useful as our life, fire and marine insurance companies; in fact they should be regarded as among the greatest insurance institutions in existence. Here, by means of short-selling, a type of risk is assumed by speculators so dangerous that no private insurance company has ever ventured to underwrite it.

Dr. Huebner crystallized his teachings about the stock market in a book of that title which appeared first in 1922. That quickly became a widely used text and increased his reputation as an authority in a field of growing interest to the whole nation. Soon the booming stock market was front-page news. Dow-Jones averages were common conversation among people who had little understanding of their meaning. Herbert Hoover campaigned during the 1928 election with the prophecy of two chickens in every pot and two cars in every garage as the picture of what was soon to be normal living for American families. Schoolteachers and taxi drivers, as well as bankers and industrialists, thought prosperity was permanent. Possibly some college professors had their misgivings.

Surely neither Dr. Huebner nor anybody else knew it when the stock market passed its peak one day in September, 1929.

Everybody knew, however, when panic struck on October 24. United States Steel, which had been as high as 261¾, opened that day at 205½ and went down to 193½. General Electric, which had been above 400, opened at 315 and dropped to 283. As the avalanche gathered speed, New York's biggest bankers quickly got together and formed a pool to support prices. Richard Whitney, vice president of the New York Stock Exchange, and known as J. P. Morgan's broker, acted for the pool. He went out on the floor and bid a spectacular 205 for U.S. Steel, 15 points above the market at that moment. That bold action temporarily halted the destructive slide and made Whitney a popular hero. The rally did not last, however. Dr. Huebner shared the horror, but not all the surprise, of that black October 29, when more than sixteen million shares changed hands. Eight and a half billion dollars of values disappeared. The Big Bull Market was dead. In six weeks of that autumn of 1929, price quotations on all American exchanges dropped some fifty billion dollars.

The experiences of the next few years were deeply educational, if not pleasant. Dr. Huebner continued his teaching about the markets with many new exhibits to illustrate his principles. Public pressures to reform and regulate the stock market stimulated various activities in which Dr. Huebner was involved. He became a consultant for a public relations committee for the New York Stock Exchange. He urged for the securities business the development of an educational program comparable to that of the American College of Life Underwriters for life insurance. At the request of the Exchange he made an extensive survey of the then current teaching concerning stock exchange markets in American colleges and universities. The survey revealed a very limited treatment of the subject and indicated a great need for such instruction both for workers in the business and for the general public. Dr. Huebner, therefore, again at the request of the Exchange, developed a

Dr. S. S. Huebner in his Logan Hall office in the 1930's. The roll-top desk had belonged to Mr. Joseph Wharton.

complete outline of a fifteen-weeks', one-semester course with subject matter and bibliography on "The Economic Services, Principles and Practices of Organized Stock Exchange Markets."

Some progress apparently was being made when a bombshell hit Wall Street. The president of the New York Stock Exchange announced one morning in March, 1938 that Richard Whitney & Company had been suspended for "conduct apparently contrary to just and equitable principles of trade." Whitney had been the symbol of power and leadership in October, 1929. Subsequently he had served for five years as president of the Exchange. He was tall, handsome, a socialite educated at Groton and Harvard. In the course of his various services for the Exchange, Dr. Huebner knew Mr. Whitney casually. He was a pleasant and intelligent man who occasionally after a committee meeting would draw Dr. Huebner aside with "Doctor, I'd like to talk to you a moment about ...." Dr. Huebner liked him, and was flabbergasted at the bad news.

Whitney made a clean breast of his troubles. He had become involved in hundreds of thousands of dollars of debt and misappropriated trust funds in a frantic effort to save himself. He was convicted of larceny and sent to Sing Sing. Dr. Huebner, recalling his feelings as consultant for the Stock Exchange public relations committee, made a considerable understatement in his comment: "It was quite an unpleasant time. You didn't know just what to do."

In the confusions that followed, the project for collegiate-level educational courses for stock exchange workers lost its priority. Dr. Huebner felt also that there was another fundamental difficulty. The stock exchange people had shown an unwillingness to divorce the proposed professional program from the industry and to have it identified completely with educational institutions. Such separation was the basis for the success of the Certified Public Accountant program, which by then was a generation old, and of the new Chartered Life Underwriter program, which was in its thriving youth. Dr. Huebner has always stressed that a professional movement must be by examination independent of the industry involved.

Concerning professional education for workers in finance, he wrote recently:

> I have believed for years that the leading personnel in all important economic industries which use other people's money, should by examination be obliged to qualify for the public performance of their functions. Any one possessing resources can start a bank and use other people's money in most dangerous economic ways. I have often gone so far as to say that every United States Senator and Congressman, since these representatives have so much to do with the economic welfare of the nation, should qualify professionally by examination and not only by being asked to meet the voters' standard of popularity.

As Professor Huebner undergirded his teaching about stock and commodity exchanges by close personal knowledge and association with men on the exchanges, so he strengthened his life insurance teaching by getting the consumer's point of view at first hand. He constantly sought opportunities to talk to owners of large amounts of life insurance. He asked these men why they had bought. Then he made their answers the raw material for his class discussions. No wonder his courses were lively.

His students were impressed to hear about Frank A. Vanderlip. He had made a spectacular rise from midwest journalism and government service in Washington to be vice president and then president of the great National City Bank. When he came to New York he bought a very substantial life insurance estate. He told Dr. Huebner that as a bank officer his salary was many times what he had earned previously and he had raised his family's standard of living appropriately. As long as he lived and continued earning, all would be well. The hazard was what the family would lose if he died. Dr. Huebner pointed out to the students that this demonstrated vividly the economic value of a man's life, a value as rightfully insurable as any property value.

Another interesting case was of a bachelor, an engineer, who was heavily insured. Dr. Huebner asked his reasons and reported to the class that the engineer was a contractor handling long-term mining contracts running into hundreds of thousands of dollars. For these he had to give completion bonds, and he bought his life insurance to protect the bonding company. The engineer's death would have disrupted the work on the jobs which required his specialized training and experience.

A New York State bankers' convention at Lake Placid gave Dr. Huebner material for many class discussions. The meeting brought him face to face with more millionaires than he had ever before had in one lecture group. To them he recalled the practice of issuing callable sinking fund bonds to protect bondholders of an enterprise using exhaustible property, such as timberlands or a mine. Such bonds are repaid at the end of a stipulated time from a fund calculated to be built up methodically over the years out of current earnings improved at interest. These bonds may also be "called" and repaid before the final date. Then he pointed out that a man's earning power likewise is exhaustible property and that any individual life may be "called" by Providence. The parallel between a permanent life insurance policy and the bankers' callable sinking fund bond was to them a completely new idea.

After that talk the bankers crowded around Dr. Huebner with all sorts of questions and comments, which he reported to his students:

"What you're talking about is just what I as a private banker do every day in appraising property. I'm capitalizing values."

"You've set me thinking. I have $100,000 of life insurance, but if your ideas are right, that's only peanuts to what I should own."

"I know twenty-five or thirty life insurance agents, but no one of them ever told me anything like this."

Some life underwriters did use Dr. Huebner's ideas, however, and he relayed to the students the story of a spectacular experience. The salesman approached one of the best-known men in Wall Street. He said: "Mr. Banker, you are about the biggest capitalizer in the country. You capitalize everything except yourself. Why not do that too?" After some deliberation the banker bought two million dollars of life insurance.

In Philadelphia John Wanamaker was a prominent citizen who was said to be one of the most heavily insured men in the world. When asked whether his ownership of life insurance could be reported publicly, John Wanamaker said, "Shout it from the housetops, if you wish. I'm proud of it and am glad to have people know it."

Dr. Huebner sought an interview with Mr. Wanamaker who

welcomed him cordially on his first call and gave him a warm invitation to return. Subsequently Dr. Huebner enjoyed many informal visits with Mr. Wanamaker in his office, chatting about a wide variety of mutual interests. He was a hard-fisted businessman and a devoted churchman. Dr. Huebner said, "I learned a lot from him." Two statements about life insurance made by Mr. Wanamaker were widely quoted during his lifetime when everybody knew the name of the man who "invented" the department store. Dr. Huebner's strong agreement with the following quotations can be easily imagined.

> It is almost a crime to bring up a family in affluence and for its master or chief to not arrange his affairs so that they shall not be exposed to sudden and severe poverty in case of death, when, by forethought and the help of substantial insurance companies, he can put something aside out of his earnings for the mother and each child without being dishonest with his creditors. In many instances known to the writer the wife has been the best partner the man had, and helped him materially in making his business a success.

> Twenty years ago I had a capital of about a half million dollars. I then realized that a businessman with a half million of capital and a million and a half of insurance on his life would have better credit than one with a half million of capital and no insurance—so I took the insurance. I now find that trading on the credit it created I made more profit than if the money which went into insurance had gone directly into my business.

Such echoes from successful businessmen gave young college students an entirely new concept of life insurance. They easily recognized the tangible qualities of a man's earning power and followed their professor as he compared it to commonly accepted property values. They enjoyed a course which made them see life insurance as a part of exciting business operations and a protector of profits. They liked a professor who knew his way about in the market place.

CHAPTER EIGHT

Expert to the Committee

TRUST busting, so spectacular a part of the political and business picture of the early 1900's, was followed by continuing action against monopolies even without the crusading leadership of Theodore Roosevelt. In 1912 conditions in domestic and foreign shipping attracted the attention of reformers. Congress authorized an investigation by the House of Representatives Committee on the Merchant Marine and Fisheries, which was conducted by the twenty-one members with Representative Joshua W. Alexander, a Democrat from Missouri, as chairman. Seeking technical help for the Committee, Judge Alexander consulted with Dr. Emory R. Johnson of the Wharton School who had done distinguished special work for the government.

Some time later Dr. Solomon Huebner was called on the telephone by a Philadelphia news reporter. "The ticker says you have been put in charge of the United States steamship agreements investigation," said the reporter. "Is that right?"

"I've no word of it," answered Dr. Huebner.

"What do you plan to do?" pressed the reporter.

Dr. Huebner responded that he had no plans. Nevertheless the next edition of the paper carried headlines about the local professor who was set to attack the steamship lines and quoted him as saying: "I'll give it to them."

Through Dr. Johnson, Judge Alexander had indeed become

acquainted with Dr. Huebner's qualifications for work with his investigating committee. He interviewed the young professor and chose him for the job. He gave him his charge: "We know you are a Republican. You know you are serving under a Democratic administration. We are not interested in politics or in personal opinions. Your instructions are to get the facts. They will speak for themselves."

Dr. Huebner made it plain that he was not interested in being a gumshoe man. He believed that the wide waters of the world should always be free as God's great highways, but because they are free they must be controlled. He was interested to help make the oceans serve mankind and would like to bring to light the necessary information in an orderly and straightforward way. When asked what working equipment he needed, Dr. Huebner requested a quiet office, a rocking chair, and a good secretary. He got everything, although he often relinquished the chair to Judge Alexander, who enjoyed it when he came for conferences. In fact, when the investigation was completed, Judge Alexander told Dr. Huebner that it was customary for a departing expert to leave a memento of service behind, and suggested that the rocking chair would be acceptable. Dr. Huebner was agreeable to the idea. The chair was left, and Judge Alexander subsequently enjoyed it during his time as Secretary of Commerce.

The work of the steamship investigation took nearly five years. Dr. Huebner devoted more than full time to this activity during the summers and was able to arrange University work so that he could spend Fridays and Saturdays in Washington during school terms.

When Senator Boies Penrose heard that Dr. Huebner was working on the investigation he wrote the professor to come see him. At that time the Senator ran Pennsylvania politically and considered any Pennsylvania Republican in Washington subject to his supervision. Dr. Huebner consulted Judge Alexander, who told him to throw the letter away and do nothing about it. Senator Penrose sent another letter. This also Dr. Huebner referred to the Democrat from Missouri, who went to see the Republican from Pennsylvania. The latter was told that the choice of Dr. Huebner by the Committee emphasized their interest in capable development of the facts with no political implications whatsoever. So that was that, and there was no more correspondence.

Judge Alexander warned Dr. Huebner that politics might not be their only complication. They must all be very careful not to take any gifts from any source, or especially any "trips," such as generous shipping companies might offer.

The investigation was authorized by two Congressional resolutions. The following official text suggests the great variety of problems and the very wide scope of the inquiries.

> Resolved, That the Committee on the Merchant Marine and Fisheries be, and is hereby, empowered and directed to make a complete and thorough investigation of the methods and practices of the various ship lines, both domestic and foreign, engaged in carrying our oversea or foreign commerce and in the coastwise and inland commerce, and the connection between such ship lines and railroads and other common carriers, and between such lines and forwarding, ferry, towing, dock, warehouse, lighterage, or other terminal companies or firms or transportation agencies, and to investigate whether any such ship lines have formed any agreements, understandings, working arrangements, conferences, pools, or other combinations among one another, or with railroads or other common carriers, or with any of the companies, firms, or transportation agencies referred to in this section, for the purpose of fixing rates and tariffs, or of giving and receiving rebates, special rates, or other special privileges or advantages, or for the purpose of pooling or dividing their earnings, losses, or traffic, or for the purpose of preventing or destroying competition; also to investigate as to what methods, if any, are used by such ship lines, foreign or domestic, and railroads and other common carriers, or of any of the companies, firms, or other transportation agencies referred to in this section, to prevent the publication

> of their methods, rates, and practices in the United States; also to investigate and report to what extent and in what manner any foreign nation has subsidized or may own any vessels engaged in our foreign commerce; also to investigate and report to what extent any vessel lines and companies, or any of the companies, firms, or transportataion agencies referred to in this section, engaged in our foreign or coastwise or inland commerce, are owned or controlled by railway companies, by other ship lines or companies, or by any of the companies, firms, or transportation agencies referred to in this section, or by the same interests and persons owning or controlling railroad companies, ship lines, or other common carriers, or any of the companies, firms, or transportation agencies referred to in this section.

It is apparent that the investigation covered practically all the major steamship lines of the world and every possible transportation agency (such as forwarding, dock, and terminal companies) in any way associated with foreign and domestic water carriers or with the connecting railroads. The purpose was to bring to light practices which might be considered monopolistic and in restraint of trade.

The committee decided, upon recommendation from Dr. Huebner, to get as much information as possible in writing in advance of public hearings. Dr. Huebner devised a questionnaire with comprehensive schedules which was sent to companies doing coastwise, lake, or inland commerce, to steamship lines engaged in United States foreign trade, and to all the leading American railroads. Replies came back from 470 domestic navigation companies, 187 railroads, and 88 foreign steamship lines. In addition, reports were requested and received from 94 diplomatic and consular representatives of the United States in practically every country of any importance in the import and export trade of the United States. Data came to the committee also from a great variety of business sources, such as boards of trade, shipping organizations, and trade journals.

This avalanche of material was Dr. Huebner's responsibility.

Titled officially "Expert to the Committee" he analyzed and organized the findings. Where further explanations and interpretations were needed, he decided on the witnesses to be called and held the hearings. In all, 55 witnesses were heard representing all geographic trade zones and all types of shipping operations.

It is interesting to wonder how much Dr. Huebner's inborn love of travel may have been stimulated as he lived week after week with all those reports. The names Halifax and San Francisco, Liverpool, Hamburg, Marseilles and Trieste, Casa Blanca, Port Said, Rio de Janeiro, Singapore, Rangoon, Hong Kong, and Yokohoma must have given an underlying rhythm of invitation to his paper work. As a student of economics, what visions of agriculture and industry must have come to mind as he read of exports of cotton and grains, Standard Oil products for all the lamps of the Orient, Singer sewing machines for the far places of the earth, and Baldwin locomotives for newly developing countries. How he must have wanted to see the source of the cargoes of raw silk, rice, tea, coffee, moist hides and dry hides, hemp, jute, and all the other products from beyond the seas.

Foreign trade in commodities was only a part of the picture. There was also the passenger service. This was particularly important in the North Atlantic between the United States and Europe, and dominating all was the steerage traffic. During 1912 over two million immigrants came to the North Atlantic ports of the United States and Canada, more than a million of them to New York alone. The Statue of Liberty with its inscription was indeed a symbol of that era.

> Give me your tired, your poor,
> Your huddled masses yearning to breathe free,
> The wretched refuse of your teaming shore.
> Send these, the homeless, tempest-tost, to me.
> I lift my lamp beside the golden door!

The report of the New York Committee of steamship representatives described the situation:

> The increasing passenger traffic, not only of Americans visiting Europe but of Europeans coming to this country, has enabled these most costly instruments of modern transportation to ply the Atlantic throughout the whole year. The steadily increasing immigration, together with the patronage of those who wish to revisit their homes abroad, furnishes a steady steerage traffic which demands and receives the most painstaking attention of the lines. It is the very lifeblood of the business, so far as these superior boats are concerned, without which their existence and further operation would become impossible.

The practices which the investigation had been set up to bring to light appeared clearly in connection with these floods of immigrants. The United States consul general at Hamburg reported:

> As far as Germany is concerned, the mechanism of the arrangement whereby all emigrants passing through Germany are directed to Conference Line steamers is as follows: The Prussian Government has established 10 sanitary control stations at various points along the frontier of Russia. It is a requirement of law or regulation, with ample means for making it effective, that every emigrant arriving in Prussia shall first sojourn at one of these stations, where he is routed to the United States and forwarded to the seaboard. The carrying out of the administrative and sanitary sides of this work is intrusted by the Government to the Hamburg-American Line and to the North German Lloyd Line, acting jointly as concessionnaires.
>
> All trans-Atlantic companies desiring to sell tickets to the United States must first procure a Government license, and such traffic as they secure must thereupon be passed through the control stations which the two great German steamship companies manage. The companies belonging to the pool all have such licenses, and in each control station, which is also a ticket office, there is a blackboard showing the cost of tickets on a given date over the different lines. These rates are fixed monthly. Traffic is evenly divided by increasing or decreasing the cost of transportation over a given line. The individual passenger can select his route so long as it is a pool

route, but the varying prices are so arranged that each ship in the course of the year obtains its fair share of the business.

When the immigrant reached America he was still subject to the system. This was summarized by Dr. Huebner in his five hundred-page official report* of the investigation.

> It remains to be stated that practically all the established passenger lines operating to and from Europe have entered into agreements or understandings with a number of the important railroad passenger associations of this country, whereby the steamship lines agree to turn over their steerage traffic to the railroads composing these associations, the railroads in turn paying the steamship lines a so-called "commercial allowance" (a commission) on the rail rate from the port of arrival to the point of destination.

To indicate the economic utility of the agreements between steamship lines and railroads, Dr. Huebner outlined a brief description of how the steerage traffic was handled.

> Testimony shows that the immigrant purchases transportation from a point in Europe to an interior point in the United States beyond trunk-line territory and produces at the railroad station at Ellis Island an order for the rail transportation. This order is drawn on the Ellis Island agency of the steamship line and is presented to the railroad's joint ticket office at Ellis Island.
>
> After having passed the examination at the island the immigrants come into the custody of the railroads, and their agent and his representatives arrange for their routing, both passengers and baggage being transferred by the joint agency to the respective roads. In this respect all westbound traffic is apportioned on the basis of an equal division between the eight trunk lines which are members of the joint agency at the island. Few immigrants have any discretion in the route over which they travel. . . . Probably not more than 1 per cent of the immigrants whose tickets are presented at the Ellis Island agency have any idea or interest as to what route they want to take. . . .

---

* This report was later published by the Committee for general distribution, *Report on Steamship Agreements and Affiliations in the American Foreign and Domestic Trade.* It became an important source book for students as well as for legislators.

It is a part of the understanding with the various passenger associations that the routing of the westbound immigrant traffic shall be controlled by the routing committee of these associations. The steamship companies also have nothing to do with the apportionment of the traffic, this being attended to by a joint agency of the railroads. Accounts of the movements of the passengers are kept, and the joint agency receives instructions as to the routing, and on the basis of these instructions makes the allotments. All the passengers of one ship, if convenient, might be transferred to one road. In other words, the division between the lines can not be followed invariably, nor does it happen that every road always receives its equal share. As a matter of fact, however, the division is practically even. The roads attempt to equalize the traffic as much as possible, and the deficits prevailing at a given time are made good in future routings. . . .

Many advantages are claimed for the agreements and practices as just outlined. The joint handling and clearing of the business is regarded as both economical and convenient. If each immigrant were consulted as to his preference of routes, Ellis Island would be congested for hours each day, without any compensating advantages whatsoever resulting. In fact, it is argued that the entire system has been discussed with the Interstate Commerce Commission and that its advantages have been acknowledged by that Commission. Before the inauguration of the joint control of the steerage traffic at Ellis Island the immigrant was largely at the mercy of many individuals at New York, especially boarding-house runners. The present system of organized control, on the contrary, effectively protects the immigrant and his baggage while being transferred from steamship to railroad, and in no way causes hardship or injury. It has eliminated the abuses which prevailed under the former system of demoralizing competition and has placed a traffic of huge proportions on a high and orderly basis.

In justification of the commissions paid by the railroads to the steamship lines, the railroads claim that they look to the water lines to assume the risk of the agents paying the fares and that the commercial allowance is in a sense a method of compensating the steamship lines for assuming this financial responsibility. It also appears that the steamship companies could send a large portion of the immigrant traffic by way of Canada, where the railroads pay commissions to the water lines on all classes of trans-Atlantic passenger traffic. For this reason, as well as for the agency service rendered, American railroads argue that they are justified in paying commissions to the steamship companies. On the other hand, criticism has been directed against the discriminatory features of some of these agreements, as exemplified by the contract between the conference lines and the Western Passenger Association. Special reference is made to the section which stipulates that the commercial allowance shall be paid exclusively to the contracting steamship lines and be withheld from all competitors. This provision is regarded as a means of unfair competition, in so far that the contracting lines are able to receive certain sums, which they have made the railroads agree not to pay to independent lines.

The ways of the railroads and shipping lines with their passengers differed only in detail and not in principle from their ways with freight. They had contracts, agreements, and understandings of all kinds among themselves. In some countries abroad the agreements were regularly set up under the law in writing, but many were simply oral commitments. The testimony developed that the practices had come into being to prevent a cutthroat competition that would have ruined many shippers and greatly hampered foreign trade for all nations.

The agreements aimed to regulate competition among the parties and also from lines outside the agreeing group or "conference." Among themselves they made rate agreements. There were fixed rates for certain runs, and minimum rates for most trips. Arrangements were made for pooling business. Shippers who did not get all their agreed-upon share of actual passenger or freight traffic were paid a part of the profit by the others who had more than their designated percentage. The conference lines agreed upon sailing dates and ports to be served, dividing the calendar and the map to their advantage, but with advantage also to the traveling and shipping public.

The conference lines united to kill off competition. They offered deferred rebates to shippers who patronized them exclusively. They even supported "fighting ships" in some circumstances. Fighting ships were conference line vessels assigned to sail on the same days and between the same ports as an independent, offering cutthroat rates subsidized by the conference.

The conference lines also made certain specially favorable agreements with various big shippers, such as United States Steel, and with docks and railroads for port services and connections.

The investigators were quick to see the many evidences of monopoly and restraint of trade in this situation. They recognized the possibilities of serious abuse. Nevertheless they began to realize that, practically, the agreements had many advantages. They made possible more regularity of service, a better distribution of sailings, service to developing ports, stability of rates over a long period, uniformity of rates for all merchants, greater security to capitalists investing in steamers, and, very importantly, conditions for American shipping similar to those in other parts of the world.

As the picture crystallized for Judge Alexander, Dr. Huebner, and a few leaders of the investigation, they wondered how it might be made clear as a basis for action by the whole Committee. Dr. Huebner's carefully organized report, with tables and charts, was the first step. Then the professor held "school" for the committee members. He assigned a chapter of the report for homework. The next day they discussed it. He assigned another chapter, followed by another discussion. By that process of teaching the Committee grew really to understand the situation. Eventually they united—Democrats, Republicans, and Progressives—in recommendations to Congress. Dr. Huebner drafted the text of a bill which, with some additions by President Wilson, became the United States Shipping Act of 1916.

This legislation legalized steamship agreements and affiliations under specified government supervision. For the first time the antitrust laws were superseded. The Act provided for what was technically a restraint of trade in certain respects, but essentially for the benefit of the American people. The Act also created the United States Shipping Board, none too soon for the tremendous maritime problems created by World War I.

Although recognizing agreements, pools, understandings, and other conference arrangements, the Act required that copies be filed with the Shipping Board. It gave the Board power to "disapprove, cancel, or modify any agreement" considered to be "unjustly discriminatory or unfair as between carriers, shippers, exporters, importers, or ports, . . . or to the detriment

Shipping Board experts of the World War I era. *Left to right, front row,* Capt. Irving L. Evans, Rear Admiral C. S. Williams, Meyer Lessner, Albert D. Lasker, Elmer Schlessinger, N. B. Beecher, J. B. Smull, R. T. Merrill, and Dr. S. S. Huebner. *Back row,* Admiral H. H. Hosseau, Winthrop L. Marvin, John Nicolson, Capt. E. E. O'Donnell, T. S. Rossbottom, and Daniel H. Hocks. (*Underwood and Underwood*)

of the commerce of the United States." The Act specifically outlawed deferred rebates, the use of "fighting ships," and the retaliation against shippers who filed complaints or failed to concentrate their shipping with certain lines.

Dr. Huebner was invited to become a member of the Shipping Board, but he decided that the limitations of permanent government service were not what he wanted. Also, he loved teaching. He never regretted this decision. Within the year the Board was in rough political seas, and the responsibilities which came with the war had little relation to research or education.

When the United States declared war on Germany, April 6, 1917, this country had only 50,000 shipyard workers. President Wilson challenged America:

> We must supply ships by the hundreds, out of our shipyards, to carry to the other side of the sea, submarines or no submarines, what will every day be needed there . . . not only to clothe and equip our own forces on land and sea but also to clothe and support our people for whom the gallant fellows under arms can no longer work; to help clothe and equip the Armies with which we are co-operating in Europe; and to keep the looms and manufactories there in raw material. We must send coal to keep the fires going on ships at sea; steel out of which to make arms and ammunition, both here and there; rails for worn out railways back of the fighting front; locomotives and rolling stock to take the place of those every day going to pieces; mules, horses, cattle for labor and military service; everything with which the people of England, and France, and Italy and Russia have usually supplied themselves but cannot now afford the men, the material or the machinery to make.

The little army of shipyard workers multiplied more than seven times. By the summer of 1918, new ships were being finished at the rate of one hundred a month. When the war ended there were more than two thousand American merchant ships of all kinds, and 42,000 men had been trained to handle them. Admiral Edward N. Hurley, in his *Bridge to France*, commented that if America had had any substantial merchant marine earlier Germany never would have adopted its policy of ruthless submarine warfare. On February 1, 1917, Germany announced her intention of sinking ships mercilessly, on sight, without warning or search. By this she hoped to make it impossible for Britain and France to carry on the war. During the first three months of 1917, 470 ocean cargo vessels were sunk. In the first two weeks after the United States declared war, 122 cargo vessels were sunk. Shipowners were in a panic because of the submarine losses.

It became necessary for the government to go into the marine insurance business from two aspects—first, the extraordinary perils of war; second, the ordinary perils of the sea. The Bureau of War Risk Insurance of the Treasury Department dealt with war perils only. The Shipping Board was concerned with those and also with the natural hazards of voyages. The War Risk Insurance coverage eventually exceeded two billion dollars.

The Shipping Board set up an advisory committee of marine insurance underwriters to guide them in providing the usual marine insurance coverage for ships owned, chartered, or otherwise controlled by the Shipping Board and the Fleet Corporation. The Board protected the ships themselves and their legal liability and provided prompt handling of claims arising through damage to cargo or injury to crew members.

When the war ended, the government wanted to turn its ships back to private owners and also to get out of the insurance business. It became apparent that United States companies were not in a position to take on the enormous increase of marine insurance business. The majority of these risks were going abroad, particularly to London. A Congressional investigation was set up to discover the causes of this situation and to recommend ways to overcome the difficulties. Again Dr. Huebner was called to serve as special expert to the investigating committee. His work in this connection began in 1918 and lasted for five years. Again a detailed questionnaire prepared by Dr. Huebner was submitted to all American and foreign companies transacting marine insurance business in the United States, and much additional information was assembled through public hearings and voluminous correspondence.

The inquiries aimed to find out the extent of consolidation among the companies, how much they co-operated through conferences, reinsurance pools, and other affiliations; the extent of foreign ownership and control of American companies; facts about reinsurance; the emphasis in each company on hull and freight insurance, cargo insurance, builders' risk insurance, coastwise and inland traffic, and foreign trade traffic.

The techniques developed in the shipping investigation were followed again with the marine insurance committee. Dr. Huebner prepared careful and detailed reports on the basis of which he "schooled" the committee. The reports were later published under the titles *Status of Marine Insurance in the United States* and *Legislative Obstructions to the Development of Marine Insurance in the United States.* Again clear understanding brought a unanimity of conclusion. Dr. Huebner later commented that he never had any trouble getting action through Congress because he helped people to understand facts.

The investigating committee reported a situation that "is an impossible one and must not be allowed to continue." About two thirds of the marine insurance written in the United States was controlled by foreign underwriters. Some kinds of insurance were handled hardly at all by American companies. About half of the reinsurance of American companies was being placed with foreign underwriters.

The committee expressed a vigorous condemnation of the situation:

> All evidence leads to the conclusions that a strong and independent national marine insurance institution is an absolute necessity to a nation's foreign trade equipment, that such an institution does not

> exist in the United States to-day, and that it is imperative to adopt ways and means to correct the present impossible situation if this country is to meet the strenuous international rivalry that the new era is certain to inaugurate. There can be no doubt, judging from the manner in which our competitors are now seeking to undermine this branch of underwriting, that marine insurance will be used, as probably never before, as a national commercial weapon for the acquisition and development of foreign markets. Failure to act now in strengthening our marine insurance facilities and placing them in an independent position free from foreign control, can not be regarded otherwise than as the neglect of a duty and an opportunity. The loss of the present rich opportunity will soon be bitterly regretted, but it will be too late to undo the mischief. . . . In view of the strategic importance of marine insurance in the upbuilding of foreign trade and a merchant marine, your committee regrets to report that American interests have largely lost their grip on this type of underwriting. Probably no other vital branch of American commerce has passed so extensively under foreign control.

The committee studied also the "climate" which in England had proved so favorable to marine insurance. That analysis added to the unfavorable factors discovered in the American situation and led to a threefold conclusion. Better conditions in the United States could come through *self-help* in a program of reinsurance, *government help* through turning the Shipping Board marine insurance business back to private companies, and *state help* by the removing of conflicting and paralyzing state restrictions which greatly hindered domestic companies.

The results were that the government got out of the marine insurance business, and again legal sanction was given to co-operation between companies such as might have been deemed contrary to the Sherman and Clayton Antitrust Acts.

Three American Merchant Marine Syndicates were formed with the approval and co-operation of the United States Shipping Board, and were executed on behalf of the government on June 28, 1920. Syndicate A was a service organization. For Shipping Board vessels and those of private owners it provided periodic inspection of the condition of hull, machinery, galley, crew's quarters, and all parts of the ship, damage and loss surveys and advice concerning repairs, equipment, efficiency, safety, and so on.

Syndicate B was organized to insure the government's interest in ships sold by the Shipping Board. As the various installments of the purchase price were paid, the protection under this syndicate decreased.

Through Syndicate C insurance was provided for vessels under private ownership. As protection under Syndicate B decreased, that under Syndicate C correspondingly increased. This latter included approved foreign companies, although Syndicate B was limited strictly to American insurers. Dr. Huebner commented* concerning these organizations:

> The three syndicates referred to represent a radical departure in American marine insurance practice, and their organization, it is believed, will constitute an epoch-making event in the history of American marine underwriting. They represent the first effort in our history to form a distinctly national policy in this important branch of commerce. For the first time, also, American companies have united in a comprehensive service plan for maintenance inspections and surveys, thus recognizing the importance of eliminating present waste and needless losses and costs.

The improved state legislation necessary to strengthen American marine insurance was promoted in several ways. Dr. Huebner drafted a liberal marine insurance law, which was adopted for the District of Columbia in 1922 as the Model

* In *Marine Insurance*, published in 1920. This book was written at the request of the Shipping Board and the Federal Board for Vocational Education. It had been discovered that no literature existed for use as class textbooks or for individual study to present basic information about the steamship business. The new merchant marine needed men trained to carry on the commercial and shipping activities that make use of ships, and a series of books was designed. Dr. Huebner, as usual, was an ideal author to set forth the facts about the nature and practical operation of marine insurance, with explanations of its relationship to shipping, banking, and overseas commerce. His work with the marine insurance investigation was an unusual foundation for such an assignment.

Marine Insurance Law. This served as a pattern for duplication in the various states. The Congressional committee and the Shipping Board also addressed a letter to state governors and insurance commissioners urging their action.

During Dr. Huebner's years in Washington in association with the Shipping Board he often saw Senator Robert M. La Follette. He had known the famous Bob first when he was governor of Wisconsin. Senator La Follette was very friendly to his young compatriot, though they differed strongly in regard to many subjects. He once invited Dr. Huebner to write for his paper, but the potential author reminded him with a smile that any articles from his pen might not be pleasing.

At one point legislation was pending which was very closely contested. It involved a subsidy for the Shipping Board to offset its current annual losses. It was really only a matter of bookkeeping, but the Board was anxious to have the proposed arrangement. The Board asked Dr. Huebner to see Senator La Follette and get his commitment, for his vote appeared to be one of the very few which was still undecided and it was much needed. Dr. Huebner interviewed his old friend easily enough but his answer was disappointing: "Go back and tell those men I will fight them on everything." Even with such differences of opinion, Dr. Huebner characterized the Senator as a fine old gentleman, a remarkable fighter, and strictly honest.

Following the work leading to the Marine Syndicates, Dr. Huebner was engaged in another government project relating to insurance. This was a Congressional investigation of theft and pilferage in American trade. American marine insurance companies were suffering disastrous losses in connection with the new merchant fleet. They were being forced to increase their rates drastically or to refuse risks entirely. Dr. Huebner summarized, in a speech to insurance men, the situation which had developed:

> Losses through theft, pilferage and non-delivery have reached enormous proportions within the last few years and seem to be increasing rather than decreasing. The magnitude of the problem is indicated by a comparison of rates for insurance covering marine hazards only with those for insurance covering such hazards as the risk of theft, pilferage and non-delivery. A tabulation of rates with respect to many of our foreign markets shows that insurance rates are in many instances increased from five to ten times by the inclusion of theft, pilferage and non-delivery, and in some instances twenty-fold. Our moral fiber seems to have disintegrated to a remarkable degree. The seriousness of the problem is universally admitted and there can be no doubt that present losses represent an appalling economic waste which is proving detrimental to the development of our foreign trade and a needless burden on commerce. Many underwriters have protested vigorously against existing conditions. A considerable number have withdrawn from the field altogether and others seem to show an inclination to follow the plan of making a shipper co-insurer for a portion, like a quarter of the risk . . .
>
> Consideration should be given to the advisability of adopting legislation which will make carriers more responsible for losses of this character resulting from their negligence. Under present conditions, it is argued, there is little inducement on the part of ocean carriers to exercise reasonable care and diligence. Too often the risk of theft, pilferage and non-delivery is transferred entirely to underwriters, who, it should be remembered, do not have the cargo within their custody and are thus not in a position to exercise control.

The problem was rooted in the type of bills of lading currently in use. Someone called them "documents of irresponsibility." They were written so as to relieve the carriers of any responsibility at all. Damages and losses of all kinds were completely repudiated. The carriers' attitude was "Let the insurance companies worry." In handling shipments they exercised no care in use of grappling hooks on cases and packages. Breakage was terrible. Damage because of improper loading was great. Stevedores stole. Men on shipboard helped themselves. Because of the terms of the bills of lading, shippers had no reddress. Shippers, too, were at fault to some degree. They fre-

Dr. Huebner in about 1940.

quently dispatched their goods inadequately packed and cased. They often used the package as an advertising medium, tempting men to steal products that were particularly desirable. Frequently, losses ascribed to the carriers were obviously or reasonably indicated to be losses at warehouses at the shipping or receiving ends rather than in transit. The whole shipping activity was in a turmoil and the weight of losses was falling on the insurance companies, which had no way to control conditions.

The investigation brought out the facts in the situation. Again it was discovered that British ships and some other foreign merchant fleets provided much better conditions than American vessels. It was apparent that a uniform bill of lading for international commerce which established responsibility for carriers would be very desirable. Conferences were held at The Hague and in Brussels which established agreements for recommendations to governments of the maritime nations. Eventually the United States accepted these standards, which brought great improvement of conditions for international trade, with protection for shippers, carriers, and insurers.

Dr. Huebner continued in government consulting and investigating service for the Shipping Board until 1934. This relationship, principally as insurance adviser, brought him a friendship, which he treasured greatly, with Admiral William S. Benson, who for most of the period was chairman of the Board. Admiral Benson had been one of the top naval commanders of World War I. He was a very religious man, thoughtful and honest. Dr. Huebner found him most co-operative officially in their joint efforts in maritime matters and very congenial personally. They met often at the end of the day in the Admiral's office to confer on matters of business and then to slip into relaxing conversation on a wide variety of topics of mutual interest.

Dr. Huebner's activities with the Shipping Board resulted in another campus nickname. It was said that only the dumbest freshman did not know that the S. S. in Professor Huebner's name stood for Steam Ship.

CHAPTER NINE

Foundations for the American College

THE daily associations at the Wharton School provided a stimulating atmosphere for young Dr. Huebner. There he was in constant intercourse with men who were applying the lessons of the textbook and classroom to practical problems of life. Those Midwesterners on the faculty especially were eager to make theoretical learning useful in the solving of civic problems, in major enterprises of transportation and industry, and in government programs. Huebner's own first government service in the shipping investigation was a natural result of his being associated with Dr. Johnson at Wharton.

With insurance, and life insurance particularly, becoming his greatest interest, he was in step with his colleagues when he too related his specialty to the world outside of the University. He deliberately decided at an early date "to throw in his hat," as he said, with the agents. He was challenged by the needs of that army of men and women who were the contact between the life insurance companies and the public. He was influenced in this decision by a personal relationship with an outstanding agency leader. One of his students was young Paul Clark, nephew of Ernest J. Clark, a general agent for the John Hancock Mutual Life Insurance Company at Baltimore, Maryland.

In 1912, Ernest Clark had sent his nephew to Wharton* in preparation for work with him in selling life insurance. Thus he met Dr. Huebner and invited him to make his first talk to the life underwriters in Baltimore. Dr. Huebner greatly enjoyed this association with men who were reaching the public with the story of life insurance. He welcomed the opportunity to combine his ideas with their experience.

In Dr. Huebner, Mr. Clark saw an ally. He, who had chosen a university education as his nephew's best foundation for life insurance sales work, felt strongly the general need for training in that vocation. He was active in the National Association of Life Underwriters and, as an industry leader, knew the weaknesses of the business. He realized that life insurance could not meet its potential in public service unless standards were raised for the people through whom the service was made available. Would life insurance be more than a death benefit? Would the vision that a few had glimpsed of business insurance, of income settlements and estate planning through life insurance ever come to fulfillment? Mr. Clark was among the first to see that the answer would depend upon specialized education and training for life insurance company field representatives. He recognized Dr. Huebner's potential place in the program. Repeatedly they met and talked about possibilities.

---

* In an article not yet published, but prepared for the University of Pennsylvania *Founder's Day Magazine*, Mr. Paul F. Clark, C.L.U., now chairman of the board of the John Hancock Mutual Life Insurance Company, wrote: "Probably one of the most significant things that happened to me during my years at Pennsylvania was that I began what was to become a lifelong association with the 'Dean of Life Insurance,' Dr. Solomon S. Huebner. I truly doubt if any man has contributed more to the educational development of the life insurance profession than this great man. To this day, his brilliant intellect, his keen powers of observation and deduction are guiding forces in this business which is so vital to the American way of life.

"Once I decided to major in insurance in preparation for a career in that field, I determined to take every course available under the direction of Dr. Huebner. And I have felt the benefits and been grateful for this decision throughout my entire business life."

In February, 1914, he asked Dr. Huebner again to speak to the Baltimore life underwriters and to discuss the general subject of life insurance education. On that occasion Dr. Huebner referred to the ideal of having a life insurance course of study on the collegiate level, leading to a degree comparable to that of Certified Public Accountant.

An immediate result of that talk was action by Mr. Clark, who in 1913–14 was president of the National Association of Life Underwriters. It seemed a strategic time to begin a real campaign toward the goals which he and Dr. Huebner had discussed so often. In the spring of 1914, Mr. Clark enlisted the interest of other life insurance leaders. At a meeting of the Executive Committee of the National Association of Life Underwriters, four key men became committed to the cause: Edward A. Woods, John Newton Russell, J. Stanley Edwards, and Franklin W. Ganse.

"Life Insurance Education" was determined as the theme of the 1914 convention of the National Association, and Dr. Huebner was invited to give the keynote address at that Cincinnati meeting.

To realize how great an impact Dr. Huebner's address made on his audience it is necessary to recall the climate for the life insurance agent and the status of life insurance services at that time. Generally people thought of life insurance in terms of a few thousand dollars of death benefit. The life insurance agent stood pretty low in the scale of social approval. Ignorance of life insurance was widespread and sources of life insurance information were few. In such a setting the Cincinnati audience listened to a new voice and found it welcome. To have a high-ranking university professor speak with such respect of the importance and dignity of their calling was thrilling; they were not used to it. To have their sales ideas strengthened and expanded with such authority was exciting; it was reinforcement from an unexpected source. To have the vision laid before them of the potential of educational activities was revolutionary; they had never dared to think in such terms.

Because this address contained the seeds which flowered so wonderfully in later years, generous quotations are important for this story. The text is taken from the *Proceedings* of the convention. In similar form this talk was repeated many, many times in the next few years.

> I believe that there are six main lines of thought that should be emphasized through every available channel of education. . . .
>
> (1) First and foremost, all who have assumed family responsibilities should be impressed with the sacred duty of using Life Insurance as a means to protect their loved ones against the want that may be occasioned by premature death. Life Insurance is a bulwark of the home and the only safe method of hedging it against the uncertainties of life. Men must be made to recognize the value of a human life both from the family and business standpoint (the two being nearly always closely interrelated) and to capitalize and perpetuate that value in compliance with the dictates of Christian duty. The capitalization of the value of a human life for the benefit of the dependent members of the household is a fundamental duty that should be preached from every pulpit, be taught in every school where students are old enough to comprehend, and be given the widest publicity through the press by means of articles, editorials and non-partisan advertising. Emphasis should be laid on the "crime of not insuring" and on the biblical injunction, so frequently quoted, that "If any provide not for his own, and especially for those of his own house, he hath denied the faith, and is worse than an infidel." Let it be taught that the finger of scorn should be pointed at any man who, although he has provided well while alive, has not seen fit to discount the uncertain future for the benefit of his dependent household. Let it also be known that such a man, as Dr. Talmage well said, "is a defalcation, an outrage, a swindle. He did not die, he absconded." [Dr. DeWitt Talmage was a prominent New York clergyman who had preached a famous sermon in defense of life insurance.]
>
> Life Insurance is the only sure means of changing uncertainty into certainty and is the antithesis of gambling. He who does not insure

gambles with the greatest of all chances and, if a loser, makes those dearest to him pay the forfeit. . . .

(2) Writers on Life Insurance assert over and over again that insurance is not a producer of wealth and that its function is merely to distribute funds from the fortunate to the unfortunate. I feel that the public should be shown that Life Insurance, besides protecting against misfortune, is also a powerful force in the production of wealth, and that premium payments should not be regarded merely as an expense to be grudgingly borne. Constant worry is one of the greatest curses that can fall to the lot of man, and Life Insurance, if universally used, would lift that curse from innumerable shoulders. The knowledge of an assured estate from the moment the premium is paid will enable the insured to feel freer in assuming initiative. By removing a load of care from the mind it promotes efficiency and makes life happier. In my own case my Life Insurance is my most sacred possession, and I have often felt that I would not be without it even though the premiums were twice what they are. Because of it, I eat better, sleep better, feel better, and as a result of these, work better.

(3) Agents constantly meet with those whose argument against Life Insurance is that they prefer to save. This view should be strenuously opposed in our educational program. The habit of saving should by all means be encouraged, but it should be made clear that the saving of a competence involves the necessary time to save, and that Life Insurance is the only certain method to use as a hedge against the possibilities of the saving period being cut short. It must be made clear that a policy of saving can yield only a small amount at the start, while a policy of insurance from its beginning guarantees the full face value. Moreover, the roseate views which so many have concerning their resolution and ability to accumulate and keep should be tempered by a frank statement of the harrowing facts as they actually exist. Eighty-five per cent of this country's adults leave no estate at all, and about one-third of the widows in the country lack the necessities and 90 per cent the comforts of life. Let us also emphasize the fact that, in addition to guaranteeing an estate at once, Life Insurance contains an investment feature which is absolutely safe, that it is one of the greatest forces to inculcate the saving instinct, that it is admirably adapted to put small sums of money to prompt and profitable use, and that, to use the choice expression

of one underwriter, it is "compound interest in harness." Let it also be known how easily and how frequently the competence which a husband or father has provided through saving or insurance is lost by the heir or beneficiary, and that modern income policies furnish a guarantee against such a contingency.

(4) Life Insurance also lends itself to numerous business uses and it is highly essential in an educational program that a knowledge of these should be given as wide circulation as possible. I recently received a circular from a leading company outlining no less than 25 such cases, and unfortunately the limits of an address do not permit an enumeration of the same. Suffice it to say that they are little understood today by the great mass of business men, and it is certain that a readable and illustrated explanation of the uses of insurance as a means of indemnification against the loss by death of a valued official or employe, of providing a sinking fund to meet future liabilities, of safeguarding credit, of covering a mortgage, of raising further capital without additional tangible collateral, etc., is sure to attract attention and produce results. I venture to say that there is hardly a business man who is not at one time or another confronted with some business situation the solution of which can be rendered easier and safer through the proper application of Life Insurance. . . .

But what is needed now is the immediate education of the adult population along the lines just indicated. This, I think, can be accomplished best (1) by having the great mission of Life Insurance explained, wherever possible, through the medium of the pulpit, the lecture platform and the editorial column; (2) by disseminating readable and carefully prepared information, of a strictly non-partisan and educational character and with the subject-matter so copiously and simply illustrated as to be readily grasped by the average mind, through the pages of the leading newspapers and magazines; and (3) by disseminating the same kind of information, as well as short articles explaining the specific business uses of Life Insurance through the leading trade journals of the country. . . .

Let us not forget that the student of today becomes the family head, business manager, teacher, agent and community leader in the pulpit, the press, the school and legislative hall tomorrow; and if a knowledge of the uses and sacred functions of Life Insurance is drilled into the minds of the young, and they are given the proper habit of thought, we may be sure that they will at the proper time translate that thought into action not only as regards themselves, but also in advising their fellow man.

I may be pardoned for feeling deeply on this subject, because in my own humble little way I am doing my best to teach Life Insurance to about 200 students a year. My meaning can best be expressed by a few examples. Every year an hour's lecture on the use of Life Insurance as a means of safely financing a young man without tangible collateral, except his health, good name and a willing relative or friend, has caused a number in the class to use the plan as a means of financing themselves through college, thus enabling them to give their undivided attention to the work before them. Every year, judging from the interviews, a fair percentage of the boys induce their fathers to take out insurance on their lives, and some take it themselves for the protection of a parent. Hardly a week goes by but some former student writes me concerning some type of policy and some particular use to which Life Insurance may be put, and they often add that I may still remember their having been in the class in such and such a year. Only about a month ago a student who seven years ago took the general insurance course in our Evening School of Accounts and Finance as a part of a general business education asked me to meet him to talk over some insurance matters. This young man has been eminently successful and has worked his way to a directorship in a manufacturing corporation employing some 1,200 men. At our meeting it was evident that he still remembered the explanation of the business uses of Life Insurance and that he had not only amply supplied himself with protection, but has been instrumental in convincing the directorate to hedge the company against the loss by premature death of the one man in the business who was its chief asset financially and mentally. Not only had $250,000 of insurance already been taken on this man's life in the interest of the business, but the management had just decided to take $500,000 more. This ex-student frankly told me that he was deeply concerned personally because he has his nearly all in that business. I trust I may be pardoned for making these references. They are merely mentioned as little incidents to show that the young men—the students—of today become the managers of business establishments and the heads of families tomorrow, and that if the uses of Life Insurance are forcefully brought to their attention it is not unreasonable to expect that in time that knowledge will be put to profitable use. . . .

The attitude of the average agent toward the whole broad plan of Life Insurance education will necessarily depend upon his attitude toward the professional standing of his work, i.e., does he regard his business as a profession or merely as an occupation? Life Insurance salesmanship must be given the status of a profession—a high calling—both as regards the methods pursued and the quality of the service rendered. If this is done you will certainly have the right to feel that you are identified with one of the noblest professions in existence, ranking with those of the ministry, law, medicine and teaching. . . .

The term "profession" implies expert knowledge and has been defined as "a vocation in which a professional knowledge of science or learning is used by its practice to the affairs of others, either in advising, guiding or teaching them, or in serving their interests or welfare in the practice of an art founded on it." If Life Insurance salesmanship is to have a professional standing, it is necessary for its representative in the field to meet the standards of this definition. . . .

To this end he should understand the scientific features of the business, such as the fundamental principles underlying rate making, the operation of the reserve, the sources of the surplus and their interpretation, etc. . . .

As already stated, Life Insurance salesmen should be students throughout their career. They should strive to keep abreast with the best that is said and written about Life Insurance. And permit me to make the further suggestion that, if possible, agents should acquaint themselves with the leading facts surrounding various business activities, especially in view of the growing importance of so-called "Business Life Insurance."

When Dr. Huebner had finished, the Cincinnati audience gave him overwhelming applause. By formal resolution they went "on record in the most emphatic way" to express "gratitude of this magnificent address."

In this speech Dr. Huebner did not refer to any formalized educational program. This was by definite request from Mr. Clark and the other Association leaders. They felt that any specific proposal in 1914 would be premature. Many things needed to be done and much groundwork laid before a successful beginning could be made. The period of preparation was to extend to thirteen years.

A major prerequisite for an academic program of training was books to study. The N.A.L.U. leaders in the education movement had agreed that the first step should be a textbook about life insurance, describing its principles of operation and the needs which it served. Dr. Huebner naturally was chosen as the author. Paul Clark had persuaded his uncle that his professor's manner of presentation, which was so popular with the University students, would be most appropriate also for life insurance agents. When publishers were approached they were cold to the idea. They felt there would be no great sale for a life insurance text. That did not long stop the plans of the leaders of the National Association of Life Underwriters, who had caught Dr. Huebner's vision for their industry. At the Cincinnati meeting they agreed to underwrite the new book. D. Appleton and Company, with their guarantee, agreed to publish the text. The N.A.L.U. men saw the book not only as useful for agency instruction but also as a tool for the Association's Education and Conservation Committee in work with schools and colleges. When the book was ready in 1915, the Committee undertook to promote its distribution, and profits on sales to life insurance customers were given by the publishers to that N.A.L.U. group.

Ernest J. Clark proudly introduced *Life Insurance: A Textbook* to the N.A.L.U. convention at San Francisco in August, 1915 with these words:

> None of us have, or ever have had, a textbook in the practice and principles of life insurance written from a purely disinterested point

> of view by a life insurance educator. Consequently, we have had no textbook in the past which could be accepted by a high school, a college, a university, or which could constitute the foundation for agency instruction in our various offices.

The guarantors never had to make good on their underwriting of this publication. By 1916 a profit of a thousand dollars from sales to life insurance customers had come back to the Committee on Education and Conservation, and distribution had been very satisfactory also in academic circles. Eventually that book went through five editions in the United States (the latest in 1958), and was translated into many foreign languages.

The influence of one of these translations on the other side of the world was dramatized when Dr. Huebner was in Japan in 1927. He and Mrs. Huebner were in their hotel sitting room one day when a Japanese gentleman was ushered in. He stopped just within the door, bowed deeply, and began to speak most earnestly. They quickly understood that he was talking of the textbook, which he had read in Japanese translation. He said that it was the foundation of his successful career in life insurance; he had achieved a position of some eminence in that industry in Japan. Since he felt that he owed his success to Dr. Huebner, it was fitting that he should make a gift in evidence of his gratitude. He was a member of the Samurai, the ancient and honored feudal warrior families of Japan. He was married, but he and his wife had no children. Therefore they had decided to give their greatest family treasure to the professor to whom they owed so much. Ceremoniously he extended to Dr. Huebner the samurai sword which had been owned by his ancestors through four centuries. The sword was forged to stainless brightness. It was encased in a handsome scabbard and in the hilt was a tiny hara-kiri knife for the defense of family honor. To take such a gift seemed almost a sacrilege; to refuse would have been an intolerable affront. Dr. Huebner received it with humility and saw it always as a symbol of the pricelessness of learning.

During the winter following the Cincinnati convention, Mr. Ernest Clark arranged for Dr. Huebner to speak before the Baltimore Association of Life Underwriters on the general subject of education for life underwriters and the professional aspects of life insurance selling. This was another epoch-making address, for in it Dr. Huebner first formally and publicly described the goal of a life insurance course of study leading to a degree or designation comparable to that of Certified Public Accountant, such course to be centered in a college of standing commensurate with other degree-granting educational institutions.

His definition of a profession as he expressed it in that Baltimore speech in 1915 reflected contemporary problems, some of which are still with us. This address was published as an appendix to the first edition of Dr. Huebner's *Life Insurance*. It is also quoted extensively in the brochure, *The Professional Concept of Life Underwriting*, furnished C.L.U. students currently by the American College.

Concerning the four major aspects of a profession, he spoke then:

> First, that the vocation should be so essentially useful to society and so noble in its purpose as to inspire sufficient love and enthusiasm on the part of the practitioner to make it his life's work. One cannot regard highly the services of a professional man who looks upon his vocation as a side issue and who is not willing to devote to its practice his entire time and his best thought and energy.
>
> Second, that the vocation involves a science and in its practice an expert knowledge of that science.
>
> Third, that in applying this expert knowledge the practitioner should abandon the strictly selfish commercial view and ever keep in mind the advantage of the client. Conscientious and disinterested service —proper advice and guidance—is the very essence of professional conduct, and in the long run the best policy.

Portrait of Dr. Huebner by Alice Kent Stoddard in 1950—the gift of C.L.U.'s from all over the world.

Fourth, that the individual practitioner should possess a spirit of loyalty to his fellow practitioners, of helpfulness to the common cause that they all profess and should not allow any unprofessional acts to bring shame upon the entire profession. Unfortunately the public has a habit of jumping to general conclusions, and too frequently the selfish unprofessional conduct of a few leads to a distorted and unfair view of an entire group. The Golden Rule is applicable in this respect quite as much as in individual transactions.

Dr. Huebner repeated this speech the next week for the New York City Association of Life Underwriters. The beginning of the American College of Life Underwriters and the Chartered Life Underwriter program was there, but the seed had to be planted in many other cities and in many minds before organized action was possible. Dr. Huebner did his full share of seed sowing during the next decade.

While such preparations were being made for a program of professional education for life insurance field men, great forces apart from the business were interacting to set the stage for the new development. The Hughes' Investigation in New York State, as reported in a previous chapter, had resulted in new laws for life insurance supervision, opening the way to new confidence in life insurance operations. The coming of World War I, with Government War Risk Insurance of ten thousand dollars for each doughboy, set a new standard for judging adequacy of life insurance ownership. The influenza epidemic caused countless families to thank from the depths of their hearts the life insurance agents who had persuaded healthy young men and women to buy the policies which so unexpectedly became claims.*

An outstanding life insurance salesman of the 1920's was fond of telling that when he entered the business about 1910 his mother sat down and cried. She felt that he had disgraced the family by his choice of vocation which to her was associated with high-pressure artists, shady operations, and failures from other lines of endeavor. The experiences of the war years started a definite move away from that point of view.

An editorial in a life insurance newspaper under the heading "Life Insurance Glorified" presents this changing public attitude. The mode of expression is somewhat flamboyant, but the facts have been confirmed from many sources.

---

* In the United States in 1918, the year the epidemic hit its peak in this country, the average age at death from the disease was 33 years.

> Life insurance. These words should only be uttered with respect, while many who have benefitted by its protecting mantle utter these words almost with a feeling of reverence.
>
> . . . The months just passed have thrown a halo around the business of life insurance, possessed of a magnetic power which draws all manner of men to its shrine. The first flicker came with the information to be found in the financial statements of the respective life insurance companies, in connection with its losses from influenza and pneumonia sustained by the different offices. As the losses from this terribly devastating plague are made known, men in all walks of life marvel at the disclosure. Millions of dollars are being transferred from the coffers of the great provisional storehouses of life insurance companies to the beneficiaries of the policyholders.
>
> Over one hundred millions of dollars has already been distributed over the country into the cottage of the poor and the mansion of the rich alike, according to the measure of protection secured through the agent back yonder, not now considered a pest or a bore.
>
> Though the business and social worlds have rocked almost unceasingly in the throes of pestilence and war for months, and unnumbered deaths have followed in their wake, the policy obligations of life insurance companies have been liquidated according to contract and there is not a quake in the stability of the legal reserve life insurance companies. Life insurance stands today adamant in strength, and glorified through its service.

During this same period Dr. Huebner was becoming increasingly well known and respected in life insurance circles.

The insurance journals, which served all branches of the industry, in reporting his part in the marine insurance investigations made him better known to life insurance people also. For instance, in the spring of 1920, in a series of issues, *The Eastern Underwriter* reprinted extensive parts of the official report on marine insurance. Later, an editorial with Dr. Huebner's picture stated:

> Dr. S. S. Huebner of the Wharton School of Finance and Commerce, University of Pennsylvania, is very much in the insurance eye these days by reason of the fact that he is insurance adviser of the United

States Shipping Board, and also of the Congressional Committee which has been investigating the subject of marine insurance. And he is the author of the one hundred page report on marine insurance, some of the most interesting aspects of which have been appearing in *The Eastern Underwriter*. Dr. Huebner has shown his versatility in his exhaustive review of marine insurance conditions in America because he has hitherto been known more as an author of textbooks on life insurance than as an authority on other branches of insurance. One of his books, which has been endorsed by the National Association of Life Underwriters, is a fine presentation of life insurance fundamentals which thousands of agents have found valuable.

About this time *Nation's Business* ran an article which was an interview with Dr. Huebner about marine insurance conditions. There was much controversy in the industry internationally because the foreign companies' representatives felt that Dr. Huebner was attacking them in urging Americans to deal with American companies. Dr. Huebner's patriotic motivation is reflected in a quotation from that interview.

Every year we hand over to foreign companies a grand total of insurance premiums to the tune of $250,000,000. Approximately two-thirds of all the marine insurance originating in this country is controlled directly, or by way of reinsurance, by foreign or foreign-controlled companies. With that goes all knowledge of the character of our shipments and the movements of our ships, placed confidingly in the hands of foreign interests, passing through the foreign insurance companies to the cognizance of the foreign merchant and foreign banker.

Commercially speaking, we literally "give ourselves away." Yes—and pay our chief competitors a whooping bonus for acceptance.

Dr. Huebner also talked on the subject of marine insurance at the national convention of the Chamber of Commerce of the United States, held at Atlantic City in April, 1920. There he again urged the expansion of American marine insurance operations:

American merchants and vessel owners should patronize their own home companies. The remedy for any shortcomings in this respect seems to lie in a campaign of education, not only on the part of those in the insurance business, but by Chambers of Commerce, merchant trade associations, trade journals and other similar sources.

It is interesting that at this convention where Dr. Huebner was turned to as an authority and a leader, insurance as an industry was for the first time recognized in the Chamber's organization. The man and the business were gaining stature together. *The Eastern Underwriter* spoke editorially:

Insurance now is a component part of the United States Chamber of Commerce as it should have been long ago. Without an insurance division the United States Chamber of Commerce would have been a misnomer, because it could not completely represent American commerce while it ignored insurance, the handmaiden of commerce, and one of the greatest, if not the greatest, of American business institutions.

At this period the new federal income tax and its impact on life insurance was an important subject. One of the insurance trade papers invited a number of national leaders outside of the business to express their ideas on this problem. Dr. Huebner wrote:

Insurance must pay tax bills for the mere privilege of doing business more than almost any other institution, and this in spite of the fact that insurance is the right arm of the state, taking upon itself many of the burdens which would be borne by the state were it not for insurance.

Dr. Huebner was becoming increasingly well known to the rank and file of life insurance salesmen. He was getting out among them, speaking to life underwriter associations, company conventions, and even to less formal groups. Parts of a verbatim report of an address given before the Fidelity Mutual Life agency convention in 1920 reflect his manner of speaking, his convictions, and the quality of thinking which he was bringing to the life insurance agents of the country. He continued to combine in his talks sales ideas, new concepts about needs for life insurance, and always the message about the professional status of the competent life insurance salesman.

> Viewing life insurance from the insured's own personal standpoint, we hear two objections very frequently raised. One is to the effect: "I do not believe in life insurance, I believe in saving"; and, secondly, where the value of life insurance from the standpoint of saving is recognized, this objection: "I can save more in other ways." The first objection is positively foolish; and the second, in the overwhelming mass of instances, untrue. The answer to the first objection is that life insurance alone makes saving feasible. If possible, both insurance and saving in other ways should be practiced; but to start on a policy of saving, where a dependent family exists, without hedging against the uncertainty of having the saving period cut short by death, is an act of wanton foolishness. How foolish to argue thus when a dependent household is at stake. What does it profit a man to say: "I will save $5,000 in twenty years," when he does not know that that number of years, or even one year, will be given him? Life insurance, on the contrary, guarantees the full face value of the policy as soon as the first premium is paid. Let us not forget that a resolution to save, even eliminating the chances of premature death, is confronted by two other grave dangers. First, failure to continue the plan, the resolution being more often ended this way than by death; and, second, failure to keep intact what may have been saved, because of bad investments or tempting expenditures.
>
> It is very appropriate at this time to call attention to this aspect of life insurance in its relation to saving. At the present time, if I may be pardoned for making the assertion, about half of all the investors in this country are foolish and about half of the remainder are somewhat worse. There never has been a period in our history when savings have been so thrown away in foolish investments as they have been during the last three years. The reckoning is coming and it is going to be a terrible one. During the year 1919 the new incorporations in the Eastern States, as compiled by the New York *Journal of Commerce*, although these figures include some duplications, aggregated approximately fifteen thousand millions of dollars—an amount equal to about four times the highest previous annual record. I do not know how true it is, but I am told that ten

Recollections About the Teacher Who Changed An Industry

by DR. DAVIS W. GREGG, C.L.U.

CONVICTION, enthusiasm, strength, sturdiness, determination—these are but a few of the adjectives that flash by in the reflections of one who knew Solomon Stephen Huebner the last quarter century of his life.

He was a master teacher, already a legend when I first met him in 1939. His students affectionately referred to him as "Sunny Sol" because of his eternal optimism and pleasant disposition—precious traits he never lost.

Many persons who first met him in his office at the University of Pennsylvania came away with distinct and memorable impressions similar to mine. Nearing his office, you picked up the strong aroma of cigar smoke. Entering, you noticed a light blue haze pervading the atmosphere of his secretary's office and a heavier haze visible through the door of his office. A booming and resonant voice could be heard as he talked vigorously on the telephone.

Coming into his presence, you were struck by the man and his setting. There he sat in his large rocking chair behind an incongruously tiny table. His telephone hung on an old-fashioned extension arm within easy reach. A large roll-top desk was to his right. Both the desk and the table were

a graduate class, or 250 in a lecture section, were delighted with him—and were a delight to him. They sat transfixed through a 50-minute lecture. They would be electrified by the drama of each class. They would leave the room buzzing with excitement.

The scene shifts. Formerly a student, I now return for fifteen years of association with the teacher in a common enterprise. I get to know him as a man and a colleague. He even becomes a second father.

of his energy, drive, conviction, and capacity to articulate his thoughts.

His visitors come from throughout the world. As he talks with them, his voice can be heard resounding through Huebner Hall as in the days when he lectured at his university. He pounds his desk, grits his teeth, crashes one hand into the other, and his visitors leave delighted and inspired.

He is always current on things economic and political. He reads the headlines. He fits new historical developments into the pattern of his philosophy. He expresses his views with great enthusiasm.

He travels and absorbs. With his lovely and gracious wife, he returns to the Orient again as the teacher. They celebrate their golden wedding

The Man Who Dedicatec

by Faith

Mildred F. Stone refers to Solomon S. Huebner in her book, THE TEACHER WHO CHANGED AN INDUSTRY, as two individuals — a man with personal interests and characteristics as well as Dr. Huebner, the educator and public servant. It is altogether fitting that any acclaim we pay him be all inclusive and extol not only his fine teaching career and obvious leadership ability, but also his personal warmth, his excellent sense of humor, his essential humility, and his genuine liking for people. For these combined traits constituted Solomon S. Huebner.

Dr. Huebner's ideas changed an industry. He viewed life insurance from the standpoint of life—not death—and felt strongly that really adequate life insurance provisions and home ownership must come first for a man with a family. His students were taught that life insurance as a protector of profits is an exciting part of our economic system. Pro-

pages of the NEW YORK JOURNAL OF COMMERCE. News of insurance filled that paper—yet the subject had not found its way into the classroom. Solomon Huebner saw the need for university instruction in insurance and prompted Penn to create such courses and to permit him to teach them. His salary was a mere $500 a year, and he was only accepted for the position after promising to grow a moustache so that he could look old enough for the job. The concept of teaching insurance offered great challenge to Solomon Huebner and a wealth of possibilities for future service. Much of his inspiration came from his wife Ethel who worked with him throughout his career.

A Teaching Legend

As there were no available textbooks for the courses, Dr. Huebner wrote his own—four major volumes, each a pioneer work in its field. His

d His Life That We May Better Serve

*. Popkin**

on the collegiate level leading to a degree comparable to that of Certified Public Accountant.

Gradually ideas for a major educational undertaking, as outlined by Dr. Huebner, became crystallized and accepted. In January 1927, the Board of Trustees of NALU formally approved the creation of the American College of Life Underwriters. Officers and directors of NALU met in May for discussions and decisions. It was agreed that courses were to be standardized and highly supervised, but in other areas there was wide disagreement. Dr. Huebner's ideas prevailed and no short cuts or easing of the rigid requirements were permitted; furthermore, he insisted that winners of the coveted recognition be forbidden to commercialize upon it. So vehement was his opposition to the awarding of any honorary degrees that he even went so far as to threaten to leave the movement if one were conferred upon him or anyone else

formation of the "Committee of 1,000" under which C.L.U.s assume responsibility for personally selecting and guiding one or more prospective C.L.U.s through the program.

Continued Service and Recognition

Dr. Huebner fostered the cause of insurance education throughout the world. Often his wife accompanied him on trips to the Orient, Alaska, Canada, Mexico and the West Indies to name but a few. While in Japan in 1958, the Emperor conferred the Order of the Sacred Treasure upon Dr. Huebner for his contribution to the welfare of the Japanese Insurance Industry. This honor is especially outstanding since it is rarely given to foreigners.

Dr. Huebner continually served the industry and his country. In 1912 he was selected to head the United States steamship agreements investigation, and later he become engaged in a

ed to advance similar objectives in the property and casualty field through the C.P.C.U. program. He served as chairman of their board from 1942-1961 when he was named emeritus chairman.

Dream Fulfilled, He Works On

And the C.L.U. movement continued to advance. In 1948 College and Society headquarters were moved to their own home in West Philadelphia, adjacent to the University of Pennsylvania campus. In September 1952, Dr. Huebner stepped down from his position as president of the American College in favor of Dr. David McCahn, a long time associate and friend. Dr. Huebner was made president emeritus of the College, and a year later was made emeritus professor of insurance at his beloved U. of P.

Because of the tremendous acceptance and growth of the C.L.U. movement, it became evident that new headquarters were needed for the Col-

日本國天皇はアメリカ合衆國人
ソロモン・エス・ヒューブナーを
勲三等に叙し瑞寶章を授與する
昭和三十五年六月十四日皇居において
璽を捺させる
天皇御璽
昭和三十五年六月十四日
内閣総理大臣 岸 信介
UNITED

The Bridge Builder

Solomon Stephen Huebner, the teacher who changed an industry, was also a great bridge builder. He built a bridge of understanding between insurance and the public. He built a bridge of knowledge for insurance men and women to cross over the chasm of ignorance about the values of the insurance mechanism. He built a bridge of dignity from the commercialism of the early 20th century to the service-centered concept of professionalism a half century later. He built a bridge of cooperation between the academic community and the institution of insurance.

> "An old man going on a lone highway,
> Came, at the evening, cold and gray,
> To a chasm vast and deep and wide.
> The old man crossed in the twilight dim,
> The sullen stream had no fear for him;
> But he turned when safe on the other side
> And built a bridge, to span the tide."

The chasm Dr. Huebner saw as a young teacher was between the performance of the institution of insurance and its potential for service to mankind; between the needs of individuals, families, and businesses for informed insurance service, and the inability of most to provide that service. His bridge was knowledge and understanding. He knew that the institution would have to embrace real standards of knowledge, character, and ethical practice if it was to grow, prosper, and serve the public.

> " 'Old man,' said a fellow pilgrim near,

Your journey will end with the ending day,
You never again will pass this way;
You've crossed the chasm, deep and wide,
Why build this bridge at evening tide?' "

Dr. Huebner saw why the bridge must be built. He worked in an environment of complacency and sometimes even opposition. Accepted by his academic colleagues as a great teacher and innovator, yet privately ridiculed by some for devoting his talents to insurance, he fought with great conviction to make a place for insurance in higher education.

"The builder lifted his old gray head;
'Good friend, in the path I have come,' he said,
'There followed after me today
A youth whose feet must pass this way.
This chasm that has been as naught to me
To that fair-haired youth may a pitfall be;
He, too, must cross in the twilight dim;
Good friend, I am building this bridge for him!' "*

It was the youth for whom the good Professor toiled—two and perhaps three generations of them have crossed his bridge. New generations now use his structure and march forward together as an institution of dignity and pride.

Our bridge builder has crossed to the other side. His job is done. The chasm will never again seem so vast and deep and wide. Our job goes on.

DAVIS W. GREGG

* *Poem "The Bridge Builder" by Will Allen Dromgoole.*

In the early years of the College, Dr. Huebner traveled extensively throughout the country promoting his new educational venture. "You had to get out and meet the people face to face, or the baby wouldn't live long," he professed.

Gradually the College developed and became a strong force in the field of life insurance education. Immediately following the first C.L.U. conferment the new alumni organized themselves to advance the C.L.U. cause; out of that group evolved the American Society of Chartered Life Underwriters. In order to achieve recognition as an autonomous educational institution, the College became totally independent of NALU in 1929.

Dr. Huebner continually stressed the value of raising the standards of the industry as a whole. He felt that it was the duty of each C.L.U. to constantly encourage others to follow him, for Dr. Huebner knew that dignity and professionalism could only be applied to the industry after significant numbers of its members were highly educated and scrupulously objective in their dealings with clients. This concept ultimately led to the

drastic effect on American marine insurance companies. He was a member of the Insurance Advisory Committee to the War Department throughout World War II. Even long and serious illness did not dampen his determination to expound his beliefs. While in great pain from arthritis, Dr. Huebner showed tremendous courage and determination and continued his lecture tours to the amazement of his doctors.

As a tribute to his outstanding service to the industry, the S. S. Huebner Foundation for Insurance Education at the University of Pennsylvania was created in 1940 to further the training of teachers of insurance. More than sixty insurance companies allocated funds to provide scholarships and fellowships for graduate work for deserving students who planned to teach insurance full-time on the college level. The honor of naming the Foundation after Dr. Huebner was "as great a tribute as the life insurance business could offer a man."

Dr. Huebner was also a driving force in the formation of the American Institute for Property and Liability Underwriters which was found-

activities. Plans were formulated and in 1961 they moved to a new building in Bryn Mawr which was appropriately named Huebner Hall in honor of the "father of life insurance education". This was one of the most significant of many tributes indicative of the high esteem in which he was held by the many whose lives he had so greatly influenced.

Until the last few years, Dr. Huebner continued on active speaking tours across the country. He constantly had the opportunity to feel the stimulus of being needed and of being able to contribute to current activities. Until a week before his death, he came regularly to his office at Huebner Hall and maintained his interest in the affairs of the College and the Society.

Although Solomon Huebner "never sold a dollars worth of insurance himself . . . he gave the business a feeling for their mission as handlers of dreams and hopes—not of dollars and cents."[1] Every Chartered Life Underwriter and everyone who aspires to ever hold the designation owe an everlasting debt of gratitude to Dr. Solomon S. Huebner—the man who dedicated his life that we may better serve.

---

* Editor's note—We realize that it would not be possible to offer the complete story of Dr. S. S. Huebner's life in so short a space. For a complete and interesting narrative of his life, we highly recommend Mildred F. Stone's book, THE TEACHER WHO CHANGED AN INDUSTRY, published by Richard D. Irwin, Inc., Homewood, Ill. We have found this book extremely helpful in the preparation of this article.

1. From a national advertisement, "He ably led, we gladly followed," by the John Hancock Mutual Life Insurance Company, Boston, Mass.

to the philosophy of life insurance is "the human life value" concept, which he introduced in 1924. The public had never before attached an economic value to the human life.

"A man's family life is a business economically speaking, and should be organized, run and liquidated as one," emphasized Dr. Huebner. He directly applied this idea to his own household, purchasing a substantial amount of life insurance at the time of his marriage to Ethel Mudie. Furthermore, he was emphatic in imparting this concept to his three daughters and son (who is now senior vice president of Penn Mutual Life Insurance Company).

Early Years

Solomon Huebner grew up on a farm in Wisconsin and did his undergraduate study at the University of Wisconsin where he also received his M.L. degree. His outstanding work on the debating team as well as his scholarship abilities earned him the coveted Phi Beta Kappa key. After a bicycle tour of Europe, he attended the Wharton School of the University of Pennsylvania on a fellowship, receiving his Ph.D. by the age of 23.

The young Dr. Huebner, his student work completed at the University, received a sudden inspiration from the was made head in 1913. Frequently, Dr. Huebner selected his teachers from among his own students. He offered a challenge to capable young men and permitted his staff to express independent judgment.

Over his fifty-year teaching career, Dr. Huebner taught some 75,000 students. With clenched fist and vigorous gestures, "Sunny Sol" (as he was fondly referred to by his students) expounded the importance of life insurance. In the process he won the love and admiration of his classes and was many times voted the most popular professor at Penn.

One day a number of his students in a large lecture room did not take their seats according to the chart. They roared with laughter and quoted across the campus Dr. Huebner's attempt to correct the situation which began "Some of you seem to be sitting in empty seats."

Recognizing a Need

Dr. Huebner realized that before life insurance could meet its potential in public service, it would be necessary to offer specialized education and training for life insurance company field representatives. In 1914, in a speech to life underwriters in Baltimore, he introduced the concept of having a life insurance course of study

His leonine head crowned with a shock of unruly gray hair, and pierced with his bright and intense eyes, made an indelible impression. His warm and sincere greeting soon made you realize his humanness. What might have been fright at first soon was dissipated, and awe and affection began to take its place. He would rock and talk, and talk and rock, and talk—seemingly oblivious that others were waiting in the outer office.

His classes were legendary. On small 5 by 8 pieces of paper he had jotted in pencil the items he planned to cover in a given session. He started with his outline but soon was carried away with the enthusiasm of conveying a fabric of ideas woven around experiences. His voice alternated between the booming, shouting tone of a great evangelist and the quiet and resonant tone of a relaxed philosopher. He set his great jaw and ground his teeth as he drove home his significant points. His eyes were lit with fire. His hand would slam down on the edge of the lecture table as if it were a great oak gavel on a rostrum. Once he even paused to say, "Ouch,"—to the delight of the class.

His students, whether a dozen in

Solomon S. Huebner

Now the teacher has grown older. Soon he is to retire from his fifty years of service on the faculty of his great university. He is not ready for retirement, however. He is destined to have a full dozen additional years of exciting and fruitful activity in the educational institution he founded for persons in life and health insurance.

Now he is remembered as the perfect president emeritus. Always available for policy-level discussions, wise in his judgments, humble in his views, and determined to make a younger generation of educators feel that they have the responsibility for decision-making.

He continues to lecture to audiences, large and small. He is recognized as being older but people stand in awe

first trip to Australia and New Zealand. With infinite and interesting detail, he remembers people and places and things and ideas.

Time, and the ravages of his many illnesses, take their toll. An 80th birthday party in 1962 finds him weakened by flu. His intimate party of friends wonders if he is failing. They wondered the same 20 years before when they created a Foundation in his name as a last tribute.

His health returns. With enthusiasm he continues with his activity at the College each day. He is obsessed with an idea that men who are Chartered Life Underwriters have the personal responsibility of bringing other men into the program. He creates his Committee of 1000 for personal sponsorship of new candidates for the C.L.U. and it succeeds as has every other project with which he has been associated.

He loves Huebner Hall. He loves the great trees, the beautiful shrubs and flowers that surround it. He feels established here.

He was a lucky man. He did not suffer. He continued active to the end. In the words of his gracious lady, "He just went to sleep."

thousand oil companies have been floated during the past three years. If one out of twenty succeeds I shall be very much surprised. This year, up to date, new incorporations in the Eastern States, by way of comparison, are taking place at the rate of approximately twenty thousand millions of dollars.

The present speculative attitude that seems to possess the American people caused me recently, in a volume I edited on "Bonds and the Bond Market," to liken the situation to the race between the tortoise and the hare, of which we are told in Aesop's fable. The hare expected to leap to victory and saw fit to take a nap somewhere on the race course. The tortoise proceeded slowly, by the methodical and everlastingly stick-to-it method, and won the race. So it is in the accumulation of a competency. The average American seems to take the attitude of the hare in this race, and in the overwhelming majority of cases is put to sleep somewhere on the race course and usually continues to sleep permanently. Judicious investors will do well to follow the life insurance method. This method may be likened unto the tortoise—the slow, persistent, accumulating method, which recognizes the tremendous working force of compound interest.

All my insurance, to-day, is on the whole life and long endowment plans. These policies give me comfort, better feeling, greater happiness; and as a result of these the increased initiative that flows from a sense of permanent security at a known cost. This feeling alone is well worth the price I must pay and I should never regard these policies as something to be grudgingly borne. What I like also are the growing reserves of those policies. The other week I took occasion to add up those reserves, the savings fund of my policies. Is it possible, I thought, that I should have unconsciously saved a sum so large? The periodic driblets, the premiums, I did not particularly miss. If not so invested, I doubt whether they would have been saved; and if they had been saved I doubt whether they would have earned a fairer rate of interest elsewhere. Now these driblets have grown into a substantial sum and are available. But I do not want to use them. I have the protection and desire to see the saving fund grow larger. Granting life and ability to work, I can ascertain the value of the saving fund into the distant future and feel reasonably sure that a quarter of a century hence I shall have something substantial for old age support. One needs only to carry a reserve life insurance policy long enough to appreciate it financially. . . .

While life insurance has been used for what we call strictly business purposes as far back as 1583, it is looming up now to an enormous degree as far as that particular purpose is concerned. The use of life insurance for strictly business purposes is required throughout our life. It is needed by the young man when he prepares himself for business. Then, when he enters business, he will need life insurance throughout his business career. Finally, upon reaching what we call the economic death period, say about age 65, the business man again needs life insurance to conserve the estate which he may have succeeded in accumulating during the years of his toil. From the very beginning until death the need of life insurance is always present.

Let us take up first the need of life insurance on the part of the young men and women who wish to prepare themselves for some vocation. This subject is dear to my heart. I want the student to see it. Life insurance is the only known way of borrowing in a business-like manner without possessing any tangible collateral. I have the experience every year of seeing it work in this respect. Scores of young men are obliged to drop their college course, or are foolishly stopped from entering college, because they say they have not the means. I come in touch every year with a much larger number of young men who do have the nerve to start the course without means and who attempt to "work their way through," as the saying is. They think that is very commendable. I do not. I think that is one of the most foolish things a person can do—and I speak feelingly because I did some of it myself. A young man who prepares for business or a vocation should devote his time to the particular object he has in view. He should not serve two masters. If he goes to college he should really go to college. In the great majority of instances I find that a young man has some friend, some acquaintance, some relative to whom he could go in a business-like way and ask for a loan of the money. All that young man needs is a good name. That asset he must have; but if the lender knows that the money will be repaid, then he need protect himself against only one other serious contingency, namely, the possibility of premature death. Life insurance affords a most excellent means of raising money at a strategic time without the possession of any tangible collateral.

Now after a man enters business, life insurance is needed to protect the business against the loss of the value of the life. It is only within the last ten or fifteen years that life insurance has been recognized on a large scale as a means of protecting business and credit.

It is dawning upon us that every life has a value in business. The development of life insurance in this respect is interesting. We started out originally with the idea of insuring big lives, the leading capitalists, the guiding brains in business. Now, if the big man needs life insurance, the small capitalist needs it even more. Every mortgage ought to be "hedged" with a life insurance policy. Every building and loan association account should be "hedged," as should also a great many of the smaller bond issues. Every obligation of any kind which in any way seriously affects the financial status of an individual in business should, as a matter of good business practice, be "hedged" with a life insurance policy. What a wonderful field! It is up to the life insurance solicitors of the United States to ferret out the cases and bring the message home.

Next, the use of life insurance was extended to the protection of business against the loss of valuable employes, managers, and persons possessing scientific skill; and now the thought is taking hold that all lives, even those of the plain workers, have a value to the business. And so we are having the development of group insurance, the insurance of workers in the mass.

Now we come to the end of the business career, the close of the working life, and we again find life insurance coming in to fulfil a very useful function, namely, to conserve the estate that has been accumulated during the years of work. I merely mention some aspects that present themselves. The inheritance tax gatherer is becoming very prominent. He will be much more prominent in the future than he is to-day. Whether we like it or not, I think that is inevitable. Men who have accumulated estates will want to conserve them against undue depreciation because of possible enforced liquidation to pay the tax at a time when their securities are selling very low in the market. Think of the present, with practically all good investment securities down 25 per cent, from what they were a few years ago. But life insurance may also be used to conserve an estate against the inheritance tax itself. That is to say, an amount of insurance approximately equal to the tax might be taken out to fill up the gap. . . .

But many people are not so fortunate as to have an estate of such size that they need to protect it against the inheritance tax gatherer. They have merely succeeded in laying up an ordinary competency. Here life insurance comes in once more to protect such limited estates and make them suffice. The purpose of life insurance is to protect those who die prematurely by requiring payments from the fortunate who do not die so soon. . . .

Now I have reached the end of my talk. You are fortunate to be associated with a business that will grow with leaps and bounds. Its future is all ahead. Some day the capitalization of human life values will be accepted everywhere and then present life insurance figures will seem small indeed. You are in a profession whose services are needed by all, rich and poor, and at all times; at the beginning of one's career, during one's working years and thereafter once more to conserve the estate. You are missionaries of happiness and your service ranks with that of the doctor, clergyman and teacher. You have a right to feel real happiness every time you close a policy which has been honestly fitted to the needs of your client. Every time you write a policy you bolster up a home against misfortune. The more insurance you write the happier you should be. So God speed you all to double your quota.

CHAPTER TEN

The Human Life Value Concept

VERY early in Dr. Huebner's career the idea struck him of the parallel between life insurance and property insurance. Of course the thought was not completely original, for his great predecessor at the University of Pennsylvania, Benjamin Franklin, had said nearly two centuries before: "It is a strange anomoly that men should be careful to insure their houses, their ships, their merchandise, and yet neglect to insure their lives, surely the most important of all to their families, and more subject to loss."

Benjamin Franklin had seen the logic of that parallel, but Dr. Huebner blazoned it on a banner and led a crusade. He mentioned it briefly in his first *Life Insurance*; it was referred to also in the Cincinnati address; and in other talks to life insurance people, to general audiences, and to his students he had been developing what came to be known as "the human life value idea."

In 1924 Dr. Huebner was the keynote speaker at the annual convention of the National Association of Life Underwriters held at Los Angeles. His topic was "The Human Value in Business Compared with the Property Value." This talk was a comprehensive presentation of his concept of the human life value from the economic point of view. He discussed this in the strictly business aspect and as it relates to the family. A few quotations from that speech, which became as familiar to life underwriters of the 1920's as Lincoln's Gettysburg Address, will give the essence of his concept.

> In our economic life only two types of values exist, namely human life and property values. The life values consist of the character, industry, technical and managerial ability, power of initiative, and judgment of individuals. They have heretofore been regarded as intangible, economically indefinite, and difficult if not impossible of scientific treatment. The property values comprise land, buildings, machinery and equipment, raw materials, finished goods, and business goodwill. Being tangible in character, and thus more easily comprehended than the life values, these material things have for years been regarded as capable of scientific organization and management. They are therefore subjected to appraisal. Through the issue of stocks, bonds, warehouse receipts, bills of lading, and similar evidences of wealth, they are given perpetuity as working capital and fluidity as collateral for loans. They are also recognized as being subject to immediate or ultimate loss. Scientific use is therefore made, as a matter of ordinary business precaution, of the principles governing depreciation, sinking funds, and contracts of indemnity.
>
> Without these practices, property values—like life values—would also be indefinite economically. But with the lessons so admirably evolved for us in the field of property values and with this information to guide us, may we not ask why life values should not be treated equally scientifically and be made equally tangible and definite? Is it not ridiculous for a human being to make himself more and more valuable all the time and then all of a sudden, just when that value is greatest to his business and his family, have it disappear entirely because of death or disability? Does it seem reasonable that life values should be treated thus carelessly, especially since we owe a duty to others—to family and business associates—when the lessons of foresight, so fully prepared in connection with property values, are before us for imitation?
>
> The most important new development in economic thought will be the recognition of the economic value of human life. I confidently believe that the time is not far distant when, in wholesale fashion, we shall apply to the economic organization, management, and conservation of life values the same scientific treatment that we now

use in connection with property. We shall do so to the extent of capitalizing them with bonds to give them perpetuity as a working force and fluidity as a source of credit, of subjecting them to the principles of depreciation, and of using the sinking-fund method to assure realization of the contemplated object wherever man has a future business or family obligation to fulfill that involves the hazard of uncertainty of the duration of the working life. I also believe that Life Insurance alone affords the medium through which such scientific treatment can be applied, and that it has no competitor.

Scientific treatment of life values is justified because of their monetary importance in our economic affairs. Human life values—the factors of personal skill, industry, judgment, and driving force, that mean so much to business success—greatly exceed in importance all property values. These personal factors are after all the real source of all other economic values. Were it not for them, there would be no property values. Were I called upon to make an estimate of life values in the United States, based on the current earning capacity of our adult population, capitalized at an ordinary rate of interest, I would place the total valuation at not less than six to eight times the aggregate of the nation's material wealth. Surely, such a predominating element in our national economic wealth should be accorded scientific consideration when we have seen fit to extend it for many years to the minor element. Instead, we have from an economic standpoint largely ignored the creative force that gives rise to property values. We have emphasized the effect rather than the cause, the finished service rather than the performer of the service, the temporary products rather than the permanent producer of those products.

With respect to many classes of men, the life value constitutes practically all of their business worth. This is true of doctors, dentists, teachers, clergymen, lawyers, engineers, architects, scientists, authors, actors, salesmen and innumerable other groups engaged in professional or expert work. And the significant fact in this connection is that in many callings the greater the practitioner, the greater his skill and compensation, the more complete the loss of the business asset in the event of the passing of the life value involved. The average doctor's practice, I am advised, can possibly be sold for an amount equal to one year's income, a price appallingly small when compared with the practitioner's earning capacity spread over the normal working life. A great specialist, however, is irreplacable even to this small extent. In his case, because no substitute exists, loss of the life value is equivalent to a total loss of the business asset. In many vocations—such as teaching, the ministry, the stage, salesmanship, etc.—the loss of the life value, unless hedged with insurance, almost invariably means a total loss of the capitalized business worth, irrespective of whether the practitioner is great or mediocre. The same is also true of all persons working on a salary, be they ordinary or expert.

Often the business under consideration is chiefly concerned with contracts, the fulfillment of which involves great skill and managerial ability, much credit, and a considerable lapse of time. Here the life value clearly exceeds the value of the equipment used. This fact is attested to by the universal demand for adequate corporate surety from the contractor. And surety companies, obligating themselves to complete the contract in the event of the contractor's failure to do so for any reason, and knowing that completion of the work is more dependent upon the personal ability of the contractor than upon his property assets, are always very careful to inquire into his personal record of efficiency and the amount of Life Insurance he carries.

Many types of business, although requiring some property for their operation, have for their chief asset the good-will of clients, built up in the course of years through close personal contact, confidence, and friendship. A prominent broker in securities, when asked by me to give an opinion concerning the value of his life to his business, replied after mature deliberation that in the event of his death probably fifty per cent of the good-will, which he had worked for years to create and hold and which was the main source of the current business income, would flow elsewhere within the course of a year. He expressed surprise at the inquiry, said he hadn't thought of things in that light before, and, knowing my general bent of thought, jovially expressed his belief that he ought to be a candidate for a substantial amount of Life Insurance indemnity.

In still another type of business, such as manufacturing and mercantile establishments, the property value seems to predominate. Yet even here, the most extreme type that we can select, a careful appraisal in the light of all attending circumstances will show that in the overwhelming mass of cases the directing life values in the business exceed in importance the property value actually owned by the concern. We are too apt to overlook the fact that most of the apparent property in such concerns is not owned out-right, but represents borrowed funds, and that the balance actually owned is largely non-liquid in character and is dependent for regular income producing value on a wisely shaped and well directed policy on the part of the owner.

Moreover, this balance of property actually owned, especially if it constitutes the major part of the owner's personal estate, as is usually the case, will in the event of his death likely suffer severe impairment through the payment of post-mortem taxes and other costs connected with the settlement of the estate, a possible curtailment of credit which, as already noted, often exceeds the actual property owned, and a diminution in earning capacity resulting from the loss of the directing life value itself. Where the business is in its formative stage, the loss of the life value, unless adequately hedged with Life Insurance, is often the cause of bankruptcy. By thus striking a net balance between the life and the property values, I am confident that the first will exceed the latter in the great majority of manufacturing and mercantile establishments.

Few appreciate the far-reaching economic importance of Life Insurance. It represents the application to human life values of the applied economic sciences, now so fully prepared and so generally taught with respect to property values. . . .

A new philosophy of values is necessary to change our attitude of mind, and in turn, the trend of our text-books. Usually the subject of insurance is treated by economists in a single chapter, and often in the form of an appended one. To them, Life Insurance seems to be a problem difficult to weave into their discussion of production, exchange, distribution and consumption. Nevertheless, it is an important factor in all of these divisions of economics. Its universal and adequate use would radically alter for the better the character and amount of present consumption. Its vast accumulation of assets from the millions of our population, and its distribution of these assets by way of investment and payment of claims, are two of the most stupendous phases of modern exchange. It is also highly creative by increasing personal initiative through removal of the paralyzing effect of worry and fear, by enlarging greatly the available fund of working capital through systematic, compulsory, and profitable thrift, by increasing tremendously the amount of available business credit, and by indemnifying business against the loss of the personal factors that give it direction and force. Life values underlie all business enterprises. Where business property values exist, life values are inseparably interwoven with them. Since economics is the "science of business" and since life values greatly exceed in importance the property values and are fundamental to business success, it seems reasonable that much more space in our economic texts ought to be devoted to their business aspects and to their scientific treatment by means of Life Insurance.

In discussing life values in business, we are apt to forget that the family is also a business. We are inclined to overlook the fact that all Life Insurance is business insurance, even when effected solely for the purpose of family protection. The family should be every man's first and most important business. From the economic standpoint, it is a business partnership which, like any other partnership, is legally dissolved through the death of either partner. If business partnership insurance is desirable, and that is conceded, then certainly the bread-winning partner in the family, for the same fundamental reason, should also be insured for the benefit of the surviving dependent partners. The family should be organized and operated in accordance with business principles. Just like any other business enterprise, it should be safe-guarded against financial impairment or bankruptcy through the loss of its strategic life value.

All the principles already discussed with reference to life values in business are equally applicable to the family relationship. To permit the starting of a family partnership, when the only contributed capital is the native ability, good-will and current earning capacity of its head, is little short of a crime, unless adequate provision has been made for a guaranteed potential estate through the medium of Life Insurance.

Dr. Huebner's life value concept and quotations from his speech made the front page of the second section of the next

Dr. Huebner with the blowup of the *Los Angeles Times* article concerning his 1924 human life value speech, presented by the Los Angeles Chapter of the American Society of Chartered Life Underwriters in 1957.

morning's *Times* in Los Angeles.* They also caught fire among life underwriters. The speech in pamphlet form was distributed

* At a meeting of the Los Angeles Chapter of the American Society of Chartered Life Underwriters in March, 1957, when Dr. Huebner was a speaker, he was presented with a laminated plaque of that page, "in abiding appreciation of the tremendous contribution that he has made to the life underwriters of America over a long period of years."

widely by the National Association of Life Underwriters. Leaders everywhere began to talk and use the life value idea in selling. Those were the days when, because of the Florida real estate boom and the burgeoning stock market, it was easy to think big. It did not scare a man making twenty thousand dollars a year to be told that he represented a capital value of several hundreds of thousands of dollars. The income tax situation then was such that he could quite comfortably manage to cover his life value with life insurance, if so he desired. Many were flattered, or logically persuaded, and did. Life insurance agents saw a professor's academic idea paying off for them in sales. That did not harm his leadership in the movement for better educational programs for life insurance fieldmen. It did not, however, bring everyone flocking to the cause.

During the 1920's the pioneers were working constantly toward their goal of a collegiate program. Books were being prepared. The National Association had formally sponsored a series to be edited by Dr. Huebner. Dr. Huebner selected the topics to be covered, planned the scope of each book, chose and persuaded the authors, and worked with them to produce a collegiate-level text. He also was making contacts with colleges and universities, stimulating the introduction of courses in life insurance, sharing his experiences as a teacher, and laying the groundwork for co-operation with the projected new organization. He took every opportunity also to lecture to all kinds of audiences—bankers, accountants, lawyers, trust officers, teachers—along lines helpful to the development of the professional concept. He featured the creative side of life insurance with subjects such as "The Value of Life Insurance to the Policyholder" (to get away from the death side only); "Life Insurance and Credit"; "Life Insurance as Investment." His most commonly used topic was "The Economics of Life Insurance." He expounded his ideas about the place of life values in the creation of wealth, and the importance of the parallel between life and property values in the study of the science of wealth, that is, economics. In his nationwide presentation of that story he reminded himself of his fellow-Philadelphian Dr. Russell H. Conwell with his popular "Acres of Diamonds" lecture. He said that program committees often did not want a lecture on the professional concept, but would be hospitable to the idea of economics. So he would develop that theme and at the end apply it to the proposed professional movement. He felt that he thus made many friends for the College before it was born.

As visitor all over the land, Dr. Huebner had the experience of being passenger in many automobiles made available by admiring friends. He could tell instantly, he says, whether a man was a good driver. Regardless, the professor had to grin and bear what came, for he was always courteous and considerate of the feelings of others. About a dozen times he was in serious accidents, not always the fault of his host-chauffeur. One noteworthy experience was a double accident, still with no disastrous personal effects. It was winter in Minneapolis. He was to take a midnight train and his host suggested an evening at the theater. When the play was over they discovered that there had been a typical Minnesota sleet storm. The world was covered with ice and under a full moon everything sparkled like diamonds, while the streets were like glass. Nevertheless, Dr. Huebner's friend said they could make the train. Going down hill their car was hit by another skidding out of control. They carromed into the path of an approaching interurban car which catapulted them back across the street and into the ditch. Amazingly nobody was hurt. They got out of the automobile. The men in the trolley crowded around in curiosity and then with good-natured co-operation got the car back on the road. They went safely on their way and still caught the train.

CHAPTER ELEVEN

Establishing the American College of Life Underwriters

During these preincorporation years of the College, the various sponsors in the N.A.L.U. were thinking and working too. Finally, ideas for a major educational undertaking as outlined by Dr. Huebner became fairly well crystallized and accepted. The plan was to promote a program of five examinations on the collegiate level, covering life insurance, life insurance selling, and related business subjects. It was agreed that an organization should be brought into existence to administer the examination series and to recognize achievement by an appropriate degree. The decision was made also to require preliminary academic qualifications similar to those of other collegiate institutions. That meant that a high school diploma or its equivalent was a prerequisite to the new educational program, which aroused vigorous criticism from many successful salesmen who in those days had made good with a minimum of formal education.

Thus, many fieldmen argued that the plan for the proposed college was too bold and too revolutionary, the standards were too high, the rules unfair. The home offices also strengthened the forces of opposition. The sales managers felt that when a salesman sat down to book work that would spoil him for getting business.

The greatest support for the program came from successful general agents in the field, men like Ernest Clark, some of whom were used to viewing many matters differently from their home office executives. In January, 1927, the Board of Trustees of the National Association of Life Underwriters formally approved the creation of the American College of Life Underwriters. On March 22, 1927, the College was incorporated in Washington, under the laws of the District of Columbia. In addition to Mr. Clark and the three men whom he had committed to the cause away back in 1914, seven other leaders of the National Association were named as incorporators. The full list was George D. Alder, Franklin W. Ganse, Frank L. Jones, Hugh D. Hart, Paul F. Clark, John N. Russell, Ernest J. Clark, Edward A. Woods, J. Stanley Edwards, Guy M. MacLaughlin and Charles L. Scott. A twelfth incorporator was Edward S. Brashears, a lawyer of Washington, D.C. acting as "resident agent," to meet requirements of the law. Except for Mr. Brashears, all incorporators were members of the National Association, and that standard necessarily excluded Dr. Huebner at that time.

The original bylaws of the College, prepared by Mr. Ernest Clark and Dr. Huebner, stated its purposes:

A. To cooperate with colleges and universities in training students for the career of professional Life Underwriter.

B. To cooperate with educational institutions in general life insurance education.

C. To conduct, if occasion demands, its own institution for the training of resident students for the profession of Life Underwriting.

D. To recognize properly qualified Life Underwriters with a professional degree.

Personally Dr. Huebner strongly opposed the idea of a resident school, believing use of existent institutions throughout the country would be more effective. This provision was included as a compromise. However, the College never did establish a resident institution, and the "degree" proposed was later changed to a "designation" because of legislation limiting degrees to resident schools.

Organization and administrative expenses of the College were underwritten by the Board of Directors and a loan of two thousand dollars was made by the National Association of Life Underwriters to provide working capital.

The first officers of the American College were Edward A. Woods, president; Guy M. MacLaughlin, vice president; Ernest J. Clark, secretary; Franklin W. Ganse, treasurer; Solomon S. Huebner, dean; Everett M. Ensign, registrar.

The officers and executive committee of the College met in May, 1927 at the Mayflower Hotel in Washington for an all-day-and-half-the-night session of discussions and decisions. In many ways those were difficult hours, with loud arguments and serious differences of opinion. A particular problem was the matter of honorary degrees. Dr. Huebner, Edward A. Woods, and Ernest Clark fought hard against those, believing they would open the door to "diploma mill" operations and leave the College without standing or prestige among higher educational institutions and with little value to the life insurance world. Another serious difference of opinion came over the extent of the examination material and the character of the examinations. Some were ready to settle for what others scornfully called "a two-dollar package." Dr. Huebner had recommended a course of study involving twenty-three books and some eight thousand pages of reading. Even his strong supporter, Edward A. Woods, balked at that. He said he had had those books standing on his desk for months "trying to get used to them." The proposal was finally cut down to thirteen books and about four thousand pages. In the heat of the arguments, some people walked out and slammed the door, but they came back and agreements were reached.

Ernest Clark's summary of decisions indicates how well the

battles were fought, and how fortunate the results were for the long-range success of the program. The following quotations are from Mr. Clark's article on the history of the College in *The Journal of the American Society of Chartered Life Underwriters.*

> There was extended discussion concerning the rights of other institutions of higher learning to grant the designation of Chartered Life Underwriter (C.L.U.). It was decided, however, that the designation should be granted only by The American College of Life Underwriters on examinations prescribed by The American College, but given under the auspices of cooperating universities and colleges. While this was "blazing a new trail" in higher education, it was the most practical course of procedure and would result in standardizing the course of study wherever given and supervised. Cooperation, therefore, was to be sought of existing universities and colleges in preparing candidates for the C.L.U. examinations instead of creating a separate college in residence as authorized by the American College charter. Through this course of procedure the C.L.U. program could be developed in every State of the Union and the American College made truly national in character and not localized in the District of Columbia. . . .
>
> Qualification requirements of candidates were set up under two heads: (1) Educational background of the candidate. It was decided that the requirements for admission to the Chartered Life Underwriter Course of Study were to be the same as those of other higher educational institutions—a completed high school course or its equivalent. (2) Other requirements: age, life insurance experience and moral character.
>
> On recommendation of Dean Huebner, the following schedule of subjects for examination of candidates for the C.L.U. designation was adopted: Life Insurance including the Economics of Life Insurance, the Scientific Principles of Life Insurance, Life Insurance Salesmanship, Economics, Taxes, Commercial Law, Wills, Trusts and Estates, Corporation Finance, Commercial Credit, Banking, Investments, English and Public Speaking. . . .
>
> It was arranged at this meeting that the first C.L.U. examinations were to be held in 1928 at a central point in every state where the

number of candidates warranted such arrangement, all examinations were to be held under the supervision of a recognized institution of learning and two and one-half days were to be given to the entire series of five examinations. . . .

The C.L.U. designation, as indicated, was to require not only academic attainment and the satisfactory completion of five examinations—uniform in character wherever given and as prescribed in detail by the American College—but the candidate, before receiving the C.L.U. designation, was to complete three years of satisfactory experience as a successful life underwriter. During his three-year period the volume and character of business written must measure up to a certain standard as to volume and quality.

The Chartered Life Underwriter, therefore, whether a resident of any of the forty-eight states, Hawaii, Porto Rico, or a foreign country, will have had the same uniform preparation for professional life underwriting.

The final syllabus for study included five new books which had been written especially for the C.L.U. program, one of which was Dr. Huebner's *Economics of Life Insurance*. That was a comprehensive treatment of the human life value concept with detailed explanation of ways for applying to human values the established economic principles so commonly used with property values. These books were published by D. Appleton and Company who had taken the guarded chance with Dr. Huebner's *Life Insurance*. They were known as the Appleton Series and subsequently included seven other books, one of which was *Life Insurance as Investment* by Dr. Huebner and David McCahan. Dr. Huebner planned the series, outlined each volume, and selected and worked with each author in a program of intensive creation through several years.

A thoughtful review of the *Economics*, with an appraisal of the whole series, which appeared in a contemporary life insurance journal, indicates the effectiveness of Dr. Huebner's pioneer work.

Professor Huebner's book is valuable to every agent in the field who is trying sincerely to do his work in a professional spirit and with a professional outlook. Not one agent in ten has any conception of the benefits of life insurance such as are here presented. How could he have? Not even the most skilled agent can read it without gaining intellectual progress, which is bound to be reflected in greater financial returns. The broadened outlook alone that it will create would be well worth-while, but don't forget, that this new outlook itself cannot escape being translated, almost without one's knowing it, into larger ability and more satisfying success. . . .

The argument is built about the thought which is Professor Huebner's central contribution to the philosophy of life insurance,—namely, that the human life value, the predominating economic element in our business and family affairs, should be given the same scientific treatment that we now extend to property possessions. . . .

The publication of the books in this series provokes certain reflections on how times have changed. Imagine such a collection, written from their lofty standpoint of scholarship in general, and of knowledge of the most modern social sciences in particular, twenty-five years ago! The project would have beggared the imagination.

At the beginning of the present century the books of any value available on life insurance were practically confined to actuarial science. There, of course, the field was well represented. But whatever existed on the medical or legal or agency aspects of the subject was crude and limited and dry indeed.

As a matter of fact, the same was true of books dealing with business in general. Be it noted that this was before the days of business with a big "B." Yet look at the current book-lists of our leading publishers! The change is profound; it would be startling were we not so accustomed to it. The tremendous amount of work that has been done in the scientific study of the phenomena of business during the first quarter of this century is simply another revelation of what can be accomplished in any given field when, the time being ripe, it becomes desirable to turn on to that field the illumination that comes only from investigation conducted by competent men. . . .

At this point, let me interject a fuller statement of what science is and the way it works.

In science the facts bearing on a given problem are presented as completely as possible, and are classified with reference to their significant bearings upon the problem. . . .

Science is also a work of the imagination, and gives to the worker the same sense of satisfaction that is experienced by the creative artist. No better illustration of this could be found than Professor Huebner's book. In the working-out of a principle, and in the systematizing of many facts under a broad generalization, every scientist finds a creator's joy. He gives form and significance to the disordered materials of experience.

Ours is a generation of pioneers in this new faith. It has taken many years to create in men the understanding and the courage that will accept truth in any field,—but most of all perhaps in Life Insurance,—simply because it is the truth. And the direct influence on practical life of such a scientific study as Professor Huebner has here undertaken is enormous. The conception of life insurance that he builds up is bound to influence all his readers and followers, to the point of almost revolutionizing our conception of its social and business utilities. Such scientific work is both an instrument and a guaranty of progress, and will affect men's attitude toward experience, and thereby promote their material advance. . . .

In no part of the great field of American business has a work of larger significance been accomplished than in life insurance. In the first place, the gigantic growth of the institution is both the cause and the result of the study that men of vision and trained observation and sound reasoning have given to it. The life insurance of the era of the Armstrong investigation of 1905 holds much the same relation to the life insurance of today that the automobile of that vintage holds to the 1928 models of the best manufacturers. The distance both have come, in every detail of executive engineering and sales operations, is stupendous.

To prove this you have only to try to imagine the subject of this article, Professor Huebner's "Economics of Life Insurance," the foundation book of this new series, as having appeared in 1905.

In the first place, it could not have been written, for the reason that no one living had ever worked out anything resembling the philosophy of life insurance that it contains. In the second place, its mes-

> sage would have fallen flat on an uninterested insurance fraternity, because no person had the philosophical comprehension of the subject to form the necessary point of contact, so to speak, to mesh-in with its assumptions and ideas. And finally, so far as the public is concerned, it would have been considered, doubtless, as little more than the Utopia of a visionary, if not the empty gesture of an extravagant quixotism.
>
> But a great change has come, and the insurance world is ready and willing to absorb broad interpretations of its service in the terms of Professor Huebner's philosophy. Reading his book is like drawing back a curtain that hangs in front of a window, looking out over a far-flung panorama of natural scenery, embracing every feature of a beautiful prospect. Here in one charming view is presented an extended vista of the serviceableness of life insurance,—a vista that is as inspiring as it is novel and arresting.*

Dr. Huebner sailed for Japan in June, 1927 for a world trip that had been planned for several years, and the embryo College was left to the leaders of the National Association of Life Underwriters. In the next few months it became apparent that things were not as settled as might have appeared. When the National Association met in Memphis in October, 1927, the leaders had to defend what they were proposing, and, under pressure, had expanded their recommendations, as the following excerpts from the *Proceedings* of the meeting indicate.

Edward A. Woods was the spokesman. He outlined the plan for the College as determined by its officers at the earlier meeting in Washington. He explained how candidates for the examinations must submit elaborate applications and that their qualifications would be carefully screened before they could sit for the tests. He announced that the charge to successful candidates would be one hundred dollars. In addition he expressed some general purposes and principles:

---

* In 1959, the third edition of *The Economics of Life Insurance* was published. Over the years Dr. Huebner has constantly expanded his ideas about the human life value concept. He believes that other scholars will continue his work and that eventually a considerable volume of publications in this field will result.

The first purpose of the American College of Life Underwriters is to give a degree similar to the degree of certified public accountants to those who come up to the required tests. The second purpose of this college, or the result of it, will be that colleges throughout the country will give courses on Life Underwriting. . . .

The giving of a college degree sounds like a simple proposition, but I wish you knew the patient work that your far-flung executive committee of the college, stretching from Houston, Texas, to Boston, has given to it. We are confronted at once with the proposition that a college degree has to mean something in the college world, and that if we give it to people on standards not recognized by the outstanding colleges, these colleges will put it aside as they put aside a proposal to call a man mortician rather than undertaker, or a realtor as compared with a real estate man. . . .

In conferring with the college deans as to what they felt was sufficient qualification for this degree, we ran up against the fact that this degree should be mighty hard to get. And I tell you frankly if we get fifty people in the United States to get the college degree the first year, we will be doing mighty well.

The colleges have looked askance at any proposition without a good educational background, high school or its equivalent. The colleges, of course, require a general knowledge of the subjects that underlie the work of the Life Underwriter, and we have been working under the leadership of Dr. Huebner, who ought to be put on the payroll of Life Insurance companies, who is doing all this work for nothing. We were up against the proposition of how it is going to be possible to give this degree widely and yet have the persons qualify for it by that study that all the college deans say is necessary. . . .

At the same time, my friends, we can't make this a cheap degree. If you are going to make it a cheap degree that college men will laugh at, you are going to ruin the whole thing. . . .

I want you to understand the difficulties under which your committee has been laboring in trying to accommodate the people who will deserve it, and who will be a credit to Life Underwriters, and in establishing a curriculum that will meet the standards of the great universities all over the country. . . .

I don't want you to think we have been unmindful of the difficulty of expecting business men to get the educational background. At the same time we have had to yield to the opinion of college deans and recognize its importance. You must remember there are only 140,000 physicians in the United States, and those men paid thousands of dollars, spent some four years in college and four years in medical school and two years of interneship, and then bought hundreds of dollars of equipment to begin to practice medicine. There are 50,000 more Life Underwriters than there are physicians in the country, and if these conditions seem hard to you, think of the lawyer or the physician or the architect or the trained nurse even. My gardener spent three years in Scotland to learn to plant flowers and vegetables, and many gardeners from Scotland and Ireland and England spend more time than that in apprenticeships. My last Scotch gardener got a shilling a week for the two years he learned gardening. . . .

I don't know a man who deserves as much thanks as Dr. Huebner for the inspiring effort he has given. Furthermore, Dr. Huebner's name has carried weight with every college we have corresponded with. If we had corresponded as Life Underwriters we wouldn't have anything like the position that is coming from Dr. Huebner's standing. His name carries weight that is of exceeding value to us, and the result of this effort, whereby courses will be given in colleges in places convenient to Life Underwriters, will be much greater than we could ever accomplish by setting up one college of our own where the people of Detroit or Seattle or Los Angeles or Miami would have to go.

If in college after college Life Underwriting will be made a subject of study, in order to give a man a professional standing, that will be one of the greatest benefits that can come from this college. We had to accommodate our views to the ideas not only of Dr. Huebner but to other college deans.

Mr. Woods also reported a new proposal for Accredited Life Underwriters. This frankly was designed for those who could not meet C.L.U. standards, or who would not make the necessary effort; and also to raise money for the Association. Upon payment of fifty dollars, a member of a local life underwriters

Dr. Davis W. Gregg and Dr. Huebner before the portrait in the American College headquarters, 1959. (*Shaw*)

association, certified as outstanding in character and sales performance, could apply to the American College for recognition. Upon his approval by the College he would receive an attractive little card in a leather case, the card reading: "The National Association of Life Underwriters certifies that (name) is an Accredited National Association Life Underwriter qualified to render professional Life Underwriting service." If the Accredited Life Underwriter later passed the C.L.U. examinations, his initial fifty-dollar payment would be applied against the hundred-dollar C.L.U. fee. Both plans were approved by the Association in convention.

In the months while the various compromises had been under discussion, one member of the College board kept following Dr. Huebner through the Orient with dispairing cablegrams. Dr. Huebner recalls that his own indignation inspired a seventeen-dollar reply, a matter of more financial moment to him than the far longer and numerous messages were to his millionaire correspondent.

When Dr. Huebner returned to Philadelphia in February, 1928, one of his University associates handed him the American College announcements prepared in accordance with the convention decisions. Futilely the friend recommended: "First sit down, then read this, but do keep calm."

Dr. Huebner read the proposals, grabbed the telephone, and shouted at Ernest Clark:* "You've killed it! If you persist in this certification plan I will have nothing to do with the College. I am through." Fortunately Mr. Clark was ready to do everything possible to maintain the integrity of the C.L.U. program.

In spite of the clouds in the sky, preparations for the first examinations in June, 1928 were continued. Thirty-five candidates, from twenty-one different cities and twelve states, were accepted as qualified and took the examinations. A young pro-

---

* Mr. Woods had died suddenly late in 1927, and Mr. Clark was to succeed him as president of the College.

fessor, Dr. David McCahan, was paid two hundred dollars for grading their papers. Twenty-two people passed, including Dr. Yien Düng of Shanghai, China, a student at the University of Pennsylvania.

Dr. Düng returned to China and remained in the insurance business. Dr. and Mrs. Huebner kept in touch with him for many years, though he never achieved the necessary *life* insurance experience to qualify him for his C.L.U. His general insurance activities took precedence over life insurance work. At that time China was more like the rest of the Orient and quite different from Japan in the attitude toward life insurance. Chinese wives did not want to receive money as the result of their husbands' deaths. In fact Chinese life insurance officials told Dr. Huebner that they had difficulty often in settling claims because the widow just was not willing to accept the money.

All the Americans who passed their examinations that first year also had completed the required three years of satisfactory life insurance experience. It was decided to award their diplomas at the National Association annual convention at Detroit on September 14, 1928. This conferment was proposed by Julian S. Myrick, who that year was president of N.A.L.U. He commented that it would "constitute an occasion of dignity and ceremony that will not only impress the recipients, but those who witness it." Thus began the tradition of associating the C.L.U. conferment exercises with the N.A.L.U. annual convention.

In 1928, only six of the twenty-one graduates were able to be present at Detroit. In their presence at a regular session of the convention Dr. Huebner made a report concerning the progress of the College to date. He congratulated the first qualifiers; he stressed the pioneer accomplishments of the College and indicated the basis for great hope for the academic acceptance of the C.L.U. movement. The following quotations from his talk give only a part of his enthusiastic review:

This [the record of twenty-one qualified for the designation] is more than twice the number, we are told, that qualified at the first certified public accountancy examination. The successful candidates are to be congratulated. But so, also, should be the unsuccessful ones, who showed their spirit and demonstrated their belief in a new order of things for the profession of life underwriting. The majority of the unsuccessful candidates have already said that they feel amply repaid through the benefits derived from the course of study to which they have applied themselves, and nearly all have already signified their intention of trying again next December. That represents a fine spirit and nothing has pleased me more. It is better to strive and fail in a good cause, than not to try at all. Nearly one-half of the successful candidates are associated with one company,* and that company has reason to feel proud. . . .

Inquiries thus far indicate that 125 candidates are now preparing for the next two examinations, and the correspondence has been so voluminous as to make your registrar and dean dizzy at times. Various universities and agency superintendents have also written that they are urging their prepared personnel to take the test. Several companies, through their educational departments, by way of printed literature or correspondence, are circularizing their personnel throughout the country. Nor must we overlook the activity of certain life underwriters' associations. One has advised that it expects to have 20 candidates take the examination in December, and another 10. It should be stated, also, that the C.L.U. degree has even a tendency to become international in character. . . .

For the coming December and June examinations correspondence indicates at this date that we shall have three candidates, respectively from China, Madras and Prince Rupert. Foreign insurance interests are vitally interested in our College. On my recent trip I found the Japanese and Chinese anxious to know about it and its aims. And I may add that one of the leading insurance educators of Europe has requested the preparation of an article on "Life Insurance Education in America," with emphasis upon the American College of Life Underwriters' movement, for publication in the

* The "one company" was the Equitable of New York. Nine of the qualifiers were from the E. A. Woods agency in western Pennsylvania; three were other Equitable men.

official organ of one of the world's leading educational insurance organizations with a membership in 24 nations.

Wherever I traveled this summer, attending numerous company and association conventions, I was struck by the genuine interest in the American College of Life Underwriters and by the large number who have personally assured me that they will strive for the C.L.U. degree. Everything seems to point to a total of at least 100 taking the next examination. I am now sure that the College has been successfully launched. I believe that the day is not far distant when your National Association, since education is the key to the future of successful life underwriting, will be convinced that the American College of Life Underwriters is one of the greatest, if not the greatest, factor for good that it has ever initiated and fostered....

Although we have only fairly started, general familiarity with the College and its standards and purposes already exists throughout educational circles. The correspondence shows whole-hearted interest, great enthusiasm, and is proceeding unabated. Twenty-five leading universities and colleges have already, through their deans or directors of their business schools, endorsed our College and its aims, and have given their assurance of co-operation and support. . . .

About half a dozen of these institutions have signified their willingness to offer to their students in insurance the entire range of subjects outlined for the C.L.U. degree. Others indicated their willingness to do so as fast as conditions permit. Three leading universities have stated their intention to recognize the C.L.U. degree in their circulars in a manner similar to that accorded to the C.P.A. degree. . . .

The College has had the fullest cooperation, without a single exception, from universities and colleges in the establishment of examination centers. In fact, a number that had not been approached about the matter because we had no candidates for the examination in those districts, offered their accommodations gratuitously. . . .

The future of the college seems exceedingly bright. The dean, and the same is true of his colleagues, entered the service of the college because of a profound belief in the value of education. But we entered with a little fear and trembling. We wondered whether the time was just ripe, although we were sure of the correctness of the idea. We are now feeling much better.

At the conclusion of Dr. Huebner's remarks, Ernest J. Clark, president of the American College, called the six qualified candidates to the platform and presented their diplomas tied with ribbons of the College colors (blue and gold because Dr. Huebner said blue was the color of life insurance). These six proud men were the vanguard of an army destined to grow mightily in size and influence over the years ahead.

In December, 1928, examinations were given again and fifteen* candidates were successful, making a total of thirty-six in the first year. These pioneers represented California, the District of Columbia, Indiana, Iowa, Massachusetts, Michigan, Minnesota, Ohio, New Jersey, New York, Pennsylvania, and Washington. After the first year, examinations were never again given in the winter, only in June. Surveying the results of 1928, Julian S. Myrick made the prophetic statement: "I am one of those who believes this is a move which you can visualize in years to come as constituting one of the biggest steps that has ever been taken for the development of life insurance." Through more than thirty years Mr. Myrick has worked devotedly to further the interests and influence of the College, to the great advantage of the industry.

Immediately following the first C.L.U. conferments, the new alumni of the College formally organized themselves to advance the C.L.U. cause. The first president was C. Vivian Anderson of Cincinnati. Originally the organization was called simply the "Alumni Association," later the "National Chapter—Chartered Life Underwriters," but since 1940, the "American Society of Chartered Life Underwriters," with local chapters throughout the country. The purposes of the organization as stated in the charter and implemented through the years are:

* The author of this book was in that group.

> To advance in every legitimate way the higher education of those engaged in the profession of life insurance and students who contemplate entering the career of professional life underwriter.
>
> To maintain at all times the dignity and high professional standards that properly attach to the Chartered Life Underwriter designation.
>
> To co-operate with the American College of Life Underwriters in extending its influence and educational program among the universities and colleges of America.
>
> To bring into social and friendly relations those engaged in the profession of life insurance who have acquired the C.L.U. designation.

It was soon apparent generally that the Accredited National Association Life Underwriter certification idea was a mistake. Moreover, Dr. Huebner's opposition was adamant, and everybody felt that he was vital to the continued development of a professional educational program for life insurance. The close connection between the College and the National Association also was seen to be a handicap to the real purposes of the College. The academic world would never recognize a college that was simply an arm of a trade association. Another factor entered the picture in an investigation of the American College by the Board of Education of the District of Columbia. Whether the educational authorities had merely developed their own interest in the procedures of the College or whether it had been maliciously stimulated is not surely known. Dr. Huebner and President Clark were called several times to Washington. They had to answer the most detailed and searching questions, first in writing and later in the cross questions of personal interview. The matter of educational prerequisites for candidates seemed to be of greatest concern. Dr. Huebner was devoutly thankful that their application blanks bringing out information along that line had always been complete. They were asked to describe examination and grading procedures. What pride Dr. Huebner and his associates felt in being able to prove that all candidates had been properly qualified for examinations and that highest standards of academic methods had been followed in every area of College operations. The American College was definitely not a "diploma mill." The C.L.U. stood for real academic and professional achievement. Apparently somebody had thought Dr. Huebner's tireless promotion of the College could not be completely without self-interest. Investigators tried to uncover something wrong there. Finally one of the Board members spoke up: "Mr. Chairman," he said, "in my opinion we are wasting a great deal of time in these inquiries. I happen to have taken my graduate education from the University of Pennsylvania. I do not know Dr. Huebner personally, but I am absolutely satisfied that his standing at the University is such that any educational program of his would be entirely up to standard." That defense quickly helped to bring a satisfactory conclusion to the investigations. The College has never been troubled again, but it has also steadfastly maintained the strictest academic standards in acceptance of candidates and in examination procedures.

Dr. Huebner was in demand as a speaker in Canada as well as in the United States. He traveled there frequently on lecture trips and often returned from Seattle or Portland by way of the Canadian Pacific Railroad to enjoy the Canadian Rockies which he loves. Soon after the founding of the American College, he and Mrs. Huebner made several long tours combining business and pleasure, covering the chief cities—Quebec, Montreal, Ottowa, Toronto, Winnepeg, Saskatoon, Regina, Calgary, Edmonton, Vancouver, and Victoria. Often these visits involved a formal welcome from the mayor of the city, dressed in his robes of office. Since Mrs. Huebner was Canadian-born, the reception given her was frequently especially gracious. Dr. Huebner was repeatedly invited to the Maritime Provinces, but the timing of the proposed meetings always conflicted with University schedules, and he has never been able to go to eastern Canada.

In 1929, the American College became completely independent of the National Association, although N.A.L.U. still continued its strong moral support of the College, and later canceled a note for two thousand dollars which the Association had loaned to the College as it was getting established. College operations, which had been decentralized in the hands of various officers, were all moved to Dr. Huebner's office in Logan Hall at the University in Philadelphia. Dr. David McCahan, professor of insurance at the University and one of the new C.L.U.'s, was elected assistant dean. Thus began a relationship of greatest value to the American College program. Every structure must have its architect and its builder. In a limited sense, because many hundreds of other people also were involved, Dr. Huebner was the architect of the American College and Dr. McCahan was the builder.

Dr. McCahan had been one of Dr. Huebner's students. He was graduated in 1920 and stayed on as instructor in the Insurance Department, getting his M.A. in 1922. After an interlude of four years with the Insurance Department of the United States Chamber of Commerce, he returned to take his Ph.D. at the University of Pennsylvania in 1928.

Dr. Huebner and Dr. McCahan were a remarkable team. Dr. McCahan's dedication to Dr. Huebner and his objectives was complete. They both were extraordinarily hard workers. Dr. Huebner pushed mountains of work over to Dr. McCahan—the organization details and office procedures, all the overwhelming amount of paper work. But he carried his own enormous load of promotion and constant face-to-face selling of the American College and the C.L.U. ideal. They operated under a real austerity program. Each man's salary at first was only fifty dollars a month, and each had half a secretary. The mutual respect and affection between the men was part of the fire in the engines of the College. Friends noted, however, that Dr. Huebner always addressed his young associate formally as Dr. McCahan. He follows that practice today even with men with whose grandfathers he is contemporary. He does not feel comfortable with the modern easy first-name habits.

Dr. McCahan was not only assistant dean of the College in the early years but also secretary and treasurer of the American Society. His careful records and devotion to the C.L.U. alumni activities were extremely important in the development of that organization which was to bring eventually a new element of dynamic leadership into the whole College program.

The C.L.U. examinations in June, 1929 drew three times the number of candidates that had come in the first year, and everybody felt that the enterprise was well established. It was the first professional movement on a collegiate level with strict uniform enforcement throughout the United States. Other professions—medicine, law, and accounting, for instance—have state standards of qualification.

In the preincorporation years of the College Dr. Emory R. Johnson had constantly advised and urged, "Make it national!" Dr. Huebner gives much credit to this man's inspiration for the vision of the College which he developed.

He thanks Dr. Johnson, too, for helping him crystallize his personal objectives in the formative years of his professional life. Naturally Dr. Huebner had many offers, some of them very tempting and well-baited with dollars, to leave Pennsylvania. Other universities wanted him. Life insurance companies tried to get him. Government and business approached him. Dr. Johnson had had much the same opportunities. Talking together they recalled brilliant men who had left teaching for business at some big salary and had dropped from sight, their real influence apparently at an end. Dr. Johnson had challenged: "You must make up your mind what you want. If you are after money, a nice rug, a handsome desk and a lot of push-buttons, business can give you that. But you won't own your own soul. You won't have the freedom to develop that you have in educational work. Talk it over with Ethel, reach a conclusion, and let me know what you decide."

Ruling out business and considering university work, Dr. and Mrs. Huebner remembered Benjamin Franklin's wise advice that a man can't be pulled up by the roots too often and still keep growing. Dr. Huebner figured that a campus midway between the nation's biggest city and its capital would never be a backwash. In Philadelphia he could have metropolitan cultural advantages and still be close to all important opportunities in business and government. So quite early he and Mrs. Huebner decided that his permanent attachment would be to the University of Pennsylvania. That commitment freed him from much waste of time and the mental distraction involved in considering the offers that were so frequently advanced to him.

Although the Wharton School was his home base, Dr. Huebner welcomed the floods of invitations which came to him to visit all over the country. After the launching of the C.L.U. movement, he became increasingly in demand as a speaker before life insurance sales groups. One such talk was made at Swampscott, Massachusetts, for the Massachusetts Mutual Life Insurance Company. He was enthusiastically received and men gathered around to congratulate and question. On this occasion, as so frequently in his busy life, Dr. Huebner found that he must leave immediately to make a connection in Boston for his next appointment. A hearty little man pursued him, urgently wanting to talk further. Dr. Huebner tried to put him off; he just must go; his taxi was waiting. The man persisted that something must be discussed immediately. So Dr. Huebner invited him to get in the cab and make what he could of the ride to Boston. That proved to be a memorable journey because the man was Joseph C. Behan, head of the Massachusetts Mutual's agency department; and the conversation resulted in Dr. Huebner's becoming educational advisor for that company.

Beginning in 1930, each summer for five years he spent the University holiday traveling all over the country for the Massachusetts Mutual. The plan of operation was threefold. First, Dr. Huebner went to such cities as the company indicated and gave a day to the local agency. He talked about the economics of life insurance, with all the ideas which everywhere were proving so stimulating to sales. He also discussed the professional aspects of life insurance selling and finished up with a strong sales talk about the C.L.U. program.

Dr. Huebner's C.L.U. objectives with his Massachusetts Mutual friends were not limited to broad general indoctrination. He set himself a definite program of promotion with a selected group of general agents whom he had appraised as good C.L.U. material. He believed that if he could commit such leaders to the cause they would influence their own associates. In his five years' special work with that company he had the great satisfaction of having about half of his thirty picked candidates become C.L.U.'s themselves and do just as he had hoped in their promoting the program with their agents. At that period the Massachusetts Mutual was the outstanding company in C.L.U. accomplishment. For its size it had by far the largest group of C.L.U.'s. This experience was the foundation of Dr. Huebner's frequently preached philosophy that every C.L.U. should assume responsibility for encouraging others to win the designation. Particularly in the early days, he was concerned by the generally limited vision of salesmen interested in the C.L.U. program. They wanted the designation to set themselves apart as professionally qualified life underwriters, but most of them did not yet have a clear concept of the value of raising the standard of the industry as a whole.

The specific Massachusetts Mutual objective accomplished, then Dr. Huebner remained a second day in each city, active directly on behalf of the American College. He had reached there free, so to speak, and the poor young College had to bear only his living expenses. On that second day he talked to the life underwriters, to civic groups, to service clubs, to the press, to local colleges—in every possible way advancing the purposes of the College with life insurance men, with educators, and with the public. These trips at the formative stage of the College were an immeasurable contribution to the cause. They were a key factor in making the C.L.U. movement a national enterprise. "You had to get out and meet the people face to face, or the baby wouldn't live long," he said, with some mixture of metaphor.

The third element in those summer trips was an occasional extra day or week for Dr. Huebner, the personal traveler. Again, he had arrived far from Philadelphia free, and so could afford a little side trip on his own. So he accomplished much of the sightseeing which he enjoyed so greatly. He thinks it was on one such trip that he and Mrs. Huebner first saw a combination of beauties which has always stood out among their favorites. In the Southwest within a radius of a hundred and fifty miles they saw the magnificent and immense view from the North Rim of the Grand Canyon, so different from the more commonly visited, lower South Rim; they marveled at the richness of color and fascinating rock formations in beautiful Bryce Canyon; they stood in awe before the majesty of the Great White Throne, that rock towering half a mile high above the valley floor in Zion National Park; and with delight they read millions of years of geology in the concentric ledges of Cedar Breaks, two miles across and half a mile deep, like a great prehistoric amphitheater, glorious in "sixty-four colors."

Dr. Huebner's eagerness to grasp opportunities for new experiences was well rewarded about this time when he was speaking at a life insurance company meeting in Miami. An agent invited him to get up very early to see something wonderful. They started before sunrise and went forty miles into the Everglades over the new Tamiami Trail, a ribbon of concrete based on limestone bedrock in the midst of the muck of the swamp, running across the tip of Florida. Paralleling the highway was the brown water of the drainage canal. On either side, as far as the eye could reach, stretched waving seas of sawgrass. No wonder the Indians called the area Pa-hay-okee, "grassy water." Occasionally there were the islands of the cypress hammocks, with their scrubby growth of pines and mangroves and palm trees. That was the setting. But what made the morning unforgettable were birds, birds, birds, especially ducks, of many kinds, and more than Dr. Huebner thought he had ever seen together in all his life. They rose in flocks from waterways unseen amidst the grass. They dropped down into the canal to swim and dive. By the water's edge, mile after mile, standing at attention or working the muck for food, were big and little herons, ibis, and egrets. On every old stump were woodpeckers of various varieties. Balancing on the bending grasses, blackbirds flashed the epaulettes of their red wings. Overhead great buzzards wheeled. It was a wilderness wonderland, completely different from anything he had ever seen. Once beside the highway they passed a Seminole Indian standing, holding a wild turkey shot through with an arrow. This reminded them of the unseen settlements, back in the swamps, of a proud people who were still asserting their inherited independence of the United States.

In the spring of 1931, Dr. Huebner toured Texas, another one of his barnstorming lecture trips. Again, being temptingly near some unknown geography, they could not resist, and he and Mrs. Huebner decided to visit Mexico. They went by rail to Mexico City, and that was a journey they never forgot. It was blue-bonnet time in Texas, and the fields of undulating flowers stretched away on either side of the track like blue water. Little islands of orange paint-brush flowers gave accents of contrasting color. In the desert country the cacti were in bloom. For a brief season their brilliant red and yellow flowers among the spines on the grotesque succulents brought wonderful life to the sands and the rocks.

In Mexico the Huebners again had a competent guide and made their sightseeing an educational experience. The Mexican pyramids, larger and older than those of Egypt, gave amazing proof of what their builders knew about engineering and astronomy. At Cuernavaca they admired the palace of Maximilian and recalled the melancholy history of that poor betrayed monarch and his beautiful Carlotta.

When Dr. Huebner had let it be known that he was traveling to Mexico, life insurance acquaintances urged him to lecture at least once at the University of Mexico. One of the professors called to give the invitation in person. Dr. Huebner agreed to go on a certain day, and waited all morning for his host to come for him. At last he gave up and went sight-seeing. The Mexican arrived while he was out and left word he would come the next day. The same experience was repeated. In frustration, Dr. Huebner told an American friend of this unusual treatment. The friend laughed and asked whether "American time" had been specified in setting the appointment. Of course it had not been, and that proved to be the trouble. In those days in Mexico it was still the land of mañana, and by Mexican time appointments were understood to mean anywhere within about a three-hour span of a designated hour. That was as strange to the punctual professor from Pennsylvania as tamales and serapes.

Such delights on these "side trips" helped to compensate for a kind of unpleasantness that was frequently encountered (other than the normal discomforts of travel in those days before air-conditioning). Usually when his train arrived at the city designated for a life insurance visit, Dr. Huebner stepped off into a welcoming group of life insurance men. Often even in that first delegation there would be somebody wanting to grab him with complaints about not passing a C.L.U. examination. "Those fellows really believed that because they could sell something they knew something. It does not follow," he often commented. To explain and justify the position of academic examiners to successful life insurance salesmen who failed in writing examinations was not easy or pleasant.

In the early 1930's the country was sliding fast to economic depths. It was a time of terrible strain and readjustment, but still the C.L.U. program moved ahead. After five years, three hundred and eighty men and women had qualified for the professional designation. Moreover, the high standards which Dr. Huebner had constantly urged had been maintained. It is easy to imagine how the difficulties of the times must have been used as arguments by those interested in short cuts and less exacting requirements. Why not make the education and experience eligibility requirements easy enough to embrace practically all life underwriters? Why not grant honorary designations without examination? Why not have the examinations focus only on life insurance, and especially selling, rather than including the allied business subjects? Why not take the personal history of the candidate into account and relax the rigid examination and grading system? The officers of the College stood firmly with Dr. Huebner in resisting all efforts to cheapen the attainment of the C.L.U. designation. Moreover, from the beginning the winner of the coveted recognition was forbidden to commercialize it, and no effort was spared by the College in detecting and stopping any laxity in this respect. The C.L.U. had been started on a level to command the respect of the professional world, and men of vision determined to keep it untarnished in prestige.

CHAPTER TWELVE

Depression Years

As the activities of the American College of Life Underwriters developed, teachers in schools and colleges across the country had been originating and expanding insurance courses. Part of this growth resulted from the promotional program of the College. Part was inspired by the demands of would-be students. Life insurance men wanted trained teachers to help them prepare for the C.L.U. examinations. College students wanted courses in insurance comparable to those which had been pioneered by Dr. Huebner at the Wharton School. The growing importance of life insurance in the economic life of the nation naturally had its influence also in bringing the subject recognition in academic circles. The life insurance industry saw its first hundred billion dollars of protection in force just before the stock market crash of 1929, and this insurance was on the lives of more than half of the population of the United States. It was a threefold increase in amount of insurance in a ten-year period when population had increased only 15 per cent. The performance of life insurance in the next few terrible years showed the stability and social importance of the business in a new way. The private life insurance companies paid out millions of dollars to policyholders who literally could not get money anywhere else.

In characteristic American fashion, the insurance professors, seeing their expanding opportunities, decided that a new organization would be helpful. It grew out of the American Economic and American Statistical Associations, and the movement was spearheaded by Frank G. Dickinson, Assistant Professor of Insurance and Statistics at the University of Illinois. In 1931 Professor Dickinson promoted the idea of an insurance teachers' round-table program at the meeting of the American Economic Association, and got Dr. Huebner to serve as chairman. The men attending the round table were favorable to the thought of an independent organization, so Dr. Huebner appointed a committee of five, with Dr. Ralph H. Blanchard as chairman, to prepare plans. The next year, 1932, at Cincinnati, a constitution was adopted and officers elected for the American Association of University Teachers of Insurance.

Not surprisingly, Dr. Huebner was made president; Dr. Blanchard, vice president; Dr. Dickinson, secretary-treasurer; and three others, members of the executive committee: A. H. Mowbray of the University of California, S. H. Nerlove of the University of Chicago, and Corliss L. Parry of the Metropolitan Life Insurance Company.

The purposes of the organization were to promote insurance teaching, research, and publications, to provide an open forum for the discussion of all kinds of insurance subjects, and to cooperate with other organizations with similar interests here and abroad. Membership was open to any one who was presently teaching, or had in the past taught, in a collegiate-level school in the United States or Canada where there was at least one full course devoted to insurance.

The first annual meeting of the Association, held in Philadelphia during the Christmas holidays of 1933, had a program of papers and discussion on life insurance topics of current interest. Authorities from the life insurance business, as well as professors, participated. That illustrated how valuable the activities of the organization could be in bringing reality to the

Portrait of Dr. Huebner by Alfred Jonniaux in 1952—gift of Wharton School students who had specialized in insurance.

academic work of the college teachers. One paper was entitled, "Some Problems Related to Life Insurance Receiverships." This was theoretically interesting, though the number of receiverships was relatively few and everybody in and out of the business was saying how wonderfully it was weathering the great economic storm. As a matter of fact, in the decade 1929–38 losses to policyholders of companies which went out of business were less than 1 per cent of the assets of all life insurance companies. Another feature of the program was a scholarly paper on the effects of inflation on life insurance and a discussion about whether there were too many insurance companies and too many agents.

A most timely report concerned life insurance operations as affected by the moratorium. The teachers realized that in 1933 they were in a year of unprecedented financial difficulties. Franklin Delano Roosevelt's first Inaugural on March 4, 1933 had challenged the country's spirit of panic with his statement, "The only thing we have to fear is fear itself." But the banks had closed across the nation and millions of life insurance policyholders turned to their assets in life insurance policies. Emergency restrictions were imposed upon the life companies by special legislation in the various states. Legislators acted upon the advice of their commissioners of insurance, who through their national association had agreed upon principles to follow. Thus, for the first time in the history of American life insurance, emergency restrictions were imposed upon solvent companies. Life insurance companies are not organized to conduct a banking business, yet following the market crash they served millions of policyholders as a very dependable bank of deposit from which to withdraw vast amounts of cash on demand.

It was important for the teachers to understand just what was happening. The restrictions imposed on the life insurance companies were on the banking features of their business. No interruption or even delay was required for the payment of death claims, maturing endowments, or contract income payments of any kind.

Policyholders wanting loans or surrender values above one

hundred dollars must, however, prove hardship or extreme need for the money. This was aimed to prevent panic withdrawal of funds, but to make money available for legitimate purposes. Many businesses were saved by the use of such life insurance money to meet payrolls. Doctors' bills and college expenses were paid, homes were purchased, new business opportunities were seized by people who could justify life insurance payments for such purposes.

To have the life insurance teachers of students all over the country get firsthand information about these important current events was a real service to them and a basis of public understanding most helpful to the industry.

For two years, Dr. Huebner served as president of the American Association of University Teachers of Insurance. In the next twenty-five years about half of his successors, also serving two-year terms, were Wharton School men, an interesting witness to the qualities of his students and also their numerical dominance in the field. Not only did Wharton train a great many good university insurance teachers, but more of them than any other school; or almost more than all other schools together. Currently the Association has about six hundred members, including several hundred training directors of life insurance companies.

The depression slowed down the progress of the C.L.U. It was harder to inspire men to spend the time and money necessary to qualify. But Dr. Huebner's efforts in promotion did not lag. Friends of the American College all over the country organized co-operative speaking tours for him. For C.L.U. meetings he always spoke without charge, although his expenses were paid by the sponsoring C.L.U. Chapter or life underwriters associations. (The great advantage of traveling in the summer as a member of the Massachusetts Mutual staff has been previously explained. This continued through 1934.) Bankers or other groups paid a small fee and travel expenses.

For the Huebners, 1932–33 was a great travel year. They went far north and far south. Being in the Pacific Northwest for life insurance appointments, they decided to go to Alaska. At that period before air travel was general, really seeing Alaska involved three trips, because the high mountain ranges divided the country. On that first trip, in 1932, they went by steamer from Seattle. When they reached Ketchikan, their first stop in Alaska, they were greeted by a delegation of life insurance men who had heard of their coming and wanted Dr. Huebner to talk to them. Of course he was delighted to oblige. They proceeded to Cordova and there were shown a mountain, beautifully green in the midst of the snow. It was oxidized copper, said to be the richest copper deposit in the world. They went on to Kennecott and began their encounters with prospectors. One graduate of the Massachusetts Institute of Technology showed them a heavy packet of gold dust and told them he was working to get a million dollars' worth. Then he would buy an annuity and enjoy life. Dr. Huebner questioned an annuity which would guarantee at his young age a return from interest and principal equal to only about 4 per cent. To which the miner replied that 4 per cent on a million dollars ought to provide for him pretty well.

Another old miner gave Dr. Huebner a gold nugget for his mineral collection. He refused payment, with the comment that if Dr. Huebner did not take it somebody else would get it in a poker game.

From Kennecott they went over the Richardson Highway to Fairbanks. They drove through an extensive cutover area where the denuded lands had grown brilliant with myriads of northern wild flowers. But the most outstanding feature of that trip was the sight of Mt. McKinley, the highest thing which man can see on earth. Mountains in the Himalayas of Asia are higher, but one looks at the summits from a high plateau. Mt. McKinley rises above twenty thousand feet and the traveler views it from a three-thousand-foot level. The Huebners were extraordinarily fortunate, for the mountain is veiled in mist except for a half-dozen days a year. They saw it first as a pinkish spot in the sky, a hundred miles away, and traveled ever nearer to behold the full beauty of its great mass for two full days when they reached McKinley Park.

In Fairbanks, as Dr. Huebner walked along a business street, he noticed an office window marked "New York Life Insurance Company." He went in to greet the man behind the desk, who with pride took from the bookcase beside him a copy of *Life Insurance: A Textbook* by Solomon S. Huebner.

The second visit to Alaska was in 1935. That trip was made by way of the Canadian Rockies and Jasper Park to Prince Rupert and then by steamer to Skagway. From that port they headed north through magnificent scenery of mountains and glaciers to Whitehorse beyond which were the Yukon and the Klondike gold fields of Canada. They stopped in overnight lodgings that were quite primitive and had strange meals. The largest meal they ever faced they got for a dollar a piece in a little restaurant run by a Japanese. Each person was served a whole wild duck, a bull moose steak covering the whole plate (which was good, much better than beef steak) and various kinds of potatoes and vegetables. Wonderful vegetables grow in Alaska's short summer season due to the midnight sun and moisture from the undersurface frozen ground. On this trip they shared the sorrow of all the world when Will Rogers and Wiley Post had their fatal air plane crash near Point Barrow. At one point they stood with the crowd as the plane bearing the bodies touched down on its way back to the States.

This summer they talked to men who recognized, as the people at home generally did not, what President Roosevelt had been doing with the American dollar. The Alaskans for many years had been selling an ounce of gold for $20.67. Beginning in 1934, they sold the same ounce for $35.00. Devaluation had a real meaning for them.

The Huebners did not make their third trip to Alaska until 1958. Then their plane made a refueling stop in the Aleutians on their way to the Orient.

In 1933, the Huebners took a trip to Central America. In February they were in New Orleans for Dr. Huebner to keep life insurance speaking engagements. Being "so near and curious" they planned to go to Yucatan. Not long before, Colonel Charles Lindbergh had flown over that amazing country and sparked the interest of the world. The University of Pennsylvania also had been doing archeological work in the area and they had heard fascinating reports of the almost incredible ruins of the pre-Columbus Mayan civilization.

Of course most of their time was spent at famous Chichen Itza. They hired a Mayan guide who was a college graduate, fully acquainted with the archeology of the country. He could tell them what they wanted to know and made the trip really worthwhile. That use of personally engaged, well-equipped guides was a luxury the Huebners always allowed themselves. Something Dr. Huebner cannot endure is the silly questions and superficial interest of many tourists. Travel for him is not only a great delight but a purposeful educational experience.

The most memorable place in Yucatan for them was the immense ruins of an ancient sports arena, seemingly as large as Franklin Field in Philadelphia. It had a paved floor and no roof—and miraculous acoustical qualities. Dr. Huebner stood at one end, their guide hundreds of feet away at the other, and they talked easily to each other. One "just couldn't have believed it."

Home again as the Depression deepened, Dr. Huebner thought often of his discussions in the Orient concerning the theories of Karl Marx. In Japan, he had first seen pictures of that disturbing economist and he found Japanese universities full of discussion of Marxist theories. An earnest Japanese student asked him if Karl Marx were not destined to be more important in history than Jesus Christ. Marx had confidently asserted that the capitalist system would spend itself into disaster. Although Dr. Huebner had no belief in the premises Marx set forth or in the logic which he followed, yet he could not help asking himself if the prophesied result might not be coming to pass. He was violently opposed to Roosevelt's economics of scarcity and has always asserted that prosperity rests upon production.

As a life-long Republican as well as an economist he found the developments of the period hard to take. He was generally conservative in politics in spite of the fact that he grew up at the University of Wisconsin, which was often said to be radical. One of his firm convictions was the importance of voting a straight ticket. He has always believed that to vote for a sound and popular leader and not to give him the support of the other candidates of his party is unfair and impractical.

The Depression gave Dr. Huebner one pleasant personal souvenir. That was membership in the famous Union League of Philadelphia. His name had been on the waiting list for some years and progress up the line had come very slowly as old members died. With the Depression, not only did the League have its share of premature deaths in the increase which those years brought, but economic reasons caused members to drop from the roll. Dr. Huebner's chance came, and he took his place in the stream of all the solid Republican citizens who had served Philadelphia for three quarters of a century.

Personal troubles of a different kind began to thwart Dr. Huebner's ambitions at this time. He had brought back more than happy memories from Yucatan. Traveling into the wild country among the ruins, he had been careless about ticks. He had been bitten by those tiny creatures without giving himself proper attention. In biting, a tick buries its head in human flesh in a soft part of the body and then dies. Mrs. Huebner described the bites around her husband's waist when she saw them some days later. They appeared then as little raised spots about the size of a finger nail, yellow with infection, with the dead tick about as big as a small ant in the center.

The first reaction to the tick poison was a terrible case of the hives. That developed the summer following their Yucatan trip. Dr. Huebner did his usual traveling for the Massachusetts Mutual (and the American College) in almost unbearable discomfort. The hives finally disappeared and he hoped there would be no more trouble.

The next winter Dr. and Mrs. Huebner went to the West Indies—a delightful tour including the Virgin Islands, Martinique, Barbados, Trinidad, La Guira, Caracas, and Curacao. Dr. Huebner's rugged health was definitely impaired, and he had his ups and downs as the doctors tried to help his kidneys in their battle against the infection from the ticks. Still he kept going as nearly as he could on the usual schedule. When it was necessary for him to stay at home he had his correspondence brought from the office and his secretary took dictation at his bedside. No letter went unanswered or even long delayed. Most of his friends across the country had no idea of his serious physical troubles. In 1935, as has been related, he even went to Alaska.

Sickness, curtailing his physical activity, gave Dr. Huebner the opportunity to share some common pleasures for which otherwise he would have had no time. Like all the rest of America he enjoyed the radio Amos 'n' Andy. Every evening he laughed at the partners in their million-dollar business operations or their neighborhood dilemmas. The theater had always attracted him, as time allowed. In his earliest days in Madison and in Philadelphia he had climbed to the peanut gallery to watch the great figures of the American stage playing Shakespeare or Ibsen or other contemporary drama of a lighter nature.

Later Mrs. Huebner shared this enthusiasm, and they have generally through the years had season subscriptions to the theater as well as for travelogues and concerts.

People who saw Dr. Huebner as the results of the infection developed were shocked. His moustache, which used to bristle, drooped. His blue eyes, which had always flashed, were tired and dull. The clenched fist was now too painful a gesture.

Finally the arthritis and neuritis which had been troubling him with increasing intensity grew dramatically worse. He no longer could leave the house. He could not even get out of bed, and the touch of the bed clothes was torture. Hospital care was necessary. Both legs were immobilized in plaster casts to prevent any motion and so lessen the pain. A board was put in the hospital bed to give him absolutely firm support. In those presulpha and prepenicillin days the doctors could do little but make him as comfortable as possible while his own system carried on the fight. At last he began to get gradually better.

The tenth anniversary of the American College came in the midst of Dr. Huebner's sickness. He had been made president of the College in 1934, succeeding Mr. Clark, and Dr. David McCahan took his place as dean. The progress of the C.L.U. movement was ever forward. Each year a larger group of candidates took examinations. At the end of the first decade, 1,255 people had been awarded the C.L.U. designation, 31 others held the certificate of proficiency, and 97 more had completed the examinations but were not yet qualified through experience.

Early in the College's history, Dr. Huebner had written a pledge for C.L.U.'s. It expressed very briefly the ideal to which, as professional underwriters, they committed themselves. It was an interpretation of the Golden Rule which included a point that Dr. Huebner considers of extreme importance. He believes that the greatest inequality lies in the equal treatment of unequals. To give some one what you would like is not necessarily good service, for you and another man have different needs. Therefore, he included in the pledge the concept of the client's point of view. The pledge became a traditional part of the conferment exercises for new C.L.U.'s each year. The acceptance is a solemn ceremony.

One year about this time Dr. Huebner as usual repeated the pledge, phrase by phrase, for the new graduates to follow in making their commitments: "In all my relations with clients I agree to observe the following rule of professional conduct: I shall, in the light of all of the circumstances surrounding my client, which I shall make every conscientious effort to ascertain and to understand, give him that service which, had I been in the same circumstances, I would have applied to myself." As he looked out at the men and women grouped before him with right hands upraised, he noticed a man who had been there the previous year. After the ceremony Dr. Huebner greeted this year-old C.L.U. "Weren't you here last year?"

And the man replied, "Yes I was. I took that pledge before you last September when I got my C.L.U., but I did not keep it. I did something wrong of which I am terribly ashamed. I thought I would feel better if I made the promise again, and I assure you I will live up to it this time."

Thus, the C.L.U. program not only set standards for professional service in life underwriting but provided also motivation for achievement of the ideals.

A continuing headache was lack of money. C.L.U. activities were going well, but from a financial point of view, not too well. The candidates' fees did not cover adequate costs of operations. Friends of the American College were active in the Association of Life Agency Officers and set up in that organization a committee to devise help for this problem. After careful study of the situation the committee concluded:

> It was ascertained that the College would require at least $30,000 additional income annually if present and prospective demands were to be adequately met. It was, as a matter of fact, something of a mystery to the Committee as to how the College had been able to accomplish what it has accomplished with the limited and uncertain revenues upon which it has heretofore depended. Certainly the annual balancing of the budget, and the 10-year record of no deficits could not have been achieved except by unsparing sacrifices in time and labor by the administrative officers of the College, and members of the College Board.

To solve the difficulty the committee organized the Cooperative Fund for Underwriter Education. They approached hundreds of life insurance executives and won agreement for a plan of contributions by the companies on a formula based upon amount of insurance in force. They reported in part:

> The first-year response has approached the unanimous more nearly than any cooperative enterprise thus far sponsored by the companies....
>
> It is desirable in any cooperative appeal for funds to reduce the project to the simplest possible elements, so that demands upon the energy and time of the Committee can be kept within reasonable bounds. The companies were therefore asked for a direct contribution solely on the grounds that the work of the College is in the interest of the public and is a definite contribution to life insurance service, aside from any question as to the number of underwriters representing a given company who may have availed themselves of the facilities of the College.
>
> That the subscriptions were tendered as direct subscriptions to the College in response to that appeal, and to that appeal alone, is a splendid commentary on the broad views of life insurance executives...
>
> The Committee (raising the money) will be wholly independent of the College and having no part in management. It will act simply in the role of sponsor for the fund, of which fund the College will become the beneficiary.

The response of the business to this fund-raising project was not only a commentary on the interest of the companies in the educational program, it was also a witness to their confidence in Dr. Huebner, both to his own integrity of purpose and the high academic standards in his leadership of the College.

This financial support by the companies has continued ever since. The fund is now called the Cooperative Fund for Underwriter Training and is handled through a committee of the College trustees. Co-operating companies are entitled to issue to their representatives credit certificates which are accepted as half payment for the fifty-dollar examination fee for any C.L.U. examination. In 1958–59 there were 221 companies which contributed a total of $153,883 to the Fund.

CHAPTER THIRTEEN

The S. S. Huebner Foundation

DR. HUEBNER's terrible ordeal with his health had aroused not only sympathy but an urgency to give tangible evidence of appreciation for a lifetime of devoted service. Often a man is appreciated far from home but is "without honor in his own country." This was happily not true for Dr. Huebner. In 1937 the Philadelphia Association of Life Underwriters inaugurated an annual award, the President's Cup, and chose Dr. Huebner to receive the recognition that first year.

Throughout the country life insurance leaders discussed what they might do industry-wide to pay him tribute. There developed several guiding principles. First, the project must have to do with an objective in which the life insurance companies could have a naturally sincere interest. Secondly, it must be something so logically associated with Dr. Huebner that there would be real motivation in having his name attached to it. Finally, of course, the undertaking must be so important that having his name connected with it would be a distinct honor to Dr. Huebner.

They thought of the C.L.U. movement obviously. Could they do something in connection with that? They talked about Dr. Huebner's dedication to the expansion of life insurance teaching in the colleges and universities of America. They knew that a roadblock to the progress of both programs was the lack of qualified teachers of insurance. Somehow an idea began to develop. No one now knows just who started it. David McCahan had a part. Joseph H. Reese helped. Holgar J. Johnson and Thomas I. Parkinson were among the leaders. Many others had a share too. Soon the life insurance business was united, through the Life Insurance Association of America, the American Life Convention, and the Institute of Life Insurance to honor Dr. Huebner in raising a fund to advance life insurance education. The plan at first was designed for an experimental period of five years. With good results, that later was extended to ten years. The co-operating life insurance companies undertook to provide twenty-five thousand dollars a year for a "Huebner Educational Fund," to be used to further the training of teachers of life insurance.

The 1940 convention of the National Association of Life Underwriters in Philadelphia was chosen as the time for announcing the new program. The annual conferment dinner of the American College was planned as a great testimonial occasion, honoring Dr. Huebner and giving opportunity for presenting to him the evidence of the new undertaking in his name.

The grand ballroom of the Bellevue Stratford Hotel was crowded to overflowing with twelve hundred guests on that historic evening of September 26, 1940. The guest of honor had been under the care of two doctors all day. He had told them to do anything, just get him in shape to do and say what was appropriate for the evening. He arrived in a wheelchair to take his place at the head table. Then his great will power, aided by the doctors' drugs, asserted itself, and he played his part nobly in the ensuing hours.

Julian S. Myrick, Chairman of the Board of the American College, was toastmaster. He said in his opening remarks: "It is a privilege to preside over this great meeting tonight which has been brought together to do honor to Dr. Solomon Stephen Huebner. . . . It is the first time in all the years that I have ever known the Institution of Life Insurance to gather in such a representative way." Then he referred to the listing in the souvenir program of the sponsoring organizations with their representative members. These indeed did represent the whole life insurance industry. The men named were of such outstanding caliber that most are known even today though many are long since dead.

The Association of Life Insurance Presidents
Vincent P. Whitsitt, *Manager*
Major Thomas I. Parkinson, *Committee Chairman*

The Institute of Life Insurance
M. Albert Linton, *Chairman of the Board*
Holgar J. Johnson, *President*
John A. Stevenson, *Committee Chairman*

American Life Convention
Cornelius A. Craig, *President*
Colonel C. B. Robbins, *Manager*
Edward E. Rhodes, *Committee Chairman*

The Association of Life Agency Officers
Alexander E. Patterson, *Chairman*
Grant L. Hill, *Committee Chairman*

The National Association of Life Underwriters
Charles J. Zimmerman, *President*
Roger B. Hull, *Manager*
Theodore M. Riehle, *Committee Chairman*

The American College of Life Underwriters
Julian S. Myrick, *Chairman of the Board*
Paul F. Clark, *Committee Chairman*

The American Society of Chartered Life Underwriters
Earle W. Brailey, *President*
Benjamin Alk, *Committee Chairman*

American Association of University Teachers of Insurance
Dr. David McCahan, *President*

Association of Life Insurance Medical Directors
Dr. Harold M. Frost, *President*

Home Office Life Underwriters Association
Leigh Cruess, *President*

The Life Advertisers Association
Karl Ljung, *President*
Cyrus T. Steven, *Committee Chairman*

The Life Insurance Sales Research Bureau
Vincent B. Coffin, *Chairman of the Board*
John Marshall Holcombe, Jr., *Manager*

Dr. Huebner was called upon to give the conferment address and made a talk on the subject "Educational Progress in Life Underwriting." He emphasized the importance of the life underwriter and the general agent's responsibility in helping his associates develop to their highest potential. The old characteristic vigor appeared when he said: "So often I am told: 'Why bother educationally with the demonstrated man? He has managed to survive and is making a fair living, so leave good enough alone.' There could be no greater mistake. A good man can be made better through proper education, but a poor stick remains a poor stick, irrespective of educational endeavors." He urged better selection of fieldmen. He spoke strongly of the value to the life insurance business and to the community of giving sound insurance education in schools and colleges. The themes were not new, but his treatment of them was fitted to the thinking of the moment, and the audience was moved by the masterly way the beloved professor still marshalled his facts and ideas.

Charles J. Zimmerman, C.L.U. was currently president of the National Association of Life Underwriters. He paid tribute to Dr. Huebner on behalf of the field forces of America, whose representatives then presented a gift to Dr. and Mrs. Huebner: a sterling silver tea and coffee service, including a pair of candelabra; and rose-banded Spode after-dinner coffee cups, tea cups, and dessert plates.

Dr. Paul Musser, vice president of the University of Pennsylvania, spoke representing the University, saying in part:

> Tonight it is our good fortune to have the thrill of attending this testimonial dinner to a son of Pennsylvania who has achieved the distinction of being the world's foremost insurance educator. To many of us in this room, the rise of Dr. Huebner to his present fame is not an abstract matter. His contacts have been so close to many of us, so informal and so continuous that his development has been a part of our daily lives. The more we have seen him and the closer we have associated with him, the more his remarkable qualities amaze us.
>
> That one should possess the vision to pioneer insurance education at the university level, possess the scientific spirit to analyze and interpret fundamental principles and the social complications of one of our most important business activities; the missionary zeal to see results of his study and to make such things available not only to college students but to the insurance business and the general public, and the enthusiasm to inspire others to carry forward the work he has started, is not only phenomenal, but superhuman.
>
> Talented and gifted men like Dr. Huebner make a university great, and the University of Pennsylvania is proud and happy indeed that his distinguished career is a part of its life and a part of its achievement.
>
> However, you ladies and gentlemen in the insurance business also have a share in our pride in Dr. Huebner as you have come to know him almost as well as we at the University. His career is unique in that he has not remained an academic possession of the University. His leadership in insurance thought has not been confined to the classroom, but has served the business community and the federal government. In fact, one of Dr. Huebner's most important considerations is that of bringing the University closer to the problems of business and the realities of business and the business world closer to the student body at the University.
>
> We, the general officers of the University, take this occasion to congratulate and to extend our best wishes to one of the best loved and most dynamic teachers to ever serve on the faculty of the University

of Pennsylvania. And we shall extend to you our high regards as a great expert and as a great gentleman.

The climax of the evening came with the introduction of Major Thomas I. Parkinson, president of the Equitable Life Assurance Society of New York and chairman of the co-operative industry committee. Speaking with appreciation and affection, he announced to Dr. Huebner the fund which had been provided in his honor to advance the training of life insurance teachers.

Through the simple words of Dr. Huebner's response, preserved in the record of that night, shine the personal qualities which made him so loved and admired. His appreciation for kindness, his consideration of those who work for and with him, his essential humility, his genuine liking for people—all were there as he spoke to "Mr. Myrick and friends."

My heart is so full of happiness tonight that I hardly have words at my command to express all the gratitude that I would like to pour forth. I am afraid that I might be the victim of the greatest of all professorial faults, namely, forgetfulness, but I will try to thank the various speakers in the order in which they appeared tonight.

First of all, Mr. Myrick, I want to thank you for the very kind words that you uttered at the beginning of the evening. My association with you during the past years in connection with the American College has been most pleasant indeed. I shall never forget those years and I hope I may continue serving with you.

Mr. Zimmerman, I wish to thank you for the kind words which you spoke, and while I haven't exactly had a chance from this point to see the beautiful token presented to me from the life insurance field through you, I can see it is fine. It comes of the life insurance people and by them and is for Mrs. Huebner and me. I hope we will have many, many years to enjoy that token. We shall behold it many times and whenever we do I know where our hearts will turn. They will turn back to the great people who make up the life insurance calling. Certainly that token will be an inspiration to continue contact with the life insurance field, as it has been a pleasure of mine to do for a good many years.

Vice-President Musser, I am certainly much obliged to you for what you said. Your remarks were very kind, indeed. They bring back to me this thought tonight, that I owe the University of Pennsylvania a great deal. That is where I had my beginning as a raw teacher, and had it not been for plenty of encouragement and help I don't know whether I would have ever succeeded, but I had the good fortune of having during my career as teacher at the University six very cooperative deans. There is one dean in particular who is with us tonight, Dr. Emory R. Johnson, who was my mentor from the very beginning. He had me under his protective and guiding wing, and I want you to know that when the history of the American College of Life Underwriters is written, as I hope some day it may be, the name of Dr. Emory R. Johnson should be in that history. He certainly encouraged me. Time upon time he told me, "Be sure to have a good character for the College; keep your standards high," and he never left a stone untouched but gave me further encouragement to do what I could to make this movement a success. He believed that every business calling should have a movement of this kind and I want you to know that of all the many people who helped me to make the American College, Dr. Johnson certainly should not be forgotten. The longer I knew him the more I appreciated what he did for me, in fact, I came to regard him finally as the perfect gentleman, free from all academic blemishes.

Major Parkinson, I must thank you for the nice things you said about me. I hope I am worthy of them all. I shall never forget your remarks. What you said about research is only too true. Research is a wonderful thing. It is at the bottom of everything in the last analysis and we can have plenty of it in life insurance.

I am happy not only to be honored by what we call the "field" in life insurance with this beautiful token, but I feel equally honored that the management in life insurance should be so well represented here tonight and should favor me with so splendid a token as you presented in the Foundation.

I am deeply honored to have that Foundation named after me. It is generous, and I can assure you, Major Parkinson, that my associates and I will bend heaven and earth to make a success of what you had in mind when that Foundation was formulated. It will be our hope that this is only a beginning. But everything has to have a beginning and I trust that at the end of five years there will be no disappointment on your part as far as our efforts at the University of Pennsylvania are concerned.

Then I must not forget the great honor that is associated with this large attendance. That is one of the most moving things of everything tonight. I wonder if I am really worthy of all that has been put into this effort. I can imagine what a difficult task of organization it must have been and how many must have spent time and thought in organizing all that we have had. I am certainly just filled to overflowing with happiness.

Everything that has happened here can not help but rekindle in me the desire that I have to keep on with that which I may have been doing; to urge me on as best I may in association with many others who cooperate in planting more voluminously into the millions of homes and into the thousands of business establishments in this country the beneficient influence of life insurance. After all, these homes and these business institutions, for which life insurance can do so much, really constitute the backbone of this wonderful country of ours.

Nobody who shared the occasion will ever forget it. (This is the author's appraisal as an eye-witness.) The assemblage was nearly as moved as the man whom they honored. There was a lump in many a throat as the guests joined in singing *Auld Lang Syne* to conclude the evening.

In later years, Dr. Huebner said he felt personally that the Huebner Foundation was the greatest award the industry ever gave him. That evening one of the guests spoke of it as "as great a tribute as the life insurance business could offer a man."

Afterward one of the life insurance newspapers said:

There was general satisfaction with the tribute throughout the life insurance world. The public was getting so fed up with ballyhoos about motion picture celebrities, glamour girls, stars of the sporting world, that there is a real thrill in learning that a man who has given such brilliant devotion to education over a span from young manhood can get the recognition that he deserves while still in the saddle.

Dr. Huebner carried through that memorable evening's celebration, but for days afterward he was again flat in bed wracked with the old pains of arthritis. The doctors seemed powerless. He just lay there getting weaker. At last he asked whether it would jeopardize his recovery to get up. The physicians said no, if he could stand the pain. Each movement was excruciating, but he forced himself to it. Soon he was able to get around with two canes. He met his classes again having transferred his lectures to a room which did not require stair climbing. He resumed travel, using wheelchairs in the railroad stations. There was every excuse to relapse into inactivity, but Dr. Huebner refused to acknowledge defeat.

After a while a friend suggested that Swedish massage might be useful. The doctors said it might be helpful; in any event would do no harm. So Dr. Huebner undertook a course of treatments with a powerful masseur who had been in the German army. Almost at once he began to improve. Within a year or so he was almost himself again, and the Battle of the Ticks was over.

Meanwhile, The S. S. Huebner Foundation for Insurance Education had taken concrete form through a formal declaration on December 18, 1940. The declaration was signed by three representatives each of the American Life Convention, the Institute of Life Insurance, and the Life Insurance Association of America. Those nine men also became the first official Cooperating Committee of the Foundation. They were H. H. Armstrong, O. J. Arnold, LeRoy A. Lincoln, M. Albert Linton, E. E. Rhodes, A. A. Rydgren, John A. Stevenson, Frank C. Weidenborner, and Thomas I. Parkinson. More than sixty companies were represented in the first year's donors to the Foundation. It seemed wise to have the money-raising operations separated from the educational program. So it was decided to delegate the latter to a university. Not surprisingly, the

University of Pennsylvania was designated, at least for the beginning.

The University named an executive director for the program, Dr. David McCahan, and an administrative board to supervise the general operations. The first administrative board was:

Honorary Chairman: S. S. Huebner, Professor of Insurance and Commerce, Wharton School of Finance and Commerce, University of Pennsylvania, and President of the American College of Life Underwriters.

Chairman: Harry J. Loman, Professor of Insurance and Director of the Graduate Division of the Wharton School of Finance and Commerce, University of Pennsylvania.

Executive Director: David McCahan, Professor of Insurance, Wharton School of Finance and Commerce, University of Pennsylvania, and Dean of the American College of Life Underwriters.

Ralph H. Blanchard, Professor of Insurance, School of Business, Columbia University.

Edison L. Bowers, Associate Professor of Economics, School of Commerce, Ohio State University.

Paul H. Musser, Administrative Vice President, University of Pennsylvania.

Edwin B. Williams, Dean of the Graduate School of Arts and Sciences, University of Pennsylvania.

The first *Announcement* of the Foundation outlined the background of need for the work that was being undertaken, set forth the plan which was to be followed, and commented about the advantages of Pennsylvania as the designated university.

> The colleges and universities of the country have not, for the most part, been adequately staffed with experienced insurance teachers. . . . This is indeed not surprising when it is realized that, outside of courses in insurance law and actuarial science primarily designed for prospective lawyers and actuaries, courses in insurance are comparatively late arrivals in the curricula of our higher educational

institutions, being entirely a development of the Twentieth Century. Thus, out of 584 courses reported by 235 institutions in a recent survey made by the American College of Life Underwriters, more than one-half have been introduced within the past fifteen years. It is further significant to note that of the 384 teachers reported as conducting these 584 courses, 88 are part-time teachers whose principal vocation is not teaching. Two hundred and fifty-eight are full-time teachers who devote more than half of their teaching time to subjects other than insurance. Only 38 are full-time teachers with at least half of their teaching load in the field of insurance.

Since the quality and effectiveness of a teacher grow with his years of research and continued study, the logical method for helping to strengthen education in insurance is to strengthen the individual teacher by giving him the opportunity and the means to broaden his own understanding of the subject. To that end . . . a foundation which would provide

1. Fellowships for graduate study available to teachers now in accredited colleges or universities who desire to study for a Doctor's degree, and who now hold at least a Bachelor's degree.

2. Scholarships for graduate study available to recent graduates of accredited colleges or universities who desire to prepare for an insurance teaching career by studying for either a Master's or Doctor's degree.

3. Scholarships for graduate study available to graduates of accredited colleges or universities now associated with insurance companies who desire to prepare for educational work within their own companies by studying for either a Master's or Doctor's degree, such scholarships to be financed by specific contributions for the purpose unless the funds available from the foundation are more than sufficient to meet the need for fellowships and scholarships among persons preparing for the teaching profession as a life career.

4. For building up and maintaining a central research library in insurance books and other source material which would be available through circulating privileges to teachers in accredited colleges and universities desirous of conducting research in insurance subjects.

5. For publishing research theses and other studies which constitute a distinct contribution directly or indirectly to insurance knowledge . . .

> Selection of the University of Pennsylvania for initial administration of the funds received by this foundation was also prompted by the hope that many future teachers would thereby have an opportunity during the years to come of sharing the vision and inspiration of Dr. Huebner's teaching as well as by the fact that Dr. Huebner has gathered about him a staff of twelve experienced full-time teachers who have acquired an understanding of their subject which can come only with research, continued study and maturity. Five of his associates in Pennsylvania's Insurance Department are full professors, one is an associate professor, four are assistant professors and two are instructors. Except the two instructors, all have taught insurance at the University of Pennsylvania for at least fifteen years. Many contributions to insurance literature have been made by these associates and numerous are the constructive services which they have rendered in a great variety of responsible private and public positions.
>
> Moreover a broad range of graduate courses is now being offered by the University of Pennsylvania which enables the institution to meet the needs of all types of students. Included therein are seven full-year courses in different divisions of the insurance field as well as courses in all of the other business subjects closely related thereto. These courses have been developed over a period of time after exhaustive study and intelligent experimentation. They are designed especially for graduate work and are not open to undergraduate or special students.
>
> Dr. Huebner's department at the University of Pennsylvania is a unit of Pennsylvania's Wharton School of Finance and Commerce, a veritable laboratory of the social sciences, affording a unique opportunity for the study of modern social and economic problems by insurance experts and the coordinated research efforts of experts in all of the social sciences toward application of insurance principles to the needs of the American public.

The first awards were granted for 1941–42. There were four scholarships and five fellowships. One fellow was Dan M. McGill of Maryville College in Tennessee, who, after the interruption of the war years and the attainment of his Ph.D. in 1947, was to become director of the Foundation in 1954.

Dr. Dan M. McGill and Dr. Huebner before the portrait in the Huebner Foundation library. (*Shaw*)

When the war curtailed Dr. Huebner's activities on campus, it brought new responsibilities in government service. In 1941 he was appointed one of four members of the Insurance Advisory Committee to the War Department and served throughout the war. The other members were Dr. Ralph H. Blanchard of Columbia, his former graduate student; John S.

Van Schaick, formerly New York State Insurance Commissioner; and Dr. George K. Gardner of the Harvard Law School. This committee had no powers of action but was called upon to study a variety of problems as they developed and to recommend what might be done. Typical subjects for their attention were: the service that was given by agents and brokers in connection with insurance placed where defense contracts were involved, and the sales of life insurance to members of the Armed Forces at locations claimed to be not subject to state supervision. Unhappily the matters revealed in these problems indicated that all insurance agents were not performing according to highest ethical standards.

From 1943 to 1945 Dr. Huebner was insurance consultant to the Civil Aeronautics Board. Much of his attention in this assignment had to do with a study of reinsurance. The situation recalled his earlier work with marine insurance for he found that two thirds of all United States aviation risks were being reinsured by Lloyd's of London. In the latter part of his service his reports were all of a confidential nature. Through these various activities he felt that he was doing his part in the great task then confronting all the American people. In war as in peace insurance is an essential factor in the life of the Nation.

CHAPTER FOURTEEN

The American Institute for Property and Liability Underwriters

THE success of the C.L.U. program for life insurance very naturally suggested the desirability of a similar plan for property insurance. Dr. Huebner took every opportunity to give publicity to the idea with groups and to talk to leaders about steps to take in implementation. For instance, he spoke before the National Association of Mutual Insurance Companies at their annual convention in Los Angeles in 1930 on the subject "An Educational Program in Property and Casualty Insurance." The audience was inspired to adopt resolutions supporting the idea and to appoint a committee to develop a plan along the lines Dr. Huebner suggested. But nothing was accomplished.

Five years later Dr. Huebner was still promoting the cause. He delivered a paper entitled "The Professionalization of Insurance Brokers" before the Insurance Brokers Association of New York, and followed it up with an article in their official publication the next year, "A Professional Standard Based upon a Professional Designation." Concurrently he presented a definite program for an American College of Property and Casualty Underwriters before the Insurance Luncheon of the United States Chamber of Commerce annual meeting. That group too took favorable action, but nothing more happened.

In 1938 Dr. Huebner gave another major push against the ball which would not seem to roll in speaking to the Insurance Federation of Pennsylvania on the same theme. This talk was widely reported in the press, but still no organized action was taken.

One industry man who was much interested in the proposal was John A. North, then vice president of the Phoenix Insurance Company of Hartford. He suggested the possibility of getting something started through the American Association of University Teachers of Insurance. The war in Europe and the possibility of American participation was another cause of delay. Many people thought it was "not the time" to start anything new.

Finally, in 1941 Dr. David McCahan, as president of A.A.U.T.I., appointed a Committee on Professional Standards in Property and Casualty Insurance, with Dr. Huebner as chairman, to take leadership in promoting a program. After much groundwork they invited representatives of leading organizations in property and casualty insurance to meet with them in New York on May 16, 1941 for a thorough consideration of the possibility of an educational program comparable to the C.L.U. Organizations included were: the American Mutual Alliance, the Association of Casualty and Surety Executives, the National Board of Fire Underwriters, the National Association of Insurance Agents, the National Association of Mutual Insurance Agents, and the National Association of Insurance Brokers.

The A.A.U.T.I. committee presented a comprehensive story about the history and methods of the C.L.U. They outlined the great development of life insurance courses in colleges and universities, and the success of hundreds of life insurance men in achieving the C.L.U. designation. They assured the property and casualty men of the co-operation of the American College in such important matters as proctors and examination centers. They reviewed many problems the American College had met and solved, experiences which would smooth the way for a new program. They emphasized the advantage of the program to the public both in the exposure of laymen to the courses during their own college days and in the improvement of service through better-educated underwriters.

After a full day of discussion the insurance representatives unanimously approved in principle the proposals of the committee, for professional recognition of property and casualty underwriters by Chartered Property Underwriter and Chartered Casualty Underwriter designations. It was decided to appoint an advisory committee and four subcommittees to work respectively on the legal and financial aspects, on nomenclature, and on a definite course of study and educational procedure. Dr. Huebner was made chairman of the advisory committee. Dr. McCahan was named chairman of the committee having educational responsibilities. Dr. Huebner was ex-officio member of all committees. Membership of each committee was carefully balanced between representatives of the stock and mutual companies.

Now the ball was rolling. The central advisory committee members really worked. They traveled to meetings; they consulted by telephone; they wrote innumerable letters, so many that Dr. Huebner reported the correspondence "had long ceased to be merely a file, but has reached the proportions of a high stack." The six committee members in addition to Dr. Huebner were:

John A. North, Vice President, Phoenix Insurance Company, Hartford, Connecticut.

William Leslie, General Manager, National Bureau of Casualty and Surety Underwriters, New York City.

George W. Scott, Director, Educational Division, National Association of Insurance Agents, New York City.

A. V. Gruhn, General Manager, American Mutual Alliance, Chicago, Illinois.

John M. Breen, Chairman, Educational Committee, Kemper Insurance, Chicago, Illinois.

Philip L. Baldwin, Executive Secretary, National Association of Mutual Insurance Agents, Washington, D.C.

The thirty other insurance and university men on the other committees worked valiantly too, and by the fall of 1941 agreement had been reached on details of a definite program and working arrangements. The highlights of the conclusions were:

1. To seek financial help from the companies to carry the project for the first two years.

2. To name the new organization the American Institute for Property and Liability Underwriters, to be incorporated in Pennsylvania with headquarters in Philadelphia.

3. To have a single designation, C.P.C.U.,* Chartered Property and Casualty Underwriter.

4. To have the basic prerequisites and examination procedure comparable to those of the C.L.U., and to conduct examinations at the same places and at the same time as the C.L.U. examinations.

5. To have a fivefold division of subject matter: the first two, insurance principles and practices, both generally and specifically for each kind of coverage; then general education, including government, economics, and social legislation; commercial and insurance law; and accounting and finance.

The confidence in the financial support of the insurance companies was not misplaced. Concerning this most important part of organizational work, Dr. Huebner reported:

> As explained last year, it was agreed "to raise $50,000 to assure the operation of the Institute for two years, and that the property, casualty and surety companies be invited to contribute, as nearly as possible on the basis of premium volume, and that the agency and brokerage organizations be invited to contribute on a voluntary

---

* The original idea of C.P.U. and C.C.U. seemed upon mature consideration to be confusing for the public. Moreover, if there were this breakdown, why not further specialization? Other professional fields did not have different recognition for specialties; for example, for the lawyer who specialized in patents or in criminal law.

> basis." Mr. Otho E. Lane, Chairman, and the other members of the Finance Committee undertook to raise the aforementioned fund, with the result that the National Board of Fire Underwriters, the American Mutual Alliance, and the Association of Casualty and Surety Executives approved the arrangement and made their respective contributions for the agreed amount on the basis of premium volume. It should be noted that these three organizations participated with their selected representatives in the original committee which met on May 16, 1941, and January 16, 1942. The National Association of Mutual Insurance Agents, which was invited to contribute on a voluntary basis, made an additional contribution of $1000. The members of the National Association of Insurance Agents, also invited to participate on a voluntary basis, made another contribution of over $6000, a total largely due to the tireless effort of Mr. Sidney O. Smith, then Chairman of the Executive Committee of the National Association of Insurance Agents, who took personal charge of a fund-raising campaign among the members of this Association. Financial support of the Institute has thus been most gratifying. At its inception the Institute has been placed on a secure financial basis to do the things necessary to a successful launching of its extensive and, in many respects, difficult program.

The Institute was incorporated in Pennsylvania on April 11, 1942. The incorporators were the Advisory Committee, with J. Dewey Dorsett replacing William Leslie, and Dr. McCahan and Mr. Lane added to comply with the statute that "at least three of the incorporators must be residents of the Commonwealth of Pennsylvania." (Dr. Huebner was the third.)

The problems of keeping the stock and mutual interests nicely balanced had been many, and when the time came for election of officers, Dr. Huebner hardly slept the night before the meeting. In the morning he met James S. Kemper of Chicago, a prominent mutual man who later became American ambassador to Brazil. Mr. Kemper had been actively interested in the development of the Institute. He greeted Dr. Huebner with a question about the man to be president. Dr. Huebner turned the question back to him. Then Mr. Kemper asked who

Dr. Harry J. Loman with Dr. Huebner at the doorway of 3924 Walnut Street, Philadelphia. (*Shaw*)

had done most to bring things to a head and was told about John North's idea of working through the University Teachers. "I think he ought to be president," Dr. Huebner said, and Mr. Kemper agreed to nominate him. The elections went off beautifully with everybody happy. "Which goes to show," Dr. Huebner commented later, "that 90 per cent of the things you worry about don't happen."

The constitution of the Institute provides for a two-year term for president, with stock and mutual representatives alternating by common consent. Dr. Huebner was named chairman of the board and Dr. Harry J. Loman, dean, from the beginning. Concerning Dr. Loman's appointment, Dr. Huebner made a significant report to the American Association of University Teachers of Insurance:

> In selecting the Dean, to take full charge of the Institute's educational work, much time and effort were given by the Advisory Committee, as well as by various members of the Board of Trustees. From the outset of its deliberations concerning candidates, the Board felt that the Dean of the Institute should be one who would have among his qualifications (1) an extensive experience as a teacher and scholar in the fields of property and casualty insurance, (2) a considerable background of experience as a writer, (3) a wide acquaintance with existing literature in the field of insurance, (4) a wide administrative experience in educational matters, (5) an extensive acquaintance with the Deans, Directors and other educational officers of the nation's collegiate schools of business, and (6) a personality that would blend with respect to field work in the promotion of the Institute's co-operative activities with institutions of learning and outside study groups.
>
> Dr. Loman, it was unanimously felt by the Board, pre-eminently met the aforementioned qualifications. His teaching career in insurance at the University of Pennsylvania has extended over twenty-four years, namely, from 1919 to the present. Along with his successful teaching career in insurance, he has also had much administrative experience in educational matters, serving as Vice Dean of the Wharton School of Finance and Commerce of the University of Pennsylvania from 1933–39, as Associate Dean of the Wharton School from 1939–42, and as Director of the Post-Graduate Division of the Wharton School from 1938–42. Dr. Loman has also served both the Federal and the Pennsylvania State Governments in insurance matters, as expert in insurance to the United States Bureau of War Risk Insurance, and as insurance consultant to the Pennsylvania State Workmen's Insurance Fund. He has also held other insurance consultant positions from time to time throughout his teaching career. During 1936–38 he also served as President of the American Association of University Teachers of Insurance. His authorship, along insurance lines, has also been very substantial.

In countless ways the Institute began from the shoulders of

the American College. Like the American College, the Institute does not conduct classes. It provides a syllabus, suggested readings, and study outlines. A student may prepare as he wishes for the examinations. Like the College, however, the Institute sought to work with resident schools. Contacts with colleges and universities across the country were already established, and Dean Loman was able in the first year to set up study groups in more than a dozen cities from Dallas to New York. Such organized preparation had not at first been available for C.L.U. students. Of course the war made difficulties (in addition to travel discomforts for civilians), for the normally small supply of insurance teachers was further reduced by leaves of absence or assignments to special war service training programs.

The first C.P.C.U. examinations were given in June, 1943. In spite of the serious handicap of war conditions, ninety people sat for 209 examinations. Fifteen tried to do all five parts (contrary to the advice of the Institute), and six were successful. More than half of the candidates had at least ten years' experience in the business. The great majority also were over thirty years of age. Both factors, of course, reflected wartime necessities. The candidates came from California, Washington State, and Texas, as well as from the Middle West and the East Coast. The Institute had operated nationally in its first year of life. Because of transportation difficulties, two conferment ceremonies were held in 1943. All six of the candidates who wrote five examinations successfully also qualified on the basis of satisfactory experience. Therefore, three received the C.P.C.U. designation at Chicago, with Dr. Huebner officiating; and three in New York City at the hands of Dr. Loman. They committed themselves to a standard of business conduct and professional ethics:

> In all of my business dealings and activities I agree to abide by the following rules of professional conduct:

> I shall strive at all times to ascertain and understand the needs of those whom I serve and act as if their interests were my own; and
>
> I shall do all in my power to maintain and uphold a standard of honor and integrity that will reflect credit on the business in which I am engaged.

The 1943 holders of the C.P.C.U. designation believed in the future. While their diplomas were still very new, in January, 1944, they completed the organization of the Society of Chartered Property and Casualty Underwriters, national in scope with the purpose of establishing local chapters as soon as the number of C.P.C.U.'s would warrant. The objectives of the organization are to promote education in its insurance fields, to maintain high standards among those carrying the service to the public, and to encourage fellowship among C.P.C.U.'s.

The war years thus were busy for Dr. Huebner in this second great pioneering work as well as in the special service for the government, as was noted in Chapter 13. In addition there were department problems because of the activities on campus in connection with the Armed Services. After Pearl Harbor the University had R.O.T.C. units for the Army and the Navy. The government wanted to provide for future leadership with men having a broad university training, but in addition the students had to take specialized government studies for the Army quartermaster work, the Navy pay corps, or navigation for the Navy or the Air Corps. Naturally many insurance courses were sidetracked for others which seemed more vital to the war effort. The Insurance Department staff was inventoried to see who could teach mathematics or navigation or what not. All was supervised by the War Manpower Commission.

The University participated in the V-5 naval training program, the V-7 refresher program, and the V-12 program. The latter was for students taking a regular University course at an accelerated rate. The V-12 men were in uniform, but the purpose was to make them not next year's second lieutenants but admirals twenty years hence. Some people felt this program undemocratic, but it was an important recognition by the government of the country's continued need for leadership beyond the Armed Forces.

The Army Specialized Training Program (A.S.T.P.) was represented at Pennsylvania with enlisted men taking their work on campus. Parts of the Area and Language program, preparing men for military police, were given. Intensive courses were taught in Russian, German, Arabic, Bengali, and Japanese. As the younger men of his staff were drawn off to teach as they were able in any of these programs, Dr. Huebner carried an increasingly heavy load in insurance teaching himself.

War conditions brought interruptions for the American College activities. The annual report of 1944 stated that over four hundred C.L.U.'s were in the Armed Forces and more than seven hundred others were in service who had some examinations to their credit. The College made every effort to keep in touch with these men, sustaining their interest in life insurance and arranging for their reorientation to developments in the business. That year C.L.U. examinations were scheduled in ninety-seven educational institutions, four army camps or naval bases, and in one German prison camp. The candidate in prison camp was a thirty-one-year-old representative of the Metropolitan Life at Easton, Pennsylvania, who, as a lieutenant colonel, had been among the first American troops ashore in French Morocco. He was captured in the Tunisia campaign. His examinations were arranged through the War Prisoners Aid of the Y.M.C.A. That organization also provided him with the necessary study materials. The examinations were properly proctored by the educational officer in the prison camp.

To help the students in service and those recently released, the American College prepared monographs in the areas of each C.L.U. examination to report, as their titles stated, "recent significant developments." Pension plans, new taxes, restrictions on business and trade, developments in social security —a great variety of subjects was discussed in these valuable little leaflets, which were furnished free of charge to candidates in the Armed Forces, and they were widely used by other students also.

In the University, Dr. Huebner welcomed the wartime innovation of expanding his teaching to women. He had had occasional women in his evening courses, but beginning in 1945 for several years he taught his insurance survey course at the College for Women. He had strong ideas about women in life insurance. In his book in 1915 he said:

> She should be taught that it is not only her husband's duty adequately to protect the family, if that is at all possible, but that it is *her* duty, if necessary, to use her persuasive powers to get him to act, and if that does not avail, to insist on action as her *right.*

In his speeches to life underwriters he constantly emphasized the importance of educating women as buyers and as beneficiaries of life insurance policies. How far into the future he saw when in 1914 he said:

> Not only will women cooperate with their husbands in respect to life insurance, but the subject will soon be one of discussion in women's clubs and social circles.

Dr. Huebner often challenged the usual life insurance vocabulary. Realizing that a husband's refusal to own adequate life insurance often is based on a wife's attitude, he undoubtedly gave double emphasis in the women's classes to what he repeatedly said about the word beneficiary, for instance.

> My wife and children are *not* my beneficiaries. When I die, they do not *benefit* from my life insurance. Through my life insurance I can bequeathe to them some portion of my life value, so that they will

> continue to have some of what they get now. Not technically of course, but in effect, my life insurance policy is a last will and testament.

The young women in his classes responded as warmly as his men students. They felt his sincerity in the advice he gave along with the formal substance of his lectures. Often some newly engaged girl would bring her fiancé to Dr. Huebner so that he too might become persuaded about life insurance as the financial foundation for a happy home.

Undoubtedly he spoke very personally to such young people for he often has said that it was his own family which made him see that life insurance is a sacred family affair. He felt so strongly the sense of obligation that a father and husband should have for those dependent upon him financially that he could not help preaching that idea to others. It was to him a matter of logic and basic decency, rather than, as he said, "that tear stuff." He often observed that the family is the basis of life insurance and, in turn, life insurance is the financial basis of the family.

Possibly he took the opportunity to tell those students about other phases of his own happy marriage. He felt that any university teacher was blessed to have a wife who could grow with him mentally, who could challenge him in thought and discussion. He had seen more than one colleague who had failed for that lack at home. He appreciated deeply all that Mrs. Huebner did for him, not only by her constant encouragement and support in all his endeavors, but in the specific tasks which she undertook in connection with his work. She read each new manuscript as a guinea pig. If she, a university graduate and intelligent layman, could not understand what he wrote, he tore it up and began again. She also did the tedious and responsible job of proofreading each new book as it came along. From most happy experience Dr. Huebner could talk to his young people about marriage as a partnership.

CHAPTER FIFTEEN

A Decade of Building

WHEN the war was over, the way cleared for two important developments in the C.L.U. program. Dr. Huebner had always pointed to the ideal of continued education of life underwriters. Winning the designation was a beginning, not the end, he believed. With paper and people again available, it became possible to start a professional publication. The aim was to help life underwriters, both C.L.U.'s and others, but also to give professional life underwriting information to people doing the supplementary estate services in law, banking, accounting, and so on. Therefore, *The Journal of the American Society of Chartered Life Underwriters*, a quarterly, was launched in the fall of 1946. The new publication was fortunate in its capable and devoted editor, Walter A. Craig, C.L.U. The editorial board also was strong—men technically qualified and willing as volunteers to devote hours and hours to a professional cause in which they believed. The first board, in addition to Mr. Craig, was: James Elton Bragg, C. L.U., Karl K. Krogue, C.L.U., William S. Leighton, C.L.U. and Martin I. Scott, C.L.U. The titles of articles in the first issue and their authors indicate the quality of the publication.

New Horizons in Life Insurance—S. S. Huebner, Ph.D., Sc.D., Professor of Insurance, University of Pennsylvania

The Creation of Estate Plans—Mayo Adams Shattuck, Attorney, Boston

Life Insurance and Rising Prices—M. Albert Linton, President, Provident Mutual Life Insurance Company

Valuation of Business Interests—Deane C. Davis, Vice President and General Counsel, National Life Insurance Company of Vermont

The Search for Economic Security—Marcus Nadler, Ph.D., Professor of Banking and Finance, New York University

Collateral Assignments of Life Insurance Policies—John V. Bloys, Assistant General Counsel, Life Insurance Association of America

The Insured and Beneficiary in Common Disaster—Warner F. Haldeman, Associate Counsel, Penn Mutual Life Insurance Company

The Spendthrift Clause in Life Insurance—John Barker, Jr., Counsel, New England Mutual Life Insurance Company

Following this good beginning, *The Journal's* editorial standards continued high. The subjects chosen for articles and their treatment was consistently on the professional level. Issue after issue, the magazine went to the desks of professional men outside of life insurance, reflecting life underwriting as a calling requiring a specialized body of knowledge for its successful practice. In itself it personified one of the principles Dr. Huebner had repeatedly preached to the life insurance agents of an earlier day. The influence of *The Journal* in winning life underwriters the respect of other professional men cannot be measured. *The Journal* is received by all members of the American Society, now over five thousand; in addition, there is a subscription list of some six thousand non-C.L.U.'s.

Dr. Huebner and other American College leaders had long looked forward to continued classroom experience for C.L.U.'s. When the war was over, the American Society launched a second new project which was along this line. This was a summer seminar called the C.L.U. Institute. Howard H. Cammack, C.L.U. was chairman of the project, and Laurence J. Ackerman

American Society of Chartered Life Underwriters annual meeting, Pittsburgh, September, 1943. *Front row,* Dr. Huebner; George E. Lackey, retiring president; M. Luther Buchanan, newly elected president. *Standing, left,* Dr. David McCahan, re-elected secretary; *right,* Edward A. Krueger, re-elected treasurer. (*Frank V. Anderson*)

was dean. In late June, 1946, thirty-nine C.L.U.'s from Chicago and Houston and many cities eastward assembled at the University of Connecticut, a beautiful campus in the rolling hills of New England. There for two weeks they devoted themselves to a program of study and discussion on estate planning, business insurance, and pension and profit sharing plans. The Institute was a huge success and has been followed by similar summer schools each year. These seminars have proved so popular that since 1951 two or three sessions have been offered to serve different areas of the country. One has often been at Storrs, and other state university campuses have been used repeatedly such as Wisconsin, Colorado, and California.

The University of Pennsylvania shared the flood of released servicemen coming back to the campus. Dr. Huebner's classes again were crowded. Many of these young men delighted him especially by their maturity and serious purpose. They were more like the evening school and extension class students whom he always found a special challenge. They did not just listen, but raised points of their own and probed for reasons and additional facts. Even as a young teacher Dr. Huebner had welcomed questions which he could not answer. But he left no stone unturned to get the desired information. To have professor and students learning together pleased him.

With the country adjusting itself to postwar conditions, every radio commentator or newspaper headline made a text for the classroom. No professor of economics could ignore the spiral of increased wages and prices, all the talk of inflation. Dr. Huebner was impatient alike with the popular comments and learned interpretations. He believes that the real problem, the basic cause, of inflation lies in lack of production. The key to control is the creation of goods by *work*. "You can't make something out of nothing," he says. "Everything that *is* results from work." The labor leaders who keep preaching against work he thinks are leading people astray. We need to recognize the truth that work is part of the moral law, and all need to experience, what he has known so richly, the great joy of seeing the fruits of work well done.

Dr. Huebner says that his personal philosophy about the importance of work undoubtedly goes back to his boyhood farm upbringing. They all worked hard there. Everybody expected to work hard if they wanted to have things. When misfortune came they just worked harder. He remembers the depression of 1893 when at the village store he sold two dressed spring roosters for a quarter, when oats were sixteen cents a bushel, and when potatoes were six cents a bushel, if you could sell them. Then many a neighboring farmer stuck his hoe upright in the potato field with the sign "Help yourself, but don't steal the hoe." He recalls his father taking him to the country schoolhouse for a New England-type town meeting where the farmers together discussed their problems and how they could help each other. Of course he admits that they all had plenty to eat, which of course made a different situation from what happens when hard times hit the cities.

Dr. Huebner has from the beginning been known as a conservative member of the University faculty. He is all for private enterprise, provided it does what it should. He believes that the insurance business should recognize that a public need must be served. If private industry fails to do a job, it has no redress when the need is met some other way.

From the beginning he has been very much in favor of disability insurance, although he deplored the merchandising excesses and underwriting mistakes which led to disaster in the early 1930's. In our money economy he sees disability insurance or accident and health insurance as essential in the event of what he calls the living death. It is a logical phase of the life value idea, as has been mentioned before. Since the war he has been very much interested in the development of major medical coverage. He considers such coverage pure property insurance for many people, the protection of savings built up for constructive purposes, which may be swept away by the calamitous expenses of a major illness or accident. Insurance is not a static business. As the economic conditions of life change, the underwriters of risk must meet the changing needs, for a public necessity must be served.

The late 1940's were a catching-up time in many respects. A most gratifying event for Dr. Huebner came in 1947 when the annual John Newton Russell Memorial Award was inaugurated in the National Association of Life Underwriters and he was the first to receive it. John Newton Russell, of Los Angeles, was a prominent life underwriter of the past generation, very active in the National Association and also one of the key men in the organization of the American College. He had died in 1942 and his son proposed to the National Association the annual award in memory of his father and in recognition of outstanding service to the institution of life insurance. Acceptance of the proposal and machinery for selecting the award winners was not completed until five years later. Nominations for the award are solicited very widely from life insurance companies, organizations, editors, and public officers. The selection committee consists of some dozen people widely representative of the life insurance business. There are an elaborate screening procedure and narrowing of the nominations through several ballots, until one person receives the majority of votes. In 1947 six awards were made, retroactively to the year of Mr. Russell's

John Newton Russell Award winners: Mr. Russell, Jr. handing the engraved watch to Dr. Huebner, winner for 1942. *Continuing left to right,* Julian S. Myrick, 1943 winner; J. Stanley Edwards, 1944 winner. *Back row,* Paul F. Clark, 1945 winner; M. Albert Linton, 1946 winner; and Holgar J. Johnson, 1947 winner. (*Egan Photo*)

death. They were: for 1942, Solomon S. Huebner; 1943, Julian S. Myrick; 1944, J. Stanley Edwards; 1945, Paul F. Clark; 1946, M. Albert Linton; and 1947, Holgar J. Johnson. The winner each year is given an inscribed gold watch and a citation. At National Association headquarters there is a memorial bronze plaque honoring Mr. Russell and listing each recipient of the award, with Dr. Huebner's name first of all. This honor of course was much appreciated by Dr. Huebner, and there was a sentiment involved also in the association with his old friend who had contributed much to the American College program.

A new ally in the cause of life insurance education was welcomed by Dr. Huebner in these postwar years. A group of nationally known educators had come together, under the chairmanship of Dr. Herold C. Hunt* and with the co-operation of the Institute of Life Insurance, to form the National Committee for Education in Family Finance. The purpose of the Committee was to help meet the need for better teaching of life insurance and other fundamental money matters in the public schools. R. Wilfred Kelsey, of the Institute of Life Insurance, became executive secretary of the Committee. He immediately sought advice from Dr. Huebner and Dr. McCahan.

The result was plans for a summer workshop in family finance for schoolteachers, a co-operative project of the Wharton School and the School of Education at the University of Pennsylvania. The program aimed to give the workshop members materials and techniques for the teaching of the fundamentals of family finance. The Institute offered financial help to implement the experiment. This summer course was to carry regular academic credit.

The first course was offered in 1950, and was most success-

---

* Then president of the American Association of School Administrators and superintendent of schools in Chicago, later undersecretary in the Department of Health, Education and Welfare. Dr. Hunt has given continued leadership to this program. He is now Eliot Professor of Education at the Harvard Graduate School.

ful. Each year since, the University of Pennsylvania has had such a workshop and the program has expanded continually into universities across the country. In 1959 there were sixteen workshops on campuses from New England to the Pacific Coast. The University of Pennsylvania program has become established as the national workshop. Other universities have members generally drawn from local areas. Each summer, teachers have come to Philadelphia from all over the nation. They were social studies teachers, mathematics teachers, home economics teachers, even some elementary school teachers. From the beginning Dr. Huebner was generally scheduled for six class periods to talk on life insurance and the life value idea. He enjoyed his lectures to these groups for he had long been enthusiastic about getting life insurance teaching into the public schools, knowing that more than half of the students there never go on to college.

The satisfaction which came from the good beginning of this academic program was matched by satisfaction in another kind of progress in the affairs of the American College. This was the realization of a dream for a home of its own. Outgrowing the corner of Dr. Huebner's office in Logan Hall, the College had rented quarters in a nearby office building. They were attic rooms, hard to climb to and like an oven in summer, but not too expensive. As the College program expanded after the war, that office, too, became overcrowded. Joseph H. Reese, C.L.U. of Philadelphia, a trustee of the College and one of Dr. Huebner's former students, was made chairman of a new headquarters committee. The specifications included price, location, and size of space, for present use and expansion. Real estate people were no help. They could offer nothing that was easily accessible to the University, and which was suitable and within the price range. Mr. Reese was not a successful life insurance salesman for nothing. He knew how to prospect. So he made a personal survey of the convenient neighborhood, driving up one street and down another. At 3924 Walnut he saw something which seemed to have possibilities. He asked the realtor to make inquiries about it. They found that, though it was not on the market, it could be purchased at a reasonable price. The house was effectively remodeled to provide suitable office space both for the College and the American Society; and for the Institute and the Society of C.P.C.U. as tenants.

And so in 1948 the American College moved into a new home, in a handsome old brick and stucco residence, set behind a high iron fence in the midst of a pleasant garden. The visitor steps into a paneled entrance hall-reception room with a fireplace flanked by bookcases. Since 1950 an oil portrait of Dr. Huebner has hung against the chimney breast. It is the gift of C.L.U.'s. From all over the country and even abroad they made one-dollar contributions to buy this painting of the man whose vision and leadership made the American College possible. The artist was Alice Kent Stoddard of Philadelphia, who had also painted the provost of the University, Justice Roberts of the United States Supreme Court, and many other notables.

The American College was not the only institution that needed more and better space. After World War II, the University of Pennsylvania, like most universities, began to be bursting at the seams with the great numbers of students returning to the campus from the Armed Forces. A University development program was undertaken, looking to a greatly enlarged campus and expanded facilities. The Wharton School had been housed for many years in Logan Hall, which was old when they inherited it. Now, as the boys with the "ruptured duck" buttons in their lapels swarmed to register, conditions were worse than ever. A new building for them was an important part of the program and one of the first objectives. Since Dr. Huebner had been repeatedly recognized as a favorite professor, Harold E. Stassen, then University president, enlisted him to help rally the alumni in the campaign. His travels took on a new purpose as he circled the country with President Stassen, helping to explain the program and gain support. The groups they met were attentive to Mr. Stassen, but rose to their feet with cheers for their beloved professor. They delighted to see the familiar red necktie and to hear him talk with the familiar vigorous gestures. He was older; they were older; but they still responded to the contagion of his convictions. In many cases too a manufacturer in Ohio or a salesman in Texas made a gift that was the American counterpart of the samurai sword presented long before in Japan. Many prosperous businessmen throughout the United States recognized that Dr. Huebner had given them something during their college years that had become truly a foundation stone for their successful accomplishments.

Of course innumerable life insurance men felt the same way. A committee of fifty-four leaders, with A. C. F. Finkbiner of Philadelphia as chairman, undertook to reach representatives of the industry. In a letter to some six thousand five hundred men and women, including C.L.U.'s, Million Dollar Round Table members, managers and general agents, and many others they asked: "How many times have you wished that you could show your appreciation to Dr. Huebner in a tangible way? Here's your chance to do it . . . an opportunity to help build with bricks and mortar a Center which will give permanence and even greater impact to his work." They described the plans for a new two-million-dollar Wharton School building including an Insurance Center which would cost one hundred thousand dollars. The Center would include faculty offices, conference rooms, workshop facilities, and so on. They visualized such a center as "the finest kind of tribute to this modest but tremendously influential teacher."

The money came in, from University alumni and from life underwriters alike. *The Daily Pennsylvanian*, looking forward to the ground-breaking, reported that every generation since

1881 had heard the talk and seen sketches of a new building for the Wharton School and that the "very land upon which the new building will rise was donated by Joseph Wharton." The reporter continued:

> Tomorrow (October 28, 1950) marks the first step in the rebuilding of the undergraduate facilities under the University's redevelopment program . . . This is a red-letter day in the history of Pennsylvania and a loud trumpeting of the occasion has been rightfully prepared. The band will be present; Professor Huebner of the Insurance Department will participate in the shovel ceremony together with a student; and many prominent speakers will be heard.

Dr. Huebner, as senior member of the faculty, did wield a shining shovel tied with ribbons of University blue and

Ground breaking for Dietrich Hall, October 28, 1950. ***Left to right,*** **Dr. Huebner, digging; President Stassen; the daughter of Joseph Wharton.** ***Extreme right,*** **Dr. C. C. Balderston;** ***third from right,*** **Dr. A. H. Williams.**

red. President Stassen presided. The daughter of Joseph Wharton was present. That bright October Saturday was a day of triumph.

The needs of the students could hardly await the completion of the building. As soon as any area was habitable, people moved in. By the spring of 1952, insurance classes were being held in the new Dietrich Hall (named for their uncle, D. Wellington Dietrich, by two brothers, alumni of the University).

By routine University rules, Dr. Huebner should have retired in June, 1952. However, in the course of one of the fund-raising trips with President Stassen, Dr. Huebner had mentioned his desire to teach in the new building. Mr. Stassen thought that would be a well-earned reward and arranged to have him continue active on the faculty for a year beyond the usual retirement date. Therefore, in 1952 Dr. Huebner gave

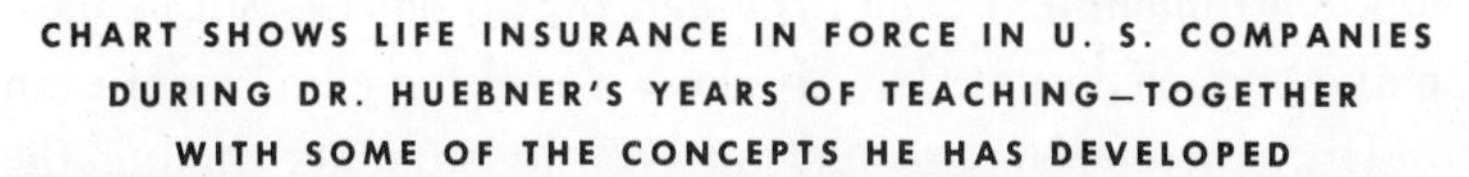

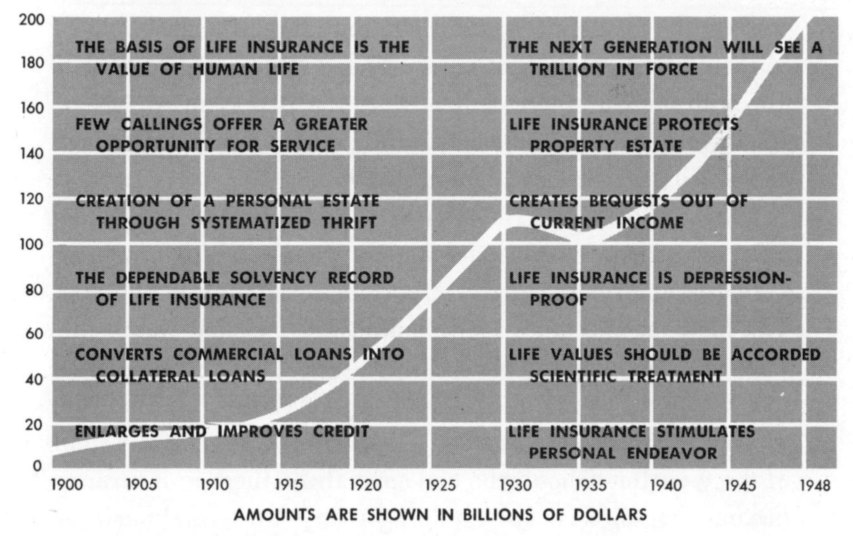

This chart was presented in the campaign material used in raising funds for the Insurance Center in Dietrich Hall.

up the department chairmanship which he had held for thirty-nine years, but remained as a teaching professor until June, 1953.

For some forty years he had had his office and done his teaching in Logan Hall. It was a part of himself, and he was a part of it. The fumes of his famous White Owl cigars (did a broadside on some long-ago Wisconsin barn account for that strange obsession?) mingled with chalk dust and the smell of old masonry to produce the characteristic odor within that campus landmark. Both he and many students recalled conference hours in his office which had changed the course of a man's life. When the time came to leave the old building Dr. Huebner admitted: "I doggone nearly wept."

The Dean had given the directive that no old furniture, no battered files, were to be taken to the new building. Completely new equipment had been provided for all offices. But he had to make one exception: Dr. Huebner's rocking chair went along.

Dr. Huebner's personal interest in students during their years at the University and his continuing relations with many of them after graduation naturally led them often to turn to him with their problems in business life. A very important result of one of these contacts was the Pension Research Council of the Wharton School, created in 1952.

During World War II, when wage levels were frozen as part of a program for industrial and financial stability, pension plans became increasingly important in employee relations. The high income taxes made employers feel that they could afford to provide pensions because a large part of the cost was, in effect, paid by the government in plans which qualified for income tax deduction. Ben S. McGiveran, C.L.U., a graduate of the Wharton School who had specialized there in insurance, became a pension consultant doing a very substantial business. As the pension idea grew in popularity, different kinds of machinery for providing pensions were developed. There were

Dr. Huebner on the steps of Logan Hall, 1959. (*Shaw*)

considerable misunderstanding and confusion about the various methods and their adaptability to different kinds of employee groups. Mr. McGiveran and other life underwriters doing pension business felt that an objective study of the problem would be helpful to them and their clients. Mr. McGiveran, therefore, approached Dr. Huebner with the proposal that funds would be provided for such an investigation.

The Wharton School had long co-operated in many kinds of research programs valuable to business and public affairs. The subject of private pensions, which were growing so phenomenally, seemed urgently to need investigation. Their economic, political, and social influences should be explored for the good of our whole American society. An impartial study of the facts and issues involved in private pensions would provide a basis for sound development of this important service.

Support was therefore provided through gifts by individuals and corporations, and the Pension Research Council began its work. Members of the Council are outstanding representatives of business, industry, finance, and the government, who serve without pay. The Council members help determine phases of the pension problem to be studied, raise the necessary funds, give guidance to the individual projects as they proceed, and in many cases actually participate in the investigations.

Dr. Dan M. McGill, professor of insurance at the Wharton School, has been director of research for the Council from the beginning. Each study has a professional research man from business or a university to head up the work and he uses Council members and other volunteers to develop the necessary materials and information.

The first study completed by the Council was published in 1955. It was written by Dr. McGill and entitled *Fundamentals of Private Pension Plans*. It has become a text in many colleges and universities and is regarded as the standard work on the subject. It won the Elizur Wright Award of the American Association of University Teachers of Insurance as the outstanding book of the year in the field of insurance.

The members of the Council at the beginning, together with

their affiliations then, indicate the caliber of the men who are giving this service. The group has changed very little in the years since 1952.

Harry Becker, Professor of Hospital Economics, Northwestern University, Chicago

Frank B. Cliffe, Vice President, H. J. Heinz Company, Pittsburgh

John K. Dyer, Jr., Vice President and Actuary, Towers, Perrin, Forster, and Crosby, Inc., Philadelphia

S. S. Huebner, Emeritus Professor of Insurance and Commerce, Wharton School of Finance and Commerce

Laflin C. Jones, Director of Insurance Services and Planning, Northwestern Mutual Life Insurance Company, Milwaukee

C. A. Kulp, Chairman, Insurance Department, Wharton School of Finance and Commerce

M. A. Linton, Chairman of the Board, Provident Mutual Life Insurance Company, Philadelphia

Ben S. McGiveran, Seefurth and McGiveran, Pension Underwriters, Chicago and Milwaukee

Fred P. McKenzie, Vice President, The Hanover Bank, New York City

J. W. Myers, Manager, Insurance and Social Security Department, Standard Oil Company of New Jersey, New York City

Ray M. Peterson, Vice President and Associate Actuary, Equitable Life Assurance Society of the United States, New York City

Otto Pollak, Associate Professor of Sociology, Wharton School of Finance and Commerce

George F. Sisler, Vice President, First National Bank, Chicago

D. N. Warters, Executive Vice President, Bankers Life Company, Des Moines

Other studies completed or in process have to do with social aspects of retirement, health care for older people, actuarial principles of pensions, tax policies related to the aged, employment of older workers, legal status and regulation of private plans, and so on. The program of the Council has become another witness to the fact that a teacher and a university can be a force far beyond the campus.

The year 1952 was the twenty-fifth anniversary of the American College. The June issue of *The Journal of the American Society of Chartered Life Underwriters* was planned as a tribute to Dr. Huebner. Harold E. Stassen, president of the University of Pennsylvania, wrote a prefatory article. In part it said:

> Rarely does one find in the life of a university—particularly a university as old as this one—an individual who has made the total contribution to it and to life outside that Dr. Solomon S. Huebner has made in his almost 50 years of service at the University of Pennsylvania . . . "Sunny Sol"—as he is affectionately known to the thousands of his students—is a pioneer in the formulation and application of insurance principles; he is the dean of insurance teachers in America; he is the founder of the business college insurance courses; and he is considered by the University of Pennsylvania as one of the greatest teachers in its two century history. Education and the life insurance business owe him a debt that can never be repaid.

The other articles in the issue were by eleven of the many outstanding men who had been his students and who took "great satisfaction in paying this unique tribute to a man whose contribution to life insurance education has been unparalleled and whose influence will continue to grow, as the years go on, through the lives of the many who have sat at his feet."

A most interesting feature of the issue was "A Collection of Huebnerian Philosophy on Life and Life Insurance—Thoughts from the Pen of Solomon Stephen Huebner" selected by Dr. McCahan and Dr. Gregg. A few items are presented here which were written not only by Dr. Huebner's pen, but in his life.

> The choice of a life's vocation is the greatest economic step that man is called upon to make. Decent remuneration must, of course, be

one of the considerations in taking this step, but it is by no means the only one. Happiness in one's labor, and love and respect for the cause represented, are also essentials. It is inconceivable how anyone can tie up with a vocation for life without wanting, in the daily practice thereof, to be constantly conscious of a feeling of happiness and of love for the work that should claim undivided attention. Such a state of feeling can only exist if we have a broad vision of our life's work.

* * * *

To be truly professional there must be continued study and conscientious practice thereafter throughout a man's working life, coupled with continuing endeavor to meet the high standards of perfection set for the calling. All worth-while professions improve from day to day in new knowledge and in new techniques. Not to continue one's studies implies a passive attitude which can only lead to mental deterioration, and disservice to clients. It marks the difference between a true professional and the individual who is only a "professional by membership." As I have often said: "he who ceases to study will soon begin to retrograde; he who retrogrades will cease to enthuse; he who ceases to enthuse about his life's work will cease to love it; and he who ceases to love his work is in an unholy mess." A true professional is one who is ever determined to keep abreast of the constant progress in knowledge and skills "in his calling."

* * * *

To be really happy in his calling, the life underwriter should decide early to be community-minded. For example, in nearly every community there are frequent fund drives for charity and welfare purposes, money-raising projects for many types of nonprofit welfare institutions, life conservation movements in the interest of better health and greater longevity. To say: "I have no time for such matters and must stick to my regular money-making work" means the missing of great opportunities. To take such an attitude is to disregard the spiritual side of a professional life. To a reasonable extent, every professional man should regard participation in community work as a duty.

* * * *

For the great mass of people with dependents, life insurance should be the first type of security to be purchased. Where a dependent family is at stake it is the height of folly to urge investment in other directions, and it is quite beside the point to offer laborious explanations of the relative merits of various classes of bonds and other types of investment. The first duty of every man is to protect his household against want in case of premature death, and this can be done only through the purchase of an adequate amount of life insurance . . . It takes time to save and, where dependents must be protected, life insurance alone guarantees the accumulation of a competency against the contingency of the saving period being cut short by an untimely death. The great mass of people live only within the life insurance stage and are removed by thousands of dollars from the point where they can judiciously become direct investors along other lines.

* * * *

The real objective of life insurance . . . is the sure and convenient accumulation of a substantial estate, on the installment plan, over the working years of life. It aims to keep the insured on the *straight road* towards his objective and seeks to safeguard him, because of his personal frailties in the field of finance, against deviations from that straight road.

* * * *

Worry and fear retard human initiative and efficiency probably more than do any other factors. To the thoughtful man, personal contentment and vocational efficiency are impossible when the curse of worry and fear is constantly exerting its dampening influence. On the contrary, the absence of this curse produces a state of mental feeling which increases man's efficiency and enables him to venture more willingly. Here we reach the heart of all insurance, irrespective of the type under consideration, namely, the creation of certainty out of the uncertainties that permeate our economic life. . . . What greater source of worry can there be to thoughtful men than the uncertainty of human longevity, and what more effective means than life insurance to remove this same anxiety?

In the first twenty-five years nearly five thousand men and women had become C.L.U.'s, and some sixty-five hundred more had taken parts of the examinations. A questionnaire sent to the C.L.U. completers of this first quarter century was filled out and returned by 85 per cent of them, answering forty very personal questions. Speaking at an agents' meeting of the Northwestern Mutual Life where Dr. Huebner was the honored guest, Grant L. Hill, then vice president and director of agents, commented on that survey. He said in part:

> First of all, let's look at the individual—what has the attainment of the C.L.U. designation meant to the C.L.U.? It is significant that the vast majority of them firmly believe it has made them better life insurance men, afforded them valuable prestige and given them the viewpoint of a professional practitioner. These are not merely the views of what other people think the attainment of the designation will do, but are the express, objective views of the C.L.U.'s themselves.
>
> As for the more tangible results to the C.L.U., there's the age-old question "Does C.L.U. study adversely affect an underwriter's production during the period of preparation?" 84% answered they had a *moderate* or a *greatly* increased income from the time of starting C.L.U. work until it was completed, and more important, 72% said that increased income could be attributed to their C.L.U studies.
>
> As agency executives, we should be particularly interested to note the advancement of C.L.U.'s into organization or management work. 7% questioned were general agents or managers in the ordinary business when they undertook their C.L.U. work. *Today* 23% are ordinary managers or general agents—nearly one in four, and 9% are presently in home offices....
>
> Has Dr. Huebner's American College helped to bring contentment to those who have followed his teaching and qualified for the designation? To be sure, contentment may not be a measurable quality, but the facts show that out of the 4,786 C.L.U. completers *only* 307 have left the business except for reasons of death, retirement or disability. This reflects a persistency of 94% over the 25-year period and proves that C.L.U.'s are certainly finding contentment and satisfaction enough in their careers to desire it above any other. They do "stay put" . . .
>
> There is also proof that the persistency of the business written by C.L.U.'s is greater than most non-C.L.U.'s. This fact is particularly

> significant because persistency is of major importance to agent, agency, company and policyholders. What is the reason, the underlying cause, for this much better persistency on the business of C.L.U.'s? The agent who has the designation has set out to do a much-better-than-ordinary-job, and his knowledge and training enable him to do it extraordinarily well.
>
> Another, and by no means minor, benefit that the American College has brought to life insurance is an improved public recognition of the growing stature of the career life underwriter....
>
> It has been my experience that most businessmen generally are so busy coping with immediate and piecemeal matters that there is a tendency to let the "long run" or future take care of itself. As one prominent educator expressed it, Americans generally "spend so much time on things that are *urgent* that we have none left to spend on those that are *important*."
>
> Twenty-five years ago Dr. Huebner saw very clearly what was of the greatest long range importance to the life insurance business. He set himself to take action, to do something about it, and how he and the American College have so brilliantly achieved their objectives is clearly proved by this survey of which I have used but a small part.

In September, 1952, Dr. Huebner relinquished his place as president of the American College to Dr. David McCahan, a former dean of the College and since the previous year executive vice president, a man to whom Dr. Huebner was wholly glad to pass the torch. Dr. Huebner was designated president emeritus, and had been elected a life trustee in 1938.

These milestones in Dr. Huebner's life seemed to inspire many groups in the industry to give him their own honors. The Insurance Society of New York elected him an honorary member, a distinction given to only two other men up to that time. The John Hancock Mutual Life Insurance Company of Boston made him the subject of one of their popular advertising series on famous Americans. Such diverse and interesting characters as Paul Revere, Abraham Lincoln, Stephen Foster, Johnny Appleseed, and Theodore Roosevelt had been presented to the readers of *Fortune*, the *Saturday Evening Post*, and many other general periodicals. Now in similar format in the life insurance magazines, John Hancock honored Dr. Huebner. Under the reproduction of the American College portrait and the heading, "He ably led, we gladly followed," was the stirring tribute:

> He's past seventy now. But time hasn't touched him inwardly. The old energy is still there, and the strong sense of calling, and the clear-eyed vision of the goal. He looks the part he's always played—a great teacher, a moulder of men.
>
> Talking to him now, you know why Dr. Solomon S. Huebner played such a hero's role in the building of today's multi-billion dollar life insurance business.
>
> He never sold a dollar's worth of life insurance himself. But he shaped the minds and inspired the men who have made the great life insurance sales records of today. He gave us a sense of our mission as handlers of dreams and hopes, not of dollars and cents. Physicians, in their moments of self-searching, think of Hippocrates. We think—or should—of Dr. Huebner.
>
> It was half a century ago when young Solomon Huebner saw the great need for *trained* young men in business. The men were available; the training was not. He resolved to change all that.
>
> He started from scratch. There were few business schools then, few textbooks, fewer teachers. So, when the Wharton School announced a course in life insurance, with Dr. Huebner as its guiding spirit, a new era had quietly begun, though not many people realized it.
>
> Teacher and students often learned together in those pioneering days. The textbooks got written; many he had to write himself. Eventually the whole country and the nations of the world began to feel the influence of Solomon S. Huebner. Some of his students became important in the business world. Some went out to teach to others what they had learned from him.
>
> That would have been enough for most men. But Dr. Huebner had just begun.
>
> For fourteen years, he had nourished a dream that was finally realized with the chartering of the American College

> of Life Underwriters. Now all young men who wished to qualify for the profession of life insurance could be tested for aptitude, integrity, and willingness to work. Here they could be trained in mind and heart for better service to themselves, their clients, their companies, and their country.
>
> Many of us have climbed to success on the ladder which S. S. Huebner built for us. To show our gratitude, we have offered him every honor at our disposal. He accepts them graciously, but being the man he is, we think he finds ample reward in knowing that his work has made thousands of other careers possible. And perhaps his greatest reward comes when he walks down a street in any American town, and sees the self-respecting families in their self-respecting houses, and knows what a part life insurance has played in the confident rhythm of their lives.

During his last year at the University, Dr. Huebner sometimes had in his lecture room an interested spectator who was not a student. That was Alfred Jonniaux, a noted Belgian artist who had been commissioned to do his portrait. He wanted to study the professor in action to get the feeling of his personality. Of course Dr. Huebner went also to the studio for sittings which lasted for hours at a time. He found Mr. Jonniaux quite different from Miss Stoddard. The gentleman from Europe insisted on working in a very warm room. The lady from Philadelphia had liked best a very cold studio. The Jonniaux portrait shows Dr. Huebner wearing his glasses, the Stoddard portrait is without them.

Like the previous painting, the Jonniaux portrait was made possible by very many small gifts, this time from the Wharton School students who had specialized in insurance. The presentation of the portrait was made at a simple but impressive ceremony. Dr. C. Canby Balderston, dean of the Wharton School, received the portrait on behalf of the School, thanking especially Mr. Paul F. Clark and Dr. McCahan, who had been leaders in the project. Mr. Robert T. McCracken, chairman of

Dr. Huebner as many students remembered him, 1952.

the University's Board of Trustees, added his tribute. The portrait was hung in the library of the Huebner Foundation, giving to the Insurance Center, as Dr. Balderston said, a record of the man "admired and respected by generations of students" and "whose stature in the industry is so great as to cast his shadow so far, far ahead."

The year 1952 was significant for the Huebner Foundation.

When the project was originated the sponsors were committed to the purpose of raising twenty-five thousand dollars a year for five years. They did not in 1940 go further than that, and they announced that the administration of the educational program by the University of Pennsylvania was a beginning, and not necessarily a permanent, arrangement.

The first fellowships and scholarships were granted for the academic year 1941–42. The program developed so well, in spite of the interruption of World War II, which called nearly all the fellows from campus, that the original five-year program was extended. By 1952 the success of the enterprise was thoroughly demonstrated and a permanent organization was judged to be justified under a permanent body of trustees. So The S. S. Huebner Foundation for Insurance Education is now continued without time limit and independent of the three industry organizations which were its original Cooperating Committee, and established in its relationship with the University of Pennsylvania.

For 1952, $39,256.48 was contributed by one hundred ten life insurance companies for the purposes of the Foundation.

The activities of the Foundation had focused on four areas of improvement of insurance education. The basic objective was to increase the number of qualified insurance teachers. The Foundation promoted interest in insurance teaching and gave financial help to selected candidates. The standards of qualification for fellowships and scholarships were high and related also to the candidate's sincere interest in making life insurance education and research his life career. Through 1952, twenty-eight teachers were added to the active staffs of colleges and universities, having taken, in most cases, three years of full-time graduate work under the Foundation grants.

A second important purpose of the Foundation was to produce study materials for insurance students in higher educational institutions. One series of publications was the *Huebner*

Foundation Lectures. These books were compilations of addresses on selected insurance topics aimed particularly to provide written sources on subjects not otherwise covered in print. The general scope of each volume was planned in consultation with experts and the lecture author for each of the various subdivisions was selected from outstanding authorities in the field. Through 1952 four volumes were prepared: *Life Insurance: Trends and Problems*; *The Beneficiary in Life Insurance*; *Life Insurance Trends at Mid-Century*; and *Investment of Life Insurance Funds*.

A second series of publications was begun called the *Huebner Foundation Studies*. This was planned to include selected doctoral dissertations of Huebner fellows, or writings of other authors working independently of the Foundation's administrative board, judged valuable for the Foundation's purpose. Through 1952 publications in this series were: *An Analysis of Government Life Insurance* by Dan M. McGill, *An Analysis of Group Life Insurance* by Davis W. Gregg, and a reprint of *The Economic Theory of Risk and Insurance* by Allan H. Willett.

The books published by the Foundation were distributed free to key educators and libraries, and to a limited number of insurance leaders. Otherwise they were sold at standard prices. Net receipts from sales nearly offset the investment in these publications so that great advantage was realized through this project, at relatively low cost.

Another project of the Foundation was the creation of a research library. With the completion of Dietrich Hall, attractive and commodious quarters were made available for the Foundation as part of the Insurance Center. The library and study room are located there, providing the best insurance literature for fellows and scholars and resources for research.

The Foundation in its first decade developed also as a service center for insurance teaching. Colleges and universities sought

Dr. Huebner at the entrance of Dietrich Hall. (*Shaw*)

help in getting teachers, in planning general programs of insurance courses and in outlining specific courses, in suggestions of textbooks, and so on. The Foundation made a survey of "College and University Courses in Insurance and Related Subjects" which was used widely by educational administrators. This survey was a follow-up of previous similar studies that had been made for some time, at intervals of about every five years, first by Dr. Huebner, later by Dr. McCahan. This activity has been continued by the Foundation.

The Foundation went far beyond the mere academic program in serving Huebner fellows and scholars. The young men were guided in field trips and discussion groups. Through the Wharton School, opportunities for practice teaching under an experienced supervisor were also made available. Of course, placement service too was provided when needed.

As Dr. Huebner enjoyed his year of teaching in Dietrich Hall, he also knew great satisfaction in the progress of the Foundation. When errands took him back and forth from his new office to the Foundation's new quarters, he surely saw it all as his friends who raised the money for the Insurance Center anticipated: as an "instrument which will continue to advance and strengthen the service rendered by education to insurance men." It must have been easy, too, to look ahead to today, when there are more than fifty thousand copies of eighteen Huebner Foundation publications in use around the world; and when more than fifty insurance teachers, trained through the Foundation, are serving in colleges and universities all over the country. Dr. Huebner sees each man and each book as a center of influence through which life insurance education will spread in ever-widening circles.

CHAPTER SIXTEEN

Money Matters

In Dr. Huebner's constant concern with financial matters he was no shoemaker who let his own children go barefoot. The convictions which he expressed about money affairs were worked out in his own life. He practiced what he preached. When he came to retirement time, he found that he had built well.

The foundation of his whole estate plan was naturally his life insurance. Just before he married, when he was only a few years removed from his starting five-hundred-dollar-a-year salary as a beginner on the University of Pennsylvania faculty, he bought a twenty-thousand-dollar life insurance policy. That was term insurance on the twenty-year renewable plan. Within about seven years that had all been converted to permanent insurance. From time to time, as his needs and potential life value increased, Dr. Huebner bought additional life insurance until he had fifteen policies. Much of this was ordinary life on which he is still paying premiums. More than half of his total has now matured as long-term endowments. With hindsight he criticizes his ownership of the ordinary life contracts. He wishes that as a young man he had exercised "just a little more thrift," for he could very easily have made all the insurance the kind that "matures when life matures," as he says. By that he means now the maturing of the working life, when it would be so pleasant to have the full face value of the policies.

Dr. Huebner regards his family financial responsibilities most seriously. To him life insurance is a unique answer to what he calls his "solemn self-assumed obligation." His own deep feelings about this made him emphasize this service as one of the most creative functions of life insurance. Freed of financial concern for his family's future, he could devote all his time, energy, and imagination to the creative activities of his life work. That is the only way his beneficiaries really benefit from his life insurance, he feels. It has made him worth more to his family while he is alive. When they receive the proceeds of his life insurance policies, that will be only a partial replacement of his life value, and not a gain at all.

Moreover, the stimulus, even with the ordinary life program, to do that "little bit more" to meet his substantial premium commitments was a factor in his broad achievements. It is not theory but experience that makes him say that owning adequate life insurance can lift a man's sights in all ways. He is apt to remark that he is a "spending animal" like most people and he has made himself save through the gentle compulsion of his life insurance contracts. Incidentally, he had the annual premiums staggered through the year so that he had a continuous monthly item in his budget. It pleased him also to have the constant monthly reminder that he was meeting his sacred self-assumed obligation.

Dr. Huebner was somewhat ahead of the industry in recognizing the need for protection against financial losses due to health problems. As he developed his ideas about disability insurance and health insurance, he applied his conclusions to himself too. His first life insurance reflected the concept of death which was current in his boyhood, simply physical death. But later he protected his own life value substantially against the living death of disability, and against the retirement death.

When he had collected a variety of life insurance contracts he realized that they included a hodgepodge of beneficiary pro-

Above, **Colonel Ralph Nemo and his wife, Margaret, the eldest daughter of Dr. and Mrs. Huebner. (*Shaw*)**

Left, **Elizabeth Ray, daughter of Mrs. Nemo.**

visions. His concept of a life insurance program is that it constitutes a life will, transmitting financial values of a life to heirs as an ordinary property will transfers property values. Therefore it was very important to him to have harmony in the terms of his two wills. Together those legal instruments would provide financial protection for his family. So he consulted with his lawyer and a good life underwriter (who, it happened,

Mr. and Mrs. John M. Huebner, with sons Bernard (*left*) and Stephen. (*Shaw*)

Dr. and Mrs. Huebner's daughters: Esther Ann (*left*) and Ethel Elizabeth. (*Shaw*)

had also graduated from a law school) who helped him bring order out of the confusion. He was a little surprised when the underwriter, refusing a fee, expressed the assurance that he would eventually profit in some other way. He did, for Dr. Huebner purchased his next life insurance from the man who had so served him in a professional spirit. In all, Dr. Huebner has had only three life insurance agents. The man who is now his underwriter in all insurance matters is both a C.L.U. and a C.P.C.U.

Dr. Huebner has convictions about the family as a unit. He has seen his children grow up and become self-supporting, but he still feels a continuing interest in their financial affairs. Whether married or unmarried his children can owe part of their financial security to their father's loving forethought. He has made adequate provision for them in both his property will and his life will.

All the Huebner children were given every help to prepare them for financial independence through their own efforts. Dr. Huebner wanted them to be able and willing to do things for themselves, not to sit waiting to see what they might get from his estate. When they were of student age he agreed to finance any education they wished. Later, believing in adult education, he further promised that he would gladly pay for any courses they wished to take leading to self-improvement. From time to time as his daughters took advanced study he was pleased to foot the bills.

Speaking specifically about his life insurance estate, he says that originally it protected only one family. Now it protects five units—himself and Mrs. Huebner, and his four children and their families, who will have no financial drain because of dependent grandparents. Writing in his latest book on this phase of life insurance ownership, Dr. Huebner said:

> Property when it becomes "obsolete" as a producer of income ceases to represent any further economic responsibility. But the

> human life value when it becomes obsolete as a producer of income at the age of retirement must already have provided for its obligations for old-age support of husband and wife as well as for the protection of their children against the heavy burden of parental financial support.

Very early Dr. Huebner transmitted his convictions about life insurance to his son. He did this more than casually. When John was in high school, Dr. Huebner asked him to study the chapter in *The Economics of Life Insurance* about the capitalizing of human life values. Then he gave the boy an examination on the subject. He did well, and showed a real understanding of the principles involved. This encouraged Dr. Huebner. If a schoolboy could master those ideas, the life underwriters of the country could also profit from the book.

Moreover, with John understanding life insurance, the time was ripe for him to be insured. Therefore, Dr. Huebner bought a fifteen-thousand-dollar policy for his son with the agreement that it would not be a complete gift. Dr. Huebner promised to pay the premiums until John wanted to take over. Then the bargain was that he would pay his father the cash value of the policy and become its sole owner. The plan worked out to the satisfaction of both, with just one little flaw. When taking over the policy, John expressed the wish that it might have been twice as big.

The Huebner girls, too, own life insurance. They have applied their father's precepts to their individual purposes. They have made up their own minds about their purchases, but his preaching about the values of thrift and the creative functions of life insurance are seen in their decisions.

Dr. Huebner's personal estate includes a number of annuities. Some were based upon life insurance policy maturities; some were direct purchases. Some are jointly with Mrs. Huebner, with no decrease in the annuity income at the first death; and some are for Dr. Huebner alone, since the life insurance still in force will provide for his wife. Incidentally, Dr. Huebner feels very strongly about the maintenance of income under a joint and last-survivor annuity without change at the first death. He asserts that the idea of a reduction in income for the last survivor came from a merchandising desire to get the cost down rather than from understanding of needs. While both husband and wife are together, he says you see them helping each other. When one is alone, deprived of companionship and cooperation in meeting life's problems, the need for the full income is as great as ever.

Dr. Huebner's ownership of real estate is limited to his home. For many years the Huebners lived in a rented dwelling, for Dr. Huebner believed that adequate life insurance ownership must come first. When he bought his first home (and subsequently when he purchased a larger one) he did not use a mortgage. He went to the bank for a call loan with the right at any time to make repayments of one-hundred dollars or more with appropriate reduction in interest. In Philadelphia in those days, call loans generally were not called. In addition, Dr. Huebner had the resource of his life insurance cash values if he should need them in an emergency. (He believed in borrowing against life insurance cash values for emergencies or opportunities, but always was very particular about repaying the loans as soon as possible.) So lecture fees, unexpected savings, or special dividends from investments continuously were applied against the call loan. It was surprising, Dr. Huebner reported, how those many little payments could eat up the debt. Moreover, Dr. Huebner says money burned holes in his pockets. He had to get rid of it to save it. To have a place always ready where he could salt it away was the best means of keeping it.

As indicated, Dr. Huebner believed that for him as a family man life insurance should come first in his estate plans. He expressed his philosophy very strongly in a foreword he wrote for a volume he edited for the American Academy of Political and Social Science, *Bonds and the Bond Market.*

> For the great mass of people with dependents, life insurance should be the first type of security to be purchased. Where a dependent family is at stake it is the height of folly to urge investments in other directions . . . The first duty of every man is to protect his household against want in case of premature death, and this can be done only through the purchase of an adequate amount of life insurance. As is well known, life insurance offers a convenient and safe method of accumulating a savings fund at a very fair rate of return. But the greatest purpose of life insurance is to protect. It takes time to save and, where dependents must be protected, life insurance alone guarantees the accumulation of a competency against the contingency of the savings period being cut short by an untimely death. The great mass of people live only within the life insurance stage and are removed by thousands of dollars from the point where they can judiciously become direct investors along other lines . . .
>
> The accumulation of a decent competency should be regarded as a duty and an act of wisdom. Yet present practices remind one of Aesop's fable of the race between the tortoise and the hare. The hare relied upon the speedy method of running the race, expected to leap to victory, and accordingly saw fit, somewhere on the race-course to take a nap. The tortoise, on the contrary, relied upon his steady, persistent and unspectacular gait, and won the race. And such is the case today in the race for a decent competency. Many seek to win by the quick method. They expect to leap to success. They assume highly speculative hazards, particularly in stocks, without possessing either the financial or educational equipment, and, as a rule, are put to sleep somewhere along the course. Others adopt the slow method. They save their surplus earnings patiently and persistently, invest the same in gilt-edged bonds, are satisfied with a fair return, allow compound interest to work its wonders, and win the race.

Dr. Huebner's ownership of securities is modest. Even a government bond may be speculative as to price under some conditions, and he remembers when Liberty bonds of World War I went down to 82. However, he says, "I still have them. The price change did not hurt me. Their basic security is beyond question."

Dr. Huebner had an interesting little experience regarding war bonds in World War II. One evening a man came to his door at home. He was serving on a local committee selling war bonds and said that the records indicated that Dr. Huebner was not buying his share. Dr. Huebner invited him in and said, "I want to tell you something and ask you something. First, I have bought war bonds through each school in which I have a child and through every organization in which I have membership where there is a bond program. You may not know that, and I assure you it represents a good share of purchasing for me.

"Now let me ask you something. How much life insurance do you own?"

The caller hedged a bit at this change of base, and said he had a lot of life insurance. Then Dr. Huebner told him the substantial figure of his own life insurance annual premiums and said: "You admit that figure is quite a lot of money. Eighty per cent of that amount has gone into war bonds. Don't you think that in proportion to my financial status I am doing a pretty fair share in buying war bonds? You must realize that bonds are bought not only directly but indirectly."

As mentioned in an earlier chapter, Dr. Huebner owns some stocks. He is interested in what they represent and he likes to have them. He feels it a duty to share in financing American industry. But he still does not count on them too much, even though they have been carefully selected. He says, "Property is fleeting in character. Don't put too much faith in equities." He has seen too many disappointments. The principle Dr. Huebner advocates in regard to stocks, and which he has followed religiously, is to buy only when you can afford to lose, and to act in the light of all obligations to dependents. His own losses in stock ownership have been negligible. He has bought chiefly in companies which furnish goods and services basic to our daily lives—such as raw materials for industry, motors, public utilities, and food.

Dr. Huebner's convictions about buying on margin have been reported previously. He strongly disapproves, and after his one early profitable experience, did not try again. He had seen too many doctors lose their practices while thinking about the market instead of their patients. He had seen too many businessmen ruin their creative thought for their own business affairs by worry over what was showing on the ticker tape. Dr. Huebner was a student of economics, "the science of wealth," and he learned many important lessons in brokers' offices.

A most unusual opportunity to practice what he preached about stock investments came to him during the collapse of the stock market in 1929. The chart of that fall looked like a jagged flash of lightning. In its ninth big decline, suddenly a man repaid Dr. Huebner one thousand dollars which he had borrowed and which Dr. Huebner had feared he would never see again. (Dr. Huebner believed he must have had some luck in short sales.) Dr. Huebner showed the check to Mrs. Huebner and said: "For once I'm going to do what I've always described to my students. Things are sinister, dark and discouraging. Now is the time to buy stocks." Mrs. Huebner wanted to use the gift from heaven and take a nice trip, but her husband overruled. He spread the thousand dollars over many stocks, buying outright, of course. He emphasized that it is better to buy one share in each of fifty corporations, than fifty shares in one company, because that gives the spread of averages. He included in his purchases Pennsylvania Railroad stock at 9. When it soon went down to 7, Mrs. Huebner chided him. They were losing that wonderful windfall and might so much better have gone traveling.

But she mourned too soon. "What money I made out of that

thousand dollars!" Dr. Huebner said. "I made so much I couldn't stand it. I sold out. My Pennsylvania was then at 50." Of course the market went higher still, but Dr. Huebner recalled what he had often told his students about Lord Rothschild. When asked how he made his fabulous fortune, that financial genius had replied: "By always buying too soon and always selling too soon."

Dr. Huebner often quoted J. P. Morgan's answer when asked to predict what the stock market would do in the coming year. He said: "It will fluctuate." Dr. Huebner observed that in the past, over an average man's lifetime, there have been half a dozen cycles during which an individual could have followed Lord Rothschild's pattern of buying before the bottom and selling before the top. The opportunity was there, but could he do it? Very few can have the courage of their intellectual convictions. We are psychological individuals not mathematical robots, and it is a rare man who can be immune to the contagion of popular emotions.

For some years Dr. Huebner has been building up savings bank accounts for Mrs. Huebner. He considers them an important emergency fund, especially in retirement. He particularly likes the comfort of knowing that Mrs. Huebner would always have plenty of ready cash available in time of need.

Dr. Huebner's University pension is a modest factor in his present financial picture. He says he was born at the wrong time for pensions because he was relatively old when plans were established. He happily is in a far different position than many college teachers of his generation who now are faced with tragic problems because they are largely dependent upon their inadequate pension incomes in an inflationary era.

Social Security too has its place in the Huebner financial house of protection. Dr. Huebner has always vigorously urged individual self-reliance in financial matters. He believes that too extensive government security systems weaken individual initiative and are a potential threat to the nation's economic health. Those who had heard his vehement statements against political economic excesses of recent years would not have been too surprised if he had made the grand gesture and refused a Social Security income. But he was too practical for that. As a student of economics he realizes that he is paying for his benefits. First he paid the relatively small price of the taxes earmarked for the purpose. He pays more importantly in the effect of the system on the whole level of prices and on economic conditions of the last twenty years.

As a man who has preached thrift all his life, Dr. Huebner is concerned about popular ignorance relating to the origin of capital. Labor today is clamoring for larger and larger shares of the profits of industry. Dr. Huebner says that a balance must come. The union spokesmen represent immediate labor. The capital in a business represents past labor. "That," Dr. Huebner says, "is the hardest labor there is: you work and don't spend." From that saving comes the tools for immediate labor to use today. It costs about fourteen thousand dollars in capital to provide a job for one worker in industry today. That past labor too must have its fair share of today's profits.

A different kind of past labor makes its contribution to Dr. Huebner's present financial picture. That is his writing. The royalties on his books are still a factor of considerable importance. Thus he has a double gratification: the monetary reward and the knowledge of the continued usefulness of his publications.

Dr. Huebner frequently has said that life insurance is the best property that any human being can own. He has pointed out that it is unique in capitalizing a man's life value and for the protection of dependents in case of premature death. He and Dr. McCahan wrote a whole book about its absolute safety and many advantages as an investment. Dr. Huebner has appreciated the convenience of its investment machinery during the saving years, and now is benefiting by the opportunity to annuitize his savings at a very favorable rate established long ago. He is comfortable also in the knowledge of income service that is available to Mrs. Huebner under his policy settlement arrangements. He has turned to his own life insurance cash values when he needed to borrow money, and it has provided useful credit in other ways. Though he hopes it never will be needed, he likes the assurance of the protection from claims of creditors for named beneficiaries under life insurance policies.

Dr. Huebner believes in life insurance, he owns life insurance, he preaches life insurance. But he appreciates that it is not the only financial tool a man can use. His own estate shows how he has built upon the life insurance foundation with wisdom and considerable good fortune.

CHAPTER SEVENTEEN

South America

Dr. Huebner became Emeritus Professor of Insurance of the University of Pennsylvania on July 1, 1953. For some men, the day of compulsory retirement from a job which has meant lifelong satisfaction brings bitterness and frustration. For Dr. Huebner, that day proved the launching platform for new achievements. Half a dozen years later one of his colleagues said, almost with wistfulness: "What turn of events could be more satisfying? He has enjoyed the ideal phase of a life of accomplishment. He has been visiting friends and former students, helping them, being entertained, seeing organizations in which he has had a formative part developing to greater usefulness, refreshing his statements of sound doctrine to eager audiences, and implanting new ideas in the minds of many who still look to him for leadership."

Dr. Huebner naturally felt the breaking of ties of a lifetime of daily associations, but his spirit of anticipation of his new career was evident at his retirement dinner. The members of the Insurance Department and their wives, with other officers of the Wharton School, met to do him honor. He delighted them with his valedictory talk. He reminisced about his half century of teaching. He poked fun at himself as a young professor. He recalled mutual moments of merriment. He drew a happy and humorous picture of what was to come. His little audience laughed and laughed, and never forgot the crowning fellowship of that evening together.

It has been estimated that through the University Dr. Huebner has had more than seventy-five thousand students. He left the touch of his personality on these men and he gave them too a lasting impression about life insurance. One student commented: "He has probably pre-sold more life insurance than any man in the world. He lectured to nearly every student who went through Wharton for two generations, and nobody went out of there without appreciating life insurance."

Recently, when the question of Dr. Huebner's wide influence was mentioned, a prominent life underwriter spoke up: "Just two weeks ago in Pittsburgh I called on a new client. I did not know anything about his background but in the first two minutes of his conversation I sensed something, and I asked him, 'Did you study at the Wharton School under Dr. Huebner?' He started in surprise and asked, 'How did you know?' I told him that the philosophy always comes out. Many, many times I have realized how men in finance, industry and business areas quite apart from life insurance, who have been conditioned by Dr. Huebner's insurance classes, respond to my sales ideas quite differently than those without that experience."

A former student, who became a C.L.U. and highly successful salesman, wrote:

> The good Doctor has sold lots of insurance without ever having an application signed. It was all indirect selling and we agents are the ones who got the orders from the people who had come in contact with "Old Sol" and his famous lectures. As a student of his in the Wharton School insurance courses as well as in the C.L.U. preparatory courses it was my good fortune to be greatly inspired and to receive basic philosophy which remains with me to this day. In addition to this philosophy and knowledge which was imparted to me and the other men who were majoring in insurance Dr. Huebner influenced the thinking of the numerous other students who were taking the required courses (Insurance I) so that they were most

Vernon Pick, uranium prospector of Grand Junction, Colorado, giving an ore specimen to Dr. Huebner in exchange for a copy of *The Economics of Life Insurance* which he is holding under his arm, October, 1954. (*Daily Sentinel* Photo)

receptive to an insurance discussion three or four years later when they were contacted by me and other agents who were endeavoring to start these people out on their insurance programs.

The point which he so vehemently drove home to us was "the important thing to insure is the goose that lays the golden egg." He would grit his teeth, get red in the face and bang loudly on the rostrum to drive home the "life value" theory and I am certain that he made it clear to every single person in the room.

It was once my good fortune to have Dr. Huebner sit in on a service interview that I had with his secretary. She owned some insurance in the Mutual Benefit Life Insurance Company and I was asked by the Philadelphia Agency of that company to provide the service which she requested. Dr. Huebner sat in the interview because he wanted to be sure that she was getting the best of advice on her personal insurance. Actually he said very little during the interview but would probably have said more had I not satisfied him and the client as to the problems and questions which she had. The point I am trying to make is that this is typical of the interest which he had taken in individuals as well as groups, and it helps to bring out the kind of a person that he is.

Dr. Huebner frequently speaks of good underwriters being humble. His feeling is that the better a man is, the more humble he should be. He himself is very modest, quiet and unassuming. His manner changes, however, when he has a chance to deal with his favorite subject of insurance, at which time his enthusiasm rises to the sky and his quietness disappears with strong verbal feeling.

A woman underwriter wrote reporting a reaction that was duplicated by life insurance men and women, experienced or novices, in all parts of the country. She said: "That man has done so much for me personally. He spoke here in Minneapolis a few years ago, and I was so excited about the Human Life Value Idea that I went right out and sold a very hard-boiled dentist and another case that very same day."

The logic of his vigorous presentation of the hazard to the human life value through "the casket death" (premature death), "the living death" (total and permanent disability), and "the economic death" (compulsory retirement) was contagious and irresistible. These were the ideas he had expounded in his earliest speeches to life insurance salesmen. He expanded and illustrated his concepts in the book *The Economics of Life Insurance,* first published in 1927 especially for the C.L.U. students, and strengthened still further in subsequent editions in 1944 and 1959. The life value idea gave life insurance a definite scientific economic basis, as he liked to say, "a track to run on," such as other applied economic subjects had.

It made possible application to the human life value of the same economic principles used for property values.

Through all the various developments in the life insurance industry, the principles still applied. At his retirement, Dr. Huebner was interested to comment about some of the innovations which he had seen come to the life insurance business. In kinds of coverage there were group life insurance, accident and health, disability and hospitalization, and all the forms of government insurance, as well as the whole Social Security program. In underwriting matters there were the development of substandard coverage, nonmedical insurance, and ordinary insurance from age 0, and the highly important change in the mid-1940's to the C.S.O. Table of Mortality for ordinary companies and the general lowering of the interest assumption in calculation of premiums. In life insurance services there were all the developments in the use of settlement options, life insurance for tax and philanthropic purposes, credit life insurance, variable annuities, and pension plans funded through life insurance.

He liked to recall the unusual experiences which stood out during his teaching career. There was one occasion when a professor in his department reported a serious charge of a student's cheating on his examination. Dr. Huebner reviewed the examination book laid before him. The words written on the page did indeed have the familiar ring of his own phraseology. He compared them with the textbook. Sentence after sentence, paragraph after paragraph were there verbatim. He summoned the student to discuss "a rather unpleasant little matter." The young man straightened in resentment at the idea of dishonesty and stated that he had a photographic mind; it was just easier to run off the answers to the questions as he saw them in his mind's eye. He told Dr. Huebner to open the book anywhere, give him the page number or a few key words, and have his own proof. When Dr. Huebner did so, the student performed as he had said he could—an amazing demonstration of a rare talent. Dr. Huebner commented, however, that although the examination showed perfection on the factual questions, the "thought questions" were below average. Years later he met the student again. He had a civil service job in Washington doing routine work excellently as a glorified clerk. His remarkable memory had not been supplemented by creative ability and leadership qualities.

Another recollection that gave Dr. Huebner great satisfaction was of an unusual result of a dependable performance of duty. An institution for the blind in a Philadelphia suburb had a program of lectures for its students. Upon one occasion Dr. Huebner had agreed to speak there on rather short notice, substituting for another man. When the night came it was horrible weather, a driving rain which made the thought of walking and waiting for the trolley, in fact of the whole idea, very unattractive compared to his comfortable rocking chair in the study at home. But he had promised, so he went. In the course of Dr. Huebner's lecture, all the lights in the room went out. They never came on again during his talk, but Dr. Huebner could discourse about his favorite subject in the dark, and night and day were the same for most of his audience. So they proceeded comfortably and with gratifying results. Two of the blind men who listened that night were inspired to go into life insurance selling. One made a success far above the average. His activities went beyond providing for his own livelihood, and he was honored by the citizens of Philadelphia for "exceptional service" to the blind. For many years his Christmas greeting reminded Dr. Huebner again that the rewards of a dedicated teacher were great.

With retirement from the University Dr. Huebner naturally gave up his office there. New quarters were made available to him in a big room on the second floor of the American College headquarters. This office was furnished by the Fidelity Mutual

Life Insurance Company of Philadelphia as a token of their appreciation for his contribution to life underwriters. The room shares the basic style of the building, which was a handsome residence in the 1920's. It has dark woodwork, a ten-foot

Dr. Huebner at his desk in his rocking chair. Picture taken by a Japanese visitor in 1956. (*Nishimoto*)

bay window with a broad sill, and a dark-green tiled fireplace with a high mantel shelf. The Fidelity provided a rich oriental rug, comfortable leather armchairs, several work tables and files, and the big desk. The desk chair, with its back to the windows, was the faithful old wooden rocker, gift from his faculty in 1927. There Dr. Huebner established himself to rock and work, the window sill behind him piled high with pamphlets and manuscripts, the desk before him full of books and correspondence. When he lifts his eyes to the right, he sees a large oil painting of Edward A. Woods, one of the men who worked with him for thirteen years to start the American College, and who lived only a few months as the College's first president. Across the room, ranged along the mantel piece, seven photographs bring to mind richest memories. These are pictures of Julian S. Myrick, David McCahan, Davis W. Gregg, the C.L.U. conferment dinner at which the Huebner Foundation was announced, Emory R. Johnson, Ernest J. Clark, and again Edward A. Woods. If Dr. Johnson in the photograph could become Dr. Johnson in person, would he remind Dr. Huebner in this beautiful room that he had promised him only austerities in life as a teacher?

Much as Dr. Huebner appreciated the new office and faithfully as he appeared there for each working day while he was in town, yet he still had keen interest in travel. The very year of his retirement was made memorable by an award from the National Board of Fire Underwriters—money for him and Mrs. Huebner to take an insurance goodwill tour of South America. It was very important that Mrs. Huebner make this trip with him, for they discovered that all business was lavishly accompanied by social affairs. They sailed from New York on the last day of September, 1953 on an Argentine liner. Dr. Huebner was quite "tuckered out" with the strain of breaking ties at the University and getting adjusted to new routines at the American College. They both welcomed the restfulness of the long sea voyage. They found that there were many industrialists and bankers aboard ship going out to assignments in South America or returning home after business in the States. When they were inclined to seek company, these people became very pleasant traveling associates.

They crossed the Equator, Mrs. Huebner's first experience, and knew that to the west was the five thousand-mile bulging coastline of Brazil. That country was to be their first stop. They recalled that, unlike the rest of South America, it had a Portuguese background, having been claimed by Portugal in 1500, and having welcomed the Portuguese royal family in exile in the early nineteenth century. Since a bloodless revolution in 1889, Brazil has been a republic. Their destination, Rio de Janeiro, the capital, is nearer to Spain than to New York City. The end of the two-week voyage was at hand. The ship passed the gigantic cone of Sugar Loaf Mountain, and they were in the harbor. They were told that all the navies of the world could ride at anchor there together. Its beauty was overwhelming. Dr. Huebner mentally compared it to the Bay of Naples which he previously had thought the loveliest of its kind, with its sparking blue water and Vesuvius rising in the distance. Rio's waters were blue too, and there were many mountains, also the beautiful city curved along the western shore between the harbor and the overhanging hills. It was an amazingly modern city. They found it had been practically rebuilt in the last fifty years. It has much striking contemporary architecture in the setting of broad streets lined by royal palms and walks lined by feathery bamboo.

In Rio they began their combination of work and play. Dr. Huebner gave half a dozen formal lectures to various associations and organizations both in the life and property fields. They were royally entertained at receptions, luncheons, and dinners. Many events were in private clubs that were artistically beautiful and luxurious beyond anything they had seen in North America. Always the ladies were a prominent part of the group, and the Huebners understood why it was important to their purpose for Dr. Huebner also to have his wife in the company. They were in Rio for about two weeks and felt that they learned much about the ways of South America that prepared them for the rest of the trip. Especially did they begin to get used to the late hours, for South American dinners followed long cocktail parties and, with their many speeches and responses, lasted until about midnight.

Incidentally, Dr. Huebner had all his life been a teetotaler so far as hard liquor was concerned. (Beer did not count for anybody raised in Wisconsin.) However, a few years before his South American trip he had begun to partake moderately. His doctor felt that a drink or two at the end of the day would be relaxing. This modification of his habits was warmly welcomed by many of his old friends who found much opportunity to tease him about his "medicine." It also proved a helpful preparation for the social activities of South America.

From Rio the Huebners went to Sao Paulo, in the highlands about forty miles from the sea, one of the world's greatest coffee markets. There Dr. Huebner gave five lectures for insurance men. They expected to have time for sightseeing but discovered that, due to a church holiday, plane schedules were disrupted. If he wanted to get to Montevideo in Uruguay for his next scheduled lecture, they would have to leave immediately, flying north to Rio in order to fly south again out of Brazil. This was Mrs. Huebner's first airplane flight. Dr. Huebner had always refused to fly before his retirement from the University. In the late summer of 1953, he had finally succumbed to Dr. Gregg's urgings and joined him in a flight to Cleveland for the annual meeting of the National Association of Life Underwriters. The day was ideally clear, the plane behaved perfectly (though it was only a *two*-engine Convair, which may have seemed meager insurance to Dr. Huebner), the United Air Lines captain came back to talk to his famous passenger, the hostess was charming. Everything combined to make Dr. Huebner feel thoroughly satisfied with his first experience of air travel. Flying in South America was, therefore, still a novelty for him also. Dr. and Mrs. Huebner enjoyed this first flight together in spite of hectic arrangements for embarkation and a take-off in a fog, which was a bit disconcerting for novices.

The lecture and friendly contacts in Montevideo were accomplished comfortably. The Huebners were impressed by the city which architecturally was so different from Rio. It was full of ancient buildings, many of a Moorish design, reflecting the early Spanish influence. Economically they admired the country. It reminded them of Switzerland for stability and industry. The currency there was sound, in striking contrast to most of the other countries.

Buenos Aires was the next stop, the largest city in South America and in all of Latin America. It had been receiving refugees from the troubled parts of all the rest of the world—Germans, French, Russians, Italians, Chinese, Japanese. There, as in many South American cities, men and women brought talents, and even property in many cases, that contributed to the creative life of the community. Essentially, the source of the country's wealth was the great fertile prairies stretching miles up the river and to the mountains—the pampas, where the waving grass often grew so high as to hide a man on horseback, and where the life on the huge cattle and grain ranches had something of the western North American flavor. Through the port of Buenos Aires streamed enormous shipments of wheat, meat, hides, wool, and flaxseed.

Dr. Huebner gave many lectures in Buenos Aires and some of their most elaborate social engagements were in this city. They were entertained lavishly at the big country estates of prominent businessmen. Their pleasure was tempered by the sense of poverty among the masses of the people. There was a law against tipping as an indignity to labor, but Dr. Huebner said he never anywhere saw so many hands out for gratuities. There was a law, too, regulating foreign exchange, but there was constant speculation in currency. In spite of themselves they made money all the time, and to them it was tragic, for the profits were in effect stolen from the people. The more pesos the Huebners got for their dollar, the less the people were getting for their work.

The Andes are the towering barrier between Argentina and Chile. In the old days the trip by boat from Buenos Aires to Valparaiso through the Straits of Magellan took eleven days. A miracle of engineering built the Trans-Andean Railroad over the mountains, part of the way so steep that cogwheel apparatus had to be used. That trip from one city to the other took forty hours. The Huebners went by air—a journey of only a few hours in transit. Their actual travel time rather spoils the story. After a start in the morning, they had engine trouble and had to turn back. Then there was a seven-hour delay before they took off again. The result was a wonderful experience: they crossed the crest of the Andes at sunset. They flew between the highest peaks, seeming almost to touch Aconcogua, the highest mountain in all the Americas, some twenty-four hundred feet higher than McKinley in Alaska. Below in the valleys was dirty snow, blackened by the October "spring" thaws. On the peaks was the snow glorified by the sunset, gold and rose in the light, purple in the shadows. They felt that this must truly be one of the wonders of all the world.

This was a glorious arrival in a most interesting country. The Huebners heard that Chile is sometimes called "The Shoestring Republic," because it stretches more than half the length of South America along the narrow strip of its Pacific Coast. If superimposed on North America, it would reach from Lower California to Alaska. The major part of its population is concentrated in the center section, about seven hundred miles long and thirty miles wide. That is a region of perpetual spring, one of the most delightful climates, where it rarely freezes or goes higher than eighty degrees. Dr. Huebner calls Santiago the most beautiful city in the world. He lectured at the University of Chile, of course, and spoke also before several other insurance audiences. Santiago is the social and educational center of Chile as well as its political capital. It is over four hundred years old and on every hand has reminders of the Spanish conquerors who founded it. There are many lovely old Spanish houses with luxuriant gardens, patios, and splashing fountains. Broad avenues are shaded by lines of poplar trees and many beautiful statues stand in the little parks where the streets cross. Everywhere there are roses and a great variety of bright flowers. Their willing hosts showed the Huebners these beauties of their city, and drove them too through the adjoining delightful valleys beneath their snow-capped mountains. Again they were lavishly entertained at formal parties.

The Huebners left Chile by boat from Valparaiso. Four hundred miles west of that port is a Chilean possession, the Juan Fernandez Island, where Alexander Selkirk once lived in solitude for four years and inspired the story of Robinson Crusoe. They passed by the famous guano islands which for many years were a great source of wealth to the Peruvians and a boon to agriculture in many parts of the world. The Huebners were going north to the port of Lima in Peru. They crossed the Humboldt Current, that turbulent, icy river sweeping out of the Antarctic which keeps northern Chile and Peru a barren desert, watered only by rivers from the high Andes. The Current is so cold that enough water cannot usually evaporate to form rain, although a heavy mist often sweeps over Lima. The Huebners learned that years sometimes go by without any rain at all, and that the record for a long period shows an average yearly rainfall of little more than an inch. They found Lima a rapidly growing metropolis, then with a population of a million people. Peru is the land of the ancient Inca Empire.

Lima was founded by the Spanish conqueror, Pizarro, who is buried in the crypt below the cathedral. There is a bull ring in the center of the city and much of the architecture has a Spanish look.

Dr. Huebner gave only one lecture in Peru, but they had much pleasure in studying the Inca ruins, in seeing the sights of the old tombs and all the beauties of the tropical city with its palm trees and flowers. Dr. Huebner remarked too upon the great numbers of mourning doves, seeming to speak always of this strange land, "Peru-u-u, Peru-u-u, Peru-u-u," while they reminded him of the faraway turtle doves of Wisconsin.

J. Victor Herd, vice president of the National Board of Fire Underwriters, presents a check to Dr. Huebner, covering the goodwill tour for him and Mrs. Huebner to South America.

The Huebner's host in Lima was a direct descendent of the first viceroy of Peru, and was president of the largest bank and biggest life insurance company in the country. He was most gracious even though he had to talk to them through an interpreter, his secretary, a young man who spoke perfect English. They discussed the economics of the country and found that the Marshall Plan was much misunderstood. The Peruvians felt that North Americans were flooding them with United States goods and would not take their products. They resented the salve of money. Peru is largely a grazing land. Their economy rests heavily upon the cattle, sheep, alpacas, llamas, and their products. Quinine is another important export, made from the cinchona tree and formerly known as "Peruvian bark." Dr. Huebner found that Bethlehem Steel and the Standard Oil were at work there. Peru is a rich country but needs much capital for development. Mrs. Huebner, the tourist, remembers Lima as the city where she walked and walked, hoping to find in the shops something not to be duplicated in Philadelphia, other than the ubiquitous silver and the shrunken human heads from the back country savages.

From Lima they took a fruit boat bound for home. They were happy to relax on deck, but alert, as always, to the sights which met their eyes. They were much interested in the fishing fleets along the coast of Peru. Some were motorized, but others were quite primitive, with sails and rigging such as had been used for centuries. The Huebners never tired of watching the many pelicans which followed the boats, flying high in great curves and dropping suddenly to dive for fish, or just to rest on the water.

Going north in the Pacific, the Huebners crossed the Equator which, two months before, they had crossed going south in the Atlantic. They were headed now for Colombia, where the ship loaded coffee. They turned south and crossed the Equator again, going back to get bananas in Ecuador at Guayaquil. They found Ecuador a typical tropical country. The Humboldt Current is shunted away from Ecuador by the bulge of the continent so that the western winds blowing over the warm sea bring rains to the "Land of the Equator." Guayaquil was formerly dreaded as one of the most deadly ports of the world, but modern knowledge of health and sanitation has prevailed over previous bad conditions. The uplands at the foot of towering mountains are a healthful country. In prehistoric times, the Huebners were interested to learn, a highly civilized people lived there long before the Incas. They built cities and temples of stone, made tools of gold, and even filled teeth with gold. Where and how and why they disappeared is still unknown.

The banana cargo was loaded in the hold, the big bunches hung on huge cables. Again they headed north, and for a fourth time crossed the Equator. They sailed past Colombia and on through the Panama Canal. They felt that was indeed a sight worth seeing, though they realized its wartime value had largely disappeared. The voyage went beautifully until they were well past Cape Hatteras. Then they ran into a raging Northeaster which lasted for two days. Nobody could stand up. Few were interested in meals. The baggage slid back and forth across the stateroom. Worse than that, the bananas on their cables tended to shift too, and the ship was constantly turned in the stormy waters to make their condition as favorable as possible. This was deemed more important than the comfort or the schedule of the passengers.

However, the Huebners reached home safely in time for a wonderful Christmas reunion. All the family was on hand except little granddaughter Elizabeth, who was going to school in Alabama and living there with her other grandmother. Elizabeth is the daughter of Margaret, the Huebners' eldest child. Margaret had been graduated from the University of Pennsylvania with a B.S. degree in education, and later took her Master's at Columbia. She and her husband, Colonel Ralph Nemo of the regular Army, were in Philadelphia for Christmas that year because he had just been released from the Army hospital at Valley Forge and was being retired from the service. Soon after the holidays they left for Florida, where they still live in St. Augustine.

John, his wife, Betty, and their schoolboy sons, Stephen and

Bernard, came from their home in nearby Wynnewood. John, who had taken his undergraduate work at Wharton, specializing in insurance, and law also at Pennsylvania, had entered the Law Department of the Penn Mutual Life Insurance Company upon leaving the University. His skills and interests had led him into underwriting work, and in 1953 he had been for some years a vice president in charge of approving and issuing new business. Currently he is senior vice president of that company.

Queenie came from Trenton, New Jersey, where she was assistant director of occupational therapy at the State Hospital. She had been graduated from Bryn Mawr College and had some years of business experience before she found her life work in the service of mentally disturbed people. She has become a leader in her field, and in 1958 was elected speaker of the House of Delegates of the American Occupational Therapy Association for a two-year term.

Esther Ann, the youngest, arrived for the holidays from New York City. She inherited her Grandfather Huebner's green thumb. She is a graduate of Antioch College and took special work at the Ambler School of Horticulture in Pennsylvania. In New York she had worked for some time with classes for children in the Brooklyn Botanical Garden and in 1953 became gardener in charge of medieval plants at The Cloisters in Fort Tryon Park, New York City, which is part of the Metropolitan Museum of Art. There she now has responsibility for all the trees and flowers and plants which make that reconstructed medieval monastery such a living monument of the past.

As Dr. and Mrs. Huebner welcomed their children home again that Christmas time, they were proud and happy for the way John and each of his sisters had made their own places in the world. The Huebners had never told their children what to do. They gave them moral standards, a good education, and encouragement to follow their own interests in life. Dr. Huebner had never helped any of them to get their jobs. Now after months of absence and thousands of miles of separation, Dr. and Mrs. Huebner looked at their assembled family with new eyes and counted themselves blessed in such children.

Dr. Huebner plunged back into life insurance activities at home. He attended the Christmas holiday meeting of the American Association of University Teachers of Insurance at Washington, D.C. He gladly spoke about his South American tour to interested audiences. He always mentioned their observations of inflation. He believes that inflation is the enemy's greatest weapon against a free economic society. He is frustrated at the blindness of many leaders in this country who seem to learn little from the appalling experiences abroad. We should not be too sure that it can not happen here.

He easily became enthusiastic about the huge economic potential of South America. He felt the surface of possibilities had hardly been scratched in that rich continent. He saw again the opportunity for education to do its wonderful work. He is convinced to the depths of his being that education is the source of power for the individual, the family, an organization, a community, a nation. Through education people grow, develop, and prosper. If educational programs like those in the United States could be carried out in South America, results would be colossal.

CHAPTER EIGHTEEN

Life Conservation

PRACTICING what he preaches about life conservation, Dr. Huebner has for many years had regular periodic physical examinations. Shortly before the South American trip he had received a clean bill of health. He habitually took good care of himself and had always been well except for the frightful experience with arthritis following the infection from the ticks of Yucatan. Without his "farm reserve," as his doctor called it, he probably never would have survived that severe disability. Early in 1954 he was speaking in Chicago to the life underwriters. The room was poorly arranged for the large audience and the microphone failed to operate. He made unusual effort to articulate his words so as to be heard. These unnatural movements caused him to notice his tongue and a queer feeling on one side. As soon as possible after the meeting he looked at the place and saw an odd spot rather like a canker. That concerned him somewhat but he said nothing to anybody, and kept his speaking dates with the C.L.U. and L.U.T.C. groups.

When he got back to Philadelphia, his wife and daughter were not alarmed but felt he was a bit worried and called the doctor. The practiced eye of the physician saw a very serious condition, and Dr. Huebner was immediately taken to the hospital for further examination and treatment.

On March 6, 1954, his seventy-second birthday, the biopsy report came back: cancer. The specialists who had come on the case in addition to Dr. Huebner's own doctor asked John Huebner: "How will your old man take it if we tell him?" To which the son replied: "I don't know exactly, but he'll find out the truth. You can't fool him, and he will not like it if you try."

Looking back, Dr. Huebner believes that he "took it" pretty philosophically. "After all," he said, "what else could you do?" He had faced death before in the depths of his arthritis troubles. He had overheard the doctors then talking outside the door of his hospital room. He knew they thought he could not get well, but he decided he would get up and fight, and he won that battle.

Speaking for himself, he believes he is a better fighter if he knows the facts. He does not have a tendency to go to pieces in the face of bad news, but rather steadfastly determines to do the best he can. He said: "I do fight mentally."

Concerning his cancer, the doctors decided the growth was about four months old, though it involved jaw, tongue, and tonsil. They were most reassuring and emphasized the possibility of cure. Dr. Huebner agreed to "be a guinea pig" for some new procedures. A mold was made and fitted into his mouth so that radium treatment could reach all the affected parts. A long series of three-hour periods of discomfort followed. But with that schedule Dr. Huebner combined a schedule of classes too, and even short trips and some public addresses. His own work went on while he returned constantly to the hospital for the doctors to do their work for him. He was studied by specialists who were learning from his case. At last the end of the course of treatments was at hand, but the doctors asked to make assurance sure with a second series half as long as the first. Finally, in July, they told their patient that they believed him cured. He reported for a monthly examination for two years and still is having a semiannual check. The trouble seems to be completely eliminated now. The cause, the doctors felt, was smoking. For years Dr. Huebner had enjoyed at least ten cigars a day and a few pipes. Dr. Huebner says that some people are still arguing about the relation between cancer and tobacco. He admits that statistics in themselves do not prove anything, but they do tell a story. And findings of ten to one chances for mouth or lung cancer in smokers as compared with nonsmokers, based on studies involving thousands of people, are more than suggestive.

One of the engagements Dr. Huebner kept that spring of 1954 was for a lecture in a series presented at the University of Connecticut sponsored by the School of Business Administration under a grant from the New York Life Insurance Company. The audience for the series was composed of students, life insurance company representatives, and others interested in life insurance, and the lectures were later published in permanent form for student use. Dr. Huebner talked on "Professional Progress in Insurance Education." He gave a masterly review of the C.L.U. and C.P.C.U. programs, of insurance courses in universities and secondary schools, and of organizations having to do with insurance teaching. He also made some pertinent remarks about how a calling becomes recognized as a profession.

> Everybody seems to want his calling to be regarded as a *profession*, if it is at all significant by way of educational preparation and, in subsequent practice, of beneficent service to humanity . . .
>
> Insurance underwriting is no exception to this general wish. Even as early as 1904, when I commenced my teaching of insurance on the collegiate level, in both the life and property fields, I found quite a few of the leaders, especially in life underwriting, speaking of their calling as a profession. . . .
>
> There is, of course, a world of difference between the professional concept attaching to the lone individual within a calling and the

> same concept for the calling as a whole—to all the trees in the forest of practitioners and not only to a limited few. I do recall very vividly how so many referred to themselves individually as professional in training and daily practice, but at the same time referred to the calling as most unprofessional for the overwhelming majority. They seemed to want public professional recognition of themselves, while the calling as a whole, even on the basis of their own statements did not merit the public commendation and dignity that we associate with the professional concept. . . .
>
> A calling cannot be made a profession by a public statement from some of its own practitioners. Nor can it be made a profession by legislative act. The professional status must be earned by the calling. A calling, viewed as a whole and not from the standpoint of lone individual practitioners, becomes recognized as a profession when it is accepted by the public as such, because of (a) a fair understanding by the public of the nobility and service-necessity of the calling, and (b) the general public understanding that high standards of knowledge and ethics are used inflexibly by all or by a very substantial proportion of the practitioners within the calling.

The next month, on a speaking trip to the Southwest, the C.L.U.'s inspired the mayor of Houston to designate a Life Insurance Day in Dr. Huebner's honor. The concluding words of his proclamation read:

> Now, therefore, I, Roy Hofheinz, Mayor of the City of Houston, in order to honor this fine old gentleman who has contributed so much to this chosen field of his life's work, and in order to commend him upon his achievements in his abundant career and in order to commend the Houston C.L.U. Chapter upon having this outstanding leader as its guiding star, do hereby proclaim Friday, April 30, 1954, as Life Insurance Day.

He was also made an admiral of the Great Navy of the State of Nebraska and a commodore of the Oklahoma Navy. The next year, again in Texas, Governor Allan Shivers made him an honorary Texan, citizen of the Lone Star State.

More serious honorary recognitions were given him also at this period. While he was in South America he had received news of nomination as an honorary member by the Japanese Society of Insurance Science. That year also he had been the first man to be named an honorary member of the Insurance Forum of San Francisco. In 1954 he was made an honorary member of the Insurance Company Education Directors' Society.

In mid-summer of 1954, Dr. Huebner personally, and many of the organizations with which he was closely associated, suffered a shocking loss. Dr. David McCahan died of a heart attack. He was only fifty-six years old and left a wife and four children. Dr. McCahan had been an officer of the American College since 1929, serving successively as assistant dean, secretary, dean, executive vice president, and president. He was secretary of the American Society from 1930 to 1945. He was executive director of the Huebner Foundation from its beginning. He was very active in his church and the board of education of Swarthmore where he lived, and had many other community, business, and professional responsibilities. He was a prodigiously hard worker, a man of sterling character, and an educator with highest academic standards. He left his enduring mark on the organizations with which he was associated, and treasured memories to his friends.

Following Dr. McCahan's death, Davis W. Gregg became president of the American College. Dr. Gregg had been dean since 1951, and had come to the College as assistant dean in 1949 from a professorship at Ohio State University. Dr. Gregg had taken his doctorate at the University of Pennsylvania as one of the early Huebner Foundation fellows. Thus Dr. Huebner was again very happy about the new leadership of the American College.

In 1955 the Wisconsin State Association of Life Underwriters celebrated the fiftieth anniversary of life insurance education, with Dr. Huebner as their honored guest at a sales congress. A feature of this occasion was the presentation to him

Life trustees of the American College, 1954. ***Left to right,*** **Ernest J. Clark, Dr. S. S. Huebner, Julian S. Myrick, J. Stanley Edwards, and Paul F. Clark.**

of a tribute signed by the governor of Wisconsin and by the presidents of the American Society of Chartered Life Underwriters, the Life Underwriters Association of Wisconsin, and the University of Wisconsin. The citation read:

> The people and organizations which we represent join in formal tribute to Solomon Stephen Huebner, B.L., M.L., Ph.D., Sc.D., distinguished native son of Wisconsin, graduate of its Public Schools and its University, and the founder and teacher of the first college course in insurance on the occasion of the Fiftieth Anniversary of Insurance Education.
>
> Internationally renowned as teacher, economist, author and lecturer, Dr. Huebner has devoted his life to the development of education in the field of insurance. As a great intellectual pioneer he conceived the ideas and wrote the books that were needed to make insurance education in college possible.
>
> His basic concept of human life values and his realization of the need for professional training and of a high standard of ethics for life underwriters were ideas that matured in the American College of Life Underwriters. His unceasing efforts to increase the opportunities for the training of teachers and the education of students of insurance, and to have life underwriting become a recognized profession, have resulted in untold benefits to his fellow man.
>
> In this scroll we record our sense of indebtedness, appreciation, respect and affection for Dr. Huebner.

Many kinds of groups seemed to vie with each other to do honor to the beloved professor. In 1956 he was called to New York City for an occasion which meant a great deal to him. The University of Pennsylvania Club there had adopted a plan of recognizing annually some individual, who had made an outstanding contribution to the University, by an honor called the Benjamin Franklin Award. Dr. Huebner was its first recipient. It was presented at a formal dinner at the club. Dr. Gaylord P. Harnwell, president of the University, and Julian S. Myrick, chairman of the board of the American College, were the evening's chief speakers. Tangible evidence of the award was a memorial scroll for the recipient, and the engraving of his name on the handsome silver trophy cup.

The next year Dr. Huebner was bracketed again with Benjamin Franklin, this time not in association with the University but through their common activity in insurance. At Ohio State University, through the Charles W. Griffith Foundation for Insurance Education, an Insurance Hall of Fame was initiated. The purpose was to honor those who from the beginning had contributed most to the thought and practice of insurance in the United States and Canada. Forty-five insurance leaders from both countries were the first Board of Electors. Their first recommendations were chosen from among one hundred thirty-five nominations, judging by seven criteria: original thinking, contributions to insurance literature, recognition as an authority, public service, previous honor awards in the profession, service of a professional character to insurance organizations, and honorary degrees. Three men were selected for the first year's honors, two pioneers of the past and a living leader.

Dr. Huebner receiving the Benjamin Franklin cup award in New York City, 1956. *Left to right,* Thomas I. Parkinson, Dr. Clay Boland, Dr. James W. Lee, Dr. Huebner, Luther Martin, III, Julian S. Myrick.

The announcements were made on March 1, 1957 at a formal luncheon with three hundred and fifty guests held as a part of the University's annual insurance conference. The first leader of the past was Benjamin Franklin, who had founded the first fire insurance company in the United States, and whose award was received by an officer of the Philadelphia Contributionship for the Insurance of Homes from Loss by Fire. The second man honored was Elizur Wright of Massachusetts, who pioneered state supervision of life insurance and whose prodigious labors made life insurance safe and fair through the legislation and nonforfeiture provisions which he promoted. His posthumus award was accepted by the Massachusetts Insurance Commissioner.

Ohio State University Insurance Hall of Fame Ceremony, 1957. ***Left to right,*** **Walter L. Smith, Jr.; Dr. Novice G. Fawcett, president of Ohio State University; Ohio's Governer C. William O'Neill; Dr. Huebner; Joseph A. Humphreys, Massachusetts' Commissioner of Insurance. (*Ohio State University Photo*)**

The living man honored was Dr. Huebner, whose citation read in part: "His untiring efforts have done more to raise the professional and ethical standards of the insurance industry than the activities of any other American."

Amidst prolonged applause, President Novice G. Fawcett of the University hung about Dr. Huebner's neck a beautiful silver medal on a ribbon of the University scarlet. The inscription on the medal read:

Awarded to Solomon S. Huebner
Leadership — Enterprise — Innovation
Integrity — Vision
1957
Ohio State University
Insurance Hall of Fame,
Presentation to
Benjamin Franklin, Elizur Wright
and S. S. Huebner, March 1st
1957

That spring Dr. and Mrs. Huebner took another long trip, speaking for life underwriter associations, C.L.U. chapters, and L.U.T.C. groups. They traveled some fifteen thousand miles in thirty-one days, during which Dr. Huebner made twenty-two major addresses.

It was six weeks of unusual happenings as well as of the habitual round of enjoyable welcomes by life insurance friends and audiences. They went by way of Chicago, Denver, and Phoenix to Los Angeles and thence to Hawaii. In Honolulu Dr. Huebner was particularly happy to renew acquaintance with the life underwriters, for he had spoken to them there in 1927 on his way to the Orient. The underwriters at that time were in the course of deciding whether to become part of the National Association of Life Underwriters. The inspiration of

Dr. and Mrs. Huebner as guests at a Japanese Tea Party in Honolulu in 1957. Notice the kimonos and Dr. Huebner's stocking feet.

Dr. Huebner's visit had its effect in increasing the Hawaiians' interest in contacts in the States, and the Honolulu Association was officially recognized in 1928.

Returning to San Francisco, they arrived on the very day of that city's most serious recent earthquakes. Dr. Huebner had met earthquakes first in Japan in 1927. While lecturing there to a most courteous audience, he had been startled to have the students suddenly all rush out the doors and through the windows. They had felt a first slight shock and expected a second severer one. It came with no damage, and the young men trouped matter-of-factly back to proceed with the lecture. Similarly, in San Francisco the earthquake was disturbing but not harmful.

With such interesting interruptions of travel and honors, Dr. Huebner was meanwhile deep in plans for the International Insurance Conference to be held in connection with the seventy-fifth anniversary of the Wharton School. He was a member of the Sponsoring Committee for the Conference. He would be one of the speakers. Of course he looked forward to renewing acquaintance at the meeting with many who had been his students and who had gone home to far countries to be leaders in the industry. He anticipated seeing again people who had been kind to him in his travels overseas.

The Wharton School in 1957 had more than two thousand undergraduate students and about five hundred and fifty graduate students. Some thirty foreign countries were represented in this enrollment by more than a hundred students. The international character of the Wharton School itself, as well as its insurance leadership, made the plan of the Conference most appropriate.

The Conference was presented in May, 1957 by the University of Pennsylvania "in recognition of the insurance industry's long and continued interest in the affairs of Wharton School as pioneer in the collegiate field of insurance education." There had been many previous international insurance meetings in the areas of marine insurance and actuarial work, but it is believed that this was the first to cover the entire field of insurance. The theme of the program was "The Role of Private Enterprise in Insuring Life and Property Values."

Dr. Davis W. Gregg and Dr. Dan M. McGill were co-directors of the conference. Co-chairmen of the Sponsoring Committee were John A. Diemand, president of the Insurance Company of North America, and M. Albert Linton, chairman of the Provident Mutual Life Insurance Company. A long list of outstanding leaders of insurance appeared on the letterhead carrying the invitation, and it was felt that the attractive possibility of meeting these men was one reason for the excellent response. A reporter cited evidence of that in quoting a man from Egypt and one from Pakistan who had each told him that they had come so far to meet the great figures in the world of insurance.

Four hundred guests assembled from all over the United States and from thirty foreign countries. The Conference was opened by an international reception at which Mayor Richardson Dilworth of Philadelphia with his wife was host. Speakers were drawn from all around the world, and all speeches were in English—a considerable tribute to the skills of the guests from overseas. There were discussions of the insurance environment of the major areas of the world where conditions of government supervision or even nationalization of the industry vary so greatly. There were talks on private and state health insurance programs, and reports about international methods of marketing insurance.

Dr. Huebner spoke on the present status and future potential of life and health insurance in the United States. With this country owning more life insurance than all the rest of the world together, it rather startled his audience to hear him refer to this country's four hundred billion dollars of life insurance in force and the five billion dollars of premiums for health and medical insurance as "pitiful" compared to real needs and possibilities.

The Conference was recognized as an international educational insurance event of much importance. Another very valuable feature was pointed out by A. S. Kirkpatrick, manager of the insurance department of the Chamber of Commerce of the United States. Appraising the Conference, he wrote:

> The insurance business in this country lives in an economic and social system in which its future—even its very existence in the years ahead—will be influenced in a major way by what happens in our international relationships as well as at home . . .
>
> The decisions which our country makes will largely depend upon the knowledge and understanding of our thinking people. This certainly includes our business executives. I strongly believe the top

Platform group at International Insurance Conference opening session with speeches by country representatives, May 21, 1957. *Left to right,* Mr. Gen Hirose (Japan), Dr. Huebner (United States), Dr. Jorge Bande (Chile), Mr. M. Albert Linton, chairman, Sir John Benn (England), Mr. Thomas B. Scott (Australia), Mr. Carl Brinier (Switzerland), Mr. Alfred Neil (United States).

> executives of our leading insurance companies have got to be prepared in the years ahead to be better informed and have a more intimate understanding of the problems, hopes and ambitions of the people of various foreign countries. And I think that the most natural lines of communication for acquiring this knowledge is through personal contact with the insurance executives from abroad.

This is an unusual way in which the insurance leaders of the world, through international understanding, may help in the conservation of life and property values. Perhaps their business friendships may help to delay the devastation and destruction of world war.

Dr. Huebner's last public contribution in 1957 was through an article in the December issue of *The Journal of Insurance,* the quarterly of the American Association of University Teachers of Insurance. He presented an educator's view of "Future Patterns of Life Insurance Distribution." The article grew out of the year's experience, as he indicated in his introduction. He had felt quite frequently, as he traveled around the country, underlying doubts about the future of life insurance activity. He acknowledged the changes that had come in life insurance, particularly with the increasing use of group coverages and of publicity about one-stop services. But he emphasized the great variety of other changes which call for increasing technical skill and professional attitude on the part of the man who serves the public. In any time of change the factors do not come into balance immediately, but he saw the solution of this situation in a great future move toward a continuing client relationship between the insured and the underwriter.

While notable progress has been made in this direction, the potential is still enormous. He summarized what had been accomplished in his lifetime to bring both underwriter and client nearer to this ideal condition.

> The main support of a client relationship between insured and underwriter is insurance education along economic lines for both the

insured and his underwriter. A program of well-organized economic education in insurance, largely absent in the 1920's, is now rapidly growing. That program is the most outstanding, forward-looking insurance movement in the United States. For this reason, the growth potential of life and health insurance (both teammates) is enormous. Many, like *Fortune* (Magazine), already predict a trillion dollars of life insurance on the books within the next ten to fifteen years. And when the first trillion dollars has been attained, the second trillion will be secured much more easily.

On the one hand, through the efforts of The American College of Life Underwriters and the American Institute for Property and Liability Underwriters, life (including health) and non-life insurance are rapidly being given a professional status on the collegiate level with their Chartered Life Underwriter (C.L.U.) and Chartered Property and Casualty Underwriter (C.P.C.U.) programs of study. The latter program (incorporated in 1940) naturally grew out of the former (incorporated in 1927), and both programs are similar in purpose and equally thorough in their respective fields. By way of illustration, the number of C.L.U. designation holders numbered nearly 6,200 in 1956; and an additional 8,700 had passed one or more, but not all, of the five professional examinations. For 1957, 7,250 life underwriters were enrolled in 352 organized study groups in 193 cities, as compared with 291 groups in 168 cities in 1956. About half of all the enrollees are in organized groups conducted solely under the auspices of a university or college or by an institution of higher learning working jointly with a C.L.U. Chapter or Life Underwriters Association.

In the case of the American Institute for Property and Liability Underwriters, nearly 2,700 separate C.P.C.U. examinations were taken by over 2,000 persons in 1956. The total designation holders in 1956 amounted to nearly 1,700, while an additional 3,300 persons have credit for passing one or more of the examinations.

In both the life and non-life areas, intermediate training and educational programs (the Life Underwriter Training Council program in life insurance and the Insurance Institute of America program in property-liability insurance) have also developed with amazing success.

On the other hand, the nation's universities and colleges are rapidly emphasizing the economics of insurance—so rapidly in fact that there is great difficulty in meeting the demand for well-trained teachers of insurance. In 1927, only 56 universities and colleges had courses emphasizing insurance economics, as distinguished from mathematics and law. Today the number is probably about 250. Under the leadership of the Life Insurance Institute and the Graduate Workshop for Family Financial Security Education, insurance education of an economic character is entering the nation's high school system at a rate of several hundred high schools per year.

The significance of the aforementioned two-fold program was recently stressed as follows by the author in an address before the International Insurance Conference held in conjunction with the 75th Anniversary of the Wharton School of the University of Pennsylvania.

> The two aforementioned insurance educational movements will mean, within the next 25 years, that a greatly enlarged educated field force of underwriters will be contacting a greatly enlarged insurance-educated and properly indoctrinated public. The result will be the development of a client relationship between the underwriter and his client, similar to what exists in medicine and law. Then "selling" will become "teaching" and "advisorship," as it should be. Then the present lack of a sense of proper family responsibility will be superseded by much higher life insurance per family than now prevails. Insurance education for both underwriters and the buying public is the great ally of the private insurance industry and insurance as an institution.

In closing, reference may again be made to the following four questions, referred to in the first section of this article—questions that clearly indicate doubt and fear:

Do you think the field of a life underwriter is narrowing?

What will be the future of the life-only underwriter in the next 25 years?

What do you think of the possibility of combining general insurance and life insurance in many of the offices?

Do you think it desirable for a man to be both a C.L.U. and a C.P.C.U.?

As regards the first two questions, this article should leave no doubt or fear that the properly-educated life underwriter, in terms of knowledge of subject matter and professional attitude, will have a narrowing field of opportunity. Even as a life-only underwriter (assuming the inclusion of health insurance) he will have expanding opportunities which tend more and more to a lasting client relationship with his insured.

With respect to the final two questions, the answers also seem clear. The growing multiple line pattern is here to stay. It is not objectionable to combine life and non-life insurance in the same office, assuming that the underwriter is properly trained and that there is no desire merely to "tack on" other forms of insurance for the sole purpose of increased commission income and greater volume. There is no harm in a man striving to be both a C.L.U. and a C.P.C.U. The double program is a difficult one, and although there are some 80 persons who have both professional designations, the author feels there will likely never be many who will seek the double goal, except among teachers of insurance. Rather, what will happen is the establishment of partnerships between C.L.U.'s and C.P.C.U.'s, as in medicine, where that procedure by doctors of different skills is already noticeable. A C.L.U., who will handle a client's life insurance affairs, will join in partnership with a C.P.C.U., who will handle the same client's property-liability insurance needs. Thus their joint action, both assuming responsibility for their respective professional fields, will establish a client relationship that will provide a service covering completely the insurance needs of the insured.

CHAPTER NINETEEN

The Far East and "Down Under"

THE year 1958 opened with the Huebner's thoughts turning to the other side of the world. The previous spring when Japanese insurance executives had attended the International Insurance Conference in Philadelphia, they had proposed that Dr. Huebner make a lecture tour to a number of Japanese universities. As consideration of the idea developed, Dr. Huebner had been asked by the State Department to undertake a broad mission of international friendship. He decided to go and to take Mrs. Huebner with him. They were getting ready to leave in May. There was much correspondence, inoculations, planning, and packing. Dr. Huebner never relaxed his usual schedule of activities, however.

In February he was slated to speak to the life underwriters of Newark, New Jersey. The morning of his meeting he awoke in his suburban home to see heavy snow. Like the honored postman, his attitude always is to let neither snow nor rain nor heat nor gloom of night stay him from the completion of his appointed rounds. So he struggled through the drifts to the local railroad station and onto a crowded train to Philadelphia. There he found himself in a maelstrom of would-be travelers awaiting trains which had not appeared, but almost immediately after his arrival the New York express came in. Dr. Huebner let himself be pushed aboard and rode quite comfortably to Newark. There again he fought the snow to reach the meet-

Birthday cake with rocking chair decoration provided for Dr. Huebner by the American College on March 6, 1958. (*Shaw*)

ing place, where a record-breaking crowd of life underwriters assembled to hear him. That audience always remembered the enthusiastic professor, still meeting his engagements at age seventy-six and delivering his message of confidence and conviction. Dr. Huebner was snowed-in at Newark until the next day. That was the famous storm which disabled all the Pennsylvania electric locomotives for more than a week.

In March his associates at the American College gave him a birthday luncheon. Since his retirement and his daily work at 3924 Walnut, the men and women there had come to know him better. The staff felt increasing pride in him, and always great affection. The morning of the luncheon, one of the men had a thought. He went down the street to a little neighborhood toy store and asked if they had any doll furniture, specifically a rocking chair. The proprietor looked at him almost as if he could not believe his ears. "What's the matter with everybody around here?" he asked. "You're the fourth person this morning who has wanted a doll's rocking chair."

Four thoughtful, but uncommunicative, people at the American College had had the same bright idea, but there was only one rocking chair on Dr. Huebner's cake that noon. He greatly appreciates such little attentions.

During those years after 1953 as new young men became members of the College staff, they naturally were particularly interested in the opportunity for daily associations with Dr. Huebner, the president emeritus. Most of them had known him from their student days. Some had been Huebner Foundation fellows. One commented that he had long been familiar with Dr. Huebner's evangelistic zeal for the professional idea in life insurance; he had regarded Dr. Huebner as a wonderful old gentleman, deservedly revered for his pioneering; but in work on the staff he saw this leader in a new light. He was impressed by Dr. Huebner's continuing power. He said that more than once he had seen a staff group in discussion begin to work toward a conclusion with which Dr. Huebner did not agree. Then, in amazement, the younger man had watched him lay facts on the line, expound principles, and by sheer force of logic and right turn the group to quite a contrary decision.

The staff men constantly go to Dr. Huebner with their current problems of the American College and Society. As he helps them reach conclusions, he stands firmly on the experience of the past, but with a forward look he applies the fundamental principles which he has tested. In contrast to so many leaders of the past, he is still definitely a man of today and tomorrow.

His younger associates feel that he is still their teacher. They value beyond measure the help which he is always ready and able to give. Their attitude toward Dr. Huebner is undoubtedly one of the reasons for his continued great capacity. The stimulus of being needed and of having the opportunity to contribute to present activities are creative forces which many older men lack.

Not only do Dr. Huebner's associates appreciate his help, but they greatly enjoy his company. When noontime approaches, some of the younger men are sure to give him a call, hoping to have him as a companion at the lunch table. At the near-by Penn-Sherwood Hotel, which is their favorite lunching place, everybody is glad to give Dr. Huebner special attention. The hat-check girl has a husband who admires him as a teacher. The hostess always makes certain he has an armchair. The head waiter, who is a refugee banker from Europe, talks to him about international economics.

Of course, in 1958 when the day of departure for the Orient drew near, there had to be a bon voyage party for Dr. Huebner. Julian Myrick from New York was host, and the farewell luncheon was attended by associates from 3924 Walnut and prominent educators and life insurance company executives of the Philadelphia area. They were proud to send out this ambassador to the insurance industry and the universities in the Far East.

Another larger group gave him farewell cheers. His son John was president that year of the Home Office Life Underwriters Association. Its annual meeting in May, at Atlantic City, attracted some three hundred members and guests. At the opening session, Mr. Huebner introduced the first speaker as follows:

> It is the custom of this Association to grant the President the privilege of selecting the guest speaker for the opening session. I would like the record to show that I am grateful for that privilege because it made it possible for me to invite a most unusual man to be with us. He is renowned throughout the insurance industry in all its branches. He is well known to your agency forces and has taught many of them . . . [Mr. Huebner gave a brief biographical sketch of Dr. Huebner and then concluded.]
>
> I would like to make one more comment on his retirement. On Monday morning at 8:00 he and Mrs. Huebner fly from Philadelphia on the first leg of a lecture tour through Japan (where he once taught and where his friends are legion), the Philippines, Australia, and New Zealand, under the auspices of the Department of State. He will

be away three months. He postponed this trip for a week to be here with us, and I shall not postpone his appearance longer. I'm proud to present to you my father, Dr. S. S. Huebner.

Dr. Huebner's pleasure in his son's proud presentation was most apparent as he responded:

I want also to say to you that I am very glad to be here. It is a privilege and a great pleasure to address your Association. I have had the opportunity in my lifetime of some 55 years in insurance education to address almost every association known in the industry, but yours happened not to come my way until this time and I am very glad indeed to add it to the list. It is like a feather in the Indian's head paraphernalia.

Then Dr. Huebner went on to make a characteristically forceful and optimistic address. He used the title "The Human Life Value Concept," and outlined again the basic principles of the idea he had preached for a lifetime. But he concluded by bringing the audience up to date in a report of progress in education and in a statement of his estimate of the future. *The Proceedings* of the meeting present his words:

Only about one student out of ten, I guess, ever gets to college, so the Workshop in Education in Family Finance, supported by the Institute of Life Insurance in New York, is preparing teachers for the high schools. That movement started in 1950 at the University of Pennsylvania, where the first pilot course was started. I have been a teacher in it every summer. I am sorry this will be the first summer that I shall not be able to do it, because I enjoyed it. Expenses of the high school teachers are paid, and they come to get an intensive course. Insurance is a part of that course, a most important part. Every year when I finish the life insurance part I ask the class, "If you have ever heard this human life value discussed before as we have done here, please raise your hand." I have yet to see the first hand after these seven years. That is a puzzle to me. We don't seem to reach the dear public.

Then, I say, "The next thing I want to ask you is: Do you believe in it?" The hands all go up.

The third question is, "What are you going to do about it? Are you going to make an effort to get it into the high schools?" The hands go up, but with some reservations. That will depend upon the school board which very frequently has a number of people who are steeped in the languages and what-not and who will say, "There isn't room for that subject no matter how vital it is to good living."

But the march is on. Last year there were 16 workshops in colleges and universities around the country, to reduce the cost of transportation, each one with about 40 "pupils." Multiply 16 by 40, and I think we can safely say that we are adding each year about 400 high schools to the list. It won't be very many years until every high school of importance will present your subject, say, to the seniors; so that when they do not go further in their educational progress, they will certainly have some fundamental ideas that will tend to augment their sense of responsibility to that most important business, the family.

I am doing my level best to have colleges and universities introduce this subject in departments other than the economics and the business departments. I want this subject, which is so fundamental, to be introduced—and there are a good many institutions where that is already being done—in the engineering school, in the law school, in the medical school and in other departments. It is fundamental.

I want it in the women's colleges.

But I want it above all in the theological seminaries and we are trying to do that now through the American College. We are visiting them. I am talking about it when I have clergymen in the audiences. They come up and say, "That is a refreshing idea of yours."

"Well," I say, "refreshing or not, what are you going to do about it? Do you believe in it?"

"Oh, yes, a good idea."

"Well, then," I say, "why don't you do something?" The Church is the greatest school I know of. Here is a semi-religious subject, if not wholly religious, the greatest thing for good, decent living and the Church ought to make it clear to the flock. Billy Graham was asked not long ago what he thought about it if a man didn't accept life insurance adequately. He said, "He is a sinner." Dr. Talmadge, who long ago gave a sermon on this subject once a year in the Brooklyn Tabernacle, put it more effectively. He said, "A man who has this explained to him and then deliberately doesn't do it, why, that fellow is an outrage. He is a scoundrel and when he dies he doesn't die, he absconds."

These are self-evident truths and I want this subject taught wherever there can be teaching, but I certainly do want to have it in the Church and it will not get into the Church unless we introduce it in the theological seminaries. Life insurance is a religious subject when you have thought it all out. It is economics given a spiritual character.

And now I have kept you a long time. With these three forces at work, the Human Life Value Concept percolating into the minds of people, the education of the field underwriter, and the education and indoctrination of the public along sound lines, we are going to have a rapid development of the client relationship. The average indoctrinated member of the public will want his insurance man as he has his accountant, his doctor, his lawyer. He will want a man who knows something. Moreover, when the field man has a client, he can begin to scold that client. Today it is sheer selling and he can't scold very much—he can be shown the door. But my doctor can sit down and tell me things that I otherwise wouldn't like—how foolish I am; my lawyer can sit down and give me a good scolding; my accountant can do it; and so the time will come when there will be a client relationship between the underwriter in the field and the buyer of the insurance. In other words, educated personnel in the field will contact a more educated group of buyers, and what an effect that will have upon the average amount of insurance per family. The $430 billion we have today on the books will be small.

I don't like to use those figures "insurance in force." I always like to know how much term insurance is included—although term insurance has some good uses—don't misunderstand me. I don't like to talk only assets, and yet we know those assets are productive assets; they really do this nation a lot of good. I think the finest key to indicate progress is the amount that is spent in premiums. When I see that figure doubled, then it means something—tripled, quadrupled, the meaning becomes stronger. So the march is on. We shall have that trillion when *Fortune* Magazine says we shall have

Above, Dr. and Mrs. Huebner board the airplane for Japan, 1958.

Left, Dr. Huebner says goodbye to Mr. Julian Myrick before leaving for Japan. (*Shaw*)

it, I am sure, and the trillion then will become $2 trillion more easily than we got the first; the $2 trillion will become $3 trillion, and we shall climb the ladder for coverage of the human life value beyond its present 10 per cent, getting it to 30 per cent, maybe 35 per cent, more in conformity with the 80 per cent coverage in fire insurance and the 95 per cent in marine insurance.

(Dr. Huebner received a rising ovation.)

On May 12, 1958, Dr. and Mrs. Huebner set out from Philadelphia, looking forward to eleven weeks of travel, mostly by air, crossing and recrossing the equator and the international date line. They flew first to Seattle, and then to Tokyo, with a refueling stop in the Aleutians, at Shemya, which gave them their taste of the third area of Alaska.

They spent five crowded and wonderful weeks in Japan. Their activities in Japan were arranged by a committee representing the Association of Life Insurance Companies, the Association of Fire and Marine Insurance Companies, the Japanese Society of Insurance Science, the Institute of Actuaries of Japan, and the University of Pennsylvania Alumni Association in Japan. Innumerable individuals were kind and helpful, but three officials were particularly gracious: Mr. Ichiro Yano, president of the Daiichi Mutual Life Insurance Company; Dr. Shozo Noguchi, executive director of the Association of Life Insurance Companies; and Mr. Gen Hirose, president of the Nippon Mutual Life Insurance Company. This Mr. Hirose was one of three generations associated with Dr. Huebner. He was the adopted son of the founder of the Nippon Life whom Dr. Huebner first met during his 1927 visit to Japan. Mr. Hirose, Senior, several times visited the Huebners in America. He was responsible for having the C.L.U. books translated into Japanese. Mr. Gen Hirose's son attended the Wharton School, specializing in foreign trade.

In addition, a charming young woman, Miss Matsuyo Naruse, niece of Dr. Huebner's long-time friend Mr. Hirose of

Dr. and Mrs. Huebner at the Kyoto Royal Palace in Japan with Mr. Hirose and Miss Naruse. (*Y. Kunizaki*)

the Nippon Life, was delegated to be Mrs. Huebner's companion, to be with her at her pleasure during all the visit in Japan. Miss Naruse added greatly to Mrs. Huebner's comfort.

Soon after their arrival in Tokyo, Dr. Huebner was interviewed by the outstanding insurance publisher there, Mr. T. H. Kaneko. Mr. Kaneko published the complete interview in his magazine and in three successive issues presented articles about Dr. Huebner and his visit written by many prominent insurance men of Japan. The magazines were made up in the Japanese style, of course, reading from back to front. Most of the material was in Japanese, but there was considerable also in English. Several excerpts are revealing.

Yutaka Kunizaki, executive vice president of the Nippon Life, reported a charming little personal experience.

> Dr. Huebner's stay in Japan coincided with rose season.
>
> On May 27 I attended the celebration of the extension of Yatsu Rosery on the Keisei Line, and presented Dr. and Mrs. Huebner with an armful of pretty roses at the hotel. Dr. Huebner had just

awaked from afternoon nap, and in the other room Mrs. Huebner was busy preparing herself for the reception to be held at Hitotsubashi University. Mrs. Huebner later wrote me to say that her husband was still half asleep and forgot to tell her that I had brought the beautiful roses, and that was why she failed to thank me when I left. According to Miss Naruse, the couple had the usual mild and pleasant exchange of words about these roses. Dr. Huebner said it was strange that Mrs. Huebner did not notice the smell of so many roses I had brought, to which Mrs. Huebner retorted saying her husband blamed her nose instead of his own idleness.

Also on the day of their departure, I sent about a hundred roses to them at the airport. I wished the roses to take my place and to accompany the couple on their journey. In a letter from Sydney, they wrote that they had arrived in Manila with the pretty roses, that they would never forget the kind friends in Japan and that they wished me to visit their mother city Philadelphia at the earliest possible opportunity.

Again according to Miss Naruse, Mrs. Huebner was telling her husband that Japanese insurance men all seemed to have some kind of hobbies, Mr. Yano fencing, Mr. Hirose painting, and Mr. Kunizaki rose gardening, and that they could still enjoy life if they had left the insurance business.

Dr. Huebner came and left when roses were in their best. "Where there is no rose, there is no affection." Dr. and Mrs. Huebner seem to be overflowing with affection; they are always in the rosery.

Chiyotaro Ono, director and chief of the education department of the Chiyoda Mutual Life Insurance Company, presented a vivid personal impression:

On May 21, I heard Dr. Huebner give a lecture at Dai-ichi Seimei Hall. I was amazed at the passion hidden in Dr. Huebner in his late seventies, with silver hair. As he gave his lecture I saw his cheeks glow like those of a youth: his fiery speech delivered from his sturdy physique simply overwhelmed the audience. The words flowed from the depth of his heart, and for a time he was oblivious of the interpreter...

For as long as 50 years, Dr. Huebner has taught insurance at universities to a total of more than fifty-thousand students. His con-

> tribution to the insurance industry is unfathomable. It would not be too much to say that without him the life insurance of the U.S. would not be enjoying the prosperity of today. We ought to remember with what force the faith and passion of one man can touch the heart of each and all of us.
>
> Mrs. Huebner, herself well along in years, is hale and healthy. She performed her part wonderfully in attending on her husband during the long journey through many countries.

Hakaru Itami, chief of archives for the Daiichi Mutual Life Insurance Company, wrote:

> For Dr. Huebner, who came to Japan after an interval of thirty-one years, conditions in present-day Japan seem to have been of special interest. He mentioned, among other things, that the Japanese people had changed their food habits by eating more bread than before, and also that wives accompany their husbands more often to various parties. However, true to the habits of a real scholar, most of his time was spent at his hotel reading, and preparing for his lectures. He left entirely in the care of Mrs. Huebner everything connected with shopping, clothes, and baggage, which she did quite willingly, saying "My husband doesn't do anything except give lectures and write." Therefore he was quite willing to meet, so far as time permitted, anyone, whether he was a scholar, a newspaper man or an insurance man, and to give detailed explanations in answer to any questions asked. Further, he gave with pleasure an unscheduled interview to the press, and, in response to their enthusiasm, he himself proposed another interview, lasting in all three hours and half. When I asked him if he was tired, I was much moved when he answered simply, "It is for these interviews and lectures on insurance that I am staying here in Japan."

Dr. Huebner's own reports of the days in Japan are available in letters he wrote during the trip for friends at the American College. These letters must be read with understanding that the men who received them were intensely interested in their beloved professor. He need feel no restraint as he reported his honors to them. He had no fear that those readers would question his modesty. He knew they would share his wonder and delight at all the gratifying experiences he was enjoying.

Tokyo, May 19, 1958. We flew the first 2,900 miles out of Seattle without stop until we reached one of the Aleutian Islands, 2 by 4 miles in area, for refueling. The next leg was 2,100 miles to Tokyo.

At the Tokyo Airport we were met by a delegation of fifty Japanese and Chinese and State Department representatives. They held a reception for us, and the press was also there for interviews. From the airport we were driven to Yokohama for luncheon, and from there we rode 60 miles to the Lake Hakone region, one of the most scenic places I have seen. We stopped at the Hakone and Fujiya Hotels, and then spent a day at the splendid home of Mr. Yano, President of the Life Insurance Association of Japan, with a view of Mt. Fujiyama . . .

University of Pennsylvania Alumni in Japan, 1958.

Mrs. Huebner and I were given a nice dinner by Mr. K. P. Chen and Mr. Bang How. Mr. Chen was the leading banker of China for many years, and Mr. How owned the largest printing and publishing establishment in the world. They are graduates of the Wharton School of the University of Pennsylvania, and I have corresponded with them for many years.

May 21, 1958. Mr. Gen Hirose (President of the Nippon Life Insurance Co.) and his niece, Miss Naruse, brought us to the Imperial Hotel . . . In the evening we were honored with a dinner by the

University of Pennsylvania Alumni at the Sanno Hotel. There are now 150 University Alumni in Japan, 70 of whom are in Tokyo. Fifty-two of these were present at the dinner, nearly all accompanied by their wives. By request, I spoke on the Insurance Department of the University of Pennsylvania. . . . Mrs. Huebner and I were presented with a large silver tray beautifully engraved . . .

Yesterday I lectured to the Life Insurance Association of Japan for two hours, with 800 in attendance . . . This was followed by a wonderful reception given to Mrs. Huebner and me by the Association in the evening. The cocktail party, with every beverage the United States possesses, was followed by a magnificent dinner with three kinds of wine. To the merriment of the gathering, I was presented with the reddest necktie you have ever seen. I had no idea my red tie had made such an international hit.

May 22, 1958. I gave a half-hour interview yesterday for Radio TV Branch U.S.J.S., American Embassy in Tokyo, which will be translated into Japanese and distributed over all the branches in Japan. At noon the official heads of the Japanese property insurance companies gave Mrs. Huebner and me a Tea Ceremonial Luncheon which lasted about two hours.

We were then taken to the Imperial Palace in Tokyo. The vast grounds are extraordinarily wonderful, the nearest similar place I have ever seen being the Vatican. The Imperial Palace is really a city with its gardens, Music Palace, Ancient Library, etc. I was particularly pleased to see the garden of dwarf trees, so many with a pedigree extending over a long historical period.

At four o'clock the same day I addressed the Marine and Fire Insurance Association and the Insurance Institute of Japan on trends in property insurance in the United States. I was glad to see again Professor K. Fujimoto, one of the earliest insurance teachers with whom I have kept up an association since 1925. He happens to beat me in age by two years . . .

Today is National Election Day with 53,000,000 voters voting for Parliamentary representatives. I think the Japanese beat us in election excitement. They have Gallups here to predict, just as we have, and I notice they even resort to decimals in their predictions.

Athletics stand high in the Orient. Yesterday the Philippine Olympic Team for the Asiatic Olympics arrived in Japan for next Saturday's contest.

Two days ago the Shah of Iran arrived with his large retinue of officers. The visit is an extraordinary one for pomp, newspaper publicity, and the bestowing of high orders on royalty both ways. Public relations-wise, Japan is working hard internationally. She is also working hard at home. She is staging a wonderful recovery.

May 23, 1958. Yesterday I talked to the Japanese Society of Insurance Science of which I am an honorary member. I suggested that the subject of economics should include not only the well-known four divisions—production, exchange, distribution, and consumption—but should include a fifth division known as "risk and risk bearing." The idea seemed to appeal, and maybe some Japanese writer of a book on economics will make an everlasting name for himself. To date, no American author has followed this suggestion although it has been made by me for many years.

In the afternoon we visited the Imperial Museum, where it is common to see paintings that are 500 or 600 years old. We were presented with two large volumes containing colored reproductions of important paintings and objects of art...

Tokyo is truly a wonderful city with a population of nearly 9,000,000, claiming to be the largest city in the world. They are now building an Eiffel Tower which I am told will exceed in height the tower in Paris.

Everywhere one sees signs of great progress in Japan. *The people work.* And work is the creative thing that counteracts inflation and the ravages of war. Hardly any signs of war damage remain. Enormous and beautiful offices and business structures are being erected. One particularly notices the following as compared with 31 years ago when I visited Japan for five months.

1. Streets are being enormously widened. Fireproof construction has been greatly advanced...
2. Motor transportation has greatly increased. Thirty years ago there were 5,000,000 bicycles. Tokyo has 200,000 automobiles. Japanese factories are turning out small cars and buses and trucks.

Above, **Dr. Huebner and party entering the Josuikaikan Club in Tokyo, with a poster advertising Dr. Huebner's lecture at the right.**

Left, **Dr. and Mrs. Huebner and friends at the Toshogu Shrine.**

3. Japan is striving desperately for foreign markets. Foreign hotels have greatly multiplied, and they seem filled with foreign guests and business men from all parts of the world. There is a light recession from the previous good times, but no one seems to consider it seriously.
4. Apparently there is a greatly improved standard of living as compared with 31 years ago. The water and sanitation systems have been greatly improved . . . The cost of meals and other services in the best hotels of Tokyo seems to be about 70 per cent of the cost in Philadelphia and New York.
5. Everywhere there is great emphasis on education of the youth. Tokyo, the university town, claims 78 universities and 69 colleges. Today I was informed that Japan has 500 universities.
6. The greatest change of all seems to be the degree to which women participate in banquets and other affairs. The men usually wear foreign clothes, but the women seem largely to prefer their Japanese costumes.

Tokyo, May 27, 1958. Visited Tokyo University the other day and spent a pleasant time with the dean and faculty of the Economics

The Huebners with guests at a reception given by the mutual insurance companies of Osaka.

Department . . . They took pains to show me their library collection of my own works, including the early editions of the 1910's and 1920's. I discovered that seven of my own volumes have been translated into Japanese, including two of my government reports on marine insurance . . .

Most recent days have been very busy with lectures, receptions, dinners, etc. . . . We were also taken to famous Nikko, the most famous place in all Japan for scenery, as well as the shrine . . .

Waseda University gave Mrs. Huebner and me a dinner and we indulged in flowery speech-making. It is the present practice in Japan to start with cocktails and much eating on the side, and then to proceed with a heavy dinner, either foreign or Japanese in character. Near the end of the dining, the speech-making starts with a welcoming talk by the Chairman, followed by a series of other talks by those who care to. At this particular dinner, as I recall, about 6 expressed their views, some with interpreters. The guest is expected to respond as best he can to meet the situation. The Japanese practice seems to follow the style used in South America and Germany.

Tokyo, May 30, 1958. May 28 was really a whopper, and I felt somewhat tired . . . We began the day with breakfast at the Daiichi Country Club with Mr. and Mrs. Yano and Miss Naruse . . . After breakfast we motored to Tokyo to visit with Ambassador MacArthur by invitation. He was very kind to us. From 1:30 to 3 I lectured to 250 students in insurance at Keio University, then Mrs. Huebner and I were taken back to the Club for dinner. Yesterday morning I met the insurance press for an hour. Thirty were present, and all the questions related to agents' commissions, the need for renewal commission (evidently not used in Japan), bonuses, salary vs. commissions, contentment of the agent in the United States, etc.

Arose at six the next morning to catch the train for Kyoto. The train trip was grand, and the mountains and agriculture seen will never be forgotten. We are having splendid weather. We shall stay two days in Kyoto, and then go to Nara for a day, and then to Osaka where I'm scheduled for four big lectures and four receptions.

Kyoto, June 2, 1958. Following the last lecture at Tokyo (at Meiji University and the reception by the University faculty) Mrs. Huebner and I traveled by train from Tokyo to Kyoto (400 miles) for a

Dr. and Mrs. Huebner with friends at the Hititsubashi University in 1958.

sightseeing trip to Kyoto and Nara, two of the oldest cities in Japan, and which were spared a bombing unlike Tokyo and Osaka which were destroyed to the extent of almost two-thirds. We saw many famous temples, palaces and gardens for two days including three Imperial Palaces for which special permits to visit were obtained. The Katsuro Detached Palace in Kyoto (350 years old) is regarded as representing Japan's foremost architecture combined with utmost art and utility of daily life. We were also glad to see again the Kinkaku-Ji Temple built in 1397 completely covered with gold-leaf. One of the temples is noted for its ground coverage by one hundred different types of moss. The gardens in all cases were superb, and some of them are three to four centuries old. They show an unmatched degree of specialization in the art of landscape gardening. I wonder why some American genius does not come to Japan for ideas to duplicate, or surpass, in the United States the establishment of really thrilling gardens.

In Kyoto, Mr. Hirose favored us with a Geisha House Dinner with a rocking chair at the dinner probably the first one used in this section of Japan.

In the evening we were accorded at the Osaka Grand Hotel a wonderful reception by the Nippon Life, the Sumitomo Life, and the Daiichi Life. All are mutual life companies with their home offices in Osaka. The American Government was represented. Local civic and university and fire insurance officers were also there . . .

Mr. Hirose presided and made a lengthy speech of a rather personal nature, and I responded in kind. Prof. K. Yoneda, Professor of Insurance at Rikkyo University, was the interpreter and did a good job. He is interpreter for me on this whole trip outside of Tokyo. The whole evening as far as lectures were concerned was devoted to educational progress in insurance. As tokens of the occasion, Mrs. Huebner received a beautiful piece of silk cloth, and to me was given a large porcelain plate of special make. A photo was taken of the entire group. Another photo was also taken of Mrs. Huebner and me to be signed some 50 to 60 times for all the guests present.

Beppu, June 6, 1958. I am writing this letter on the steamer conveying us over the great Inland Sea (300 miles) to Beppu. It is a fascinating trip with its thousands of islands, populated everywhere where there is some soil to grow food for the 90,000,000 people who must exist on an arable area of about ⅔ the size of Pennsylvania. There are also thousands of fishing boats engaged busily at all times of the day. Many of the islands are also fruit-producing, especially tangerines.

The Japanese insurance interests seem deeply interested in our C.L.U. and C.P.C.U. programs. They are not yet educating the agents professionally. Instead their emphasis is on the managers and submanagers . . .

In the afternoon for about 3 hours I conferred with Mr. Hirose and his officers in the Company on the training of their managers. Later I addressed their present class of trainees for an hour on the spirit of life underwriting. As usual many photographs were taken, and arrangements were made to have me plant a laurel tree to commemorate the occasion. I hope the tree will grow large for the present largest life insurance company in Japan, the Nippon Life.

In the evening, the President of the Nippon Mutual Life Insurance Company gave a reception for Mrs. Huebner and me at a leading Japanese restaurant, with many leading officers of the Company in attendance.

Osaka, "The Chicago of Japan," is a remarkable business center with 2½ million people, not so large as greater Osaka with nearly five million. Its main street is just like Michigan Avenue in Chicago. The city has been rebuilt with splendid buildings. Tokyo was de-

Above, Dr. Huebner and Mr. Gen Hirose crossing the Inland Sea to Beppu.

Right, Dr. Huebner planting a tree at the school of the Nippon Life Insurance Company in a suburb of Osaka, as described in his letter.

Dr. Huebner lecturing to a class of managers at the Nippon Life school. Note the lilies by the lecture platform.

stroyed to the extent of 4/5ths, Nagoya (over one million population) was devastated during the war, Osaka was destroyed by 2/3rds, and Kobe was likewise. My great wonder is how since the close of the war all these cities and others were so wonderfully rebuilt, and made grander in so short a period of time so that virtually no physical trace of the destruction is left. The Japanese deliberately chose great inflation to accomplish what, in their opinion, *had to be*. I have devoted some time to inquire into the matter. It is to me a remarkable affair. *They got away with it*, and I think the future is bright because of their industrious habits and commendable determination.

Hakata, June 10, 1958. Beppu resembles our Yellowstone, with its roaring hot springs of varied colors. We stayed here until June 7th, when we left for Bochu, near the famous volcano Mt. Aso, still afire. First by auto and then by suspended air-cable car, the largest in the world, we were taken to the very edge of the crater (5,000 ft. level), the sight will always be remembered. The walls of the crater are 750 ft. high, and the boiling lake at the bottom is clearly visible. I found that mineral collecting is still a part of me. The curator of the museum presented me with a "volcanic bomb" and representative forms of lava, and today I received collections of 24 additional types of minerals thrown out by Aso over the ages. Enormous quantities of nice yellow sulphur line the walls of the enormous crater.

We went from Bochu by auto to Kumamoto, a large beautiful city of 350,000. Upon arrival we were met by a delegation of 15 life underwriters . . . They presented me with a fine pair of Japanese cuff links, and Mrs. Huebner with very nice earrings. Everywhere the Japanese life insurance people have taken to the Human Life Value concept.

From Kumamoto, we proceeded by train (120 miles) to Fukuoka, a beautiful city of 600,000 people. The city is noted for its skilled silk-weaving and Japanese doll making industries. We visited the two outstanding industries in these two lines, and I addressed 600 students of Fukuoka University. The University presented Mrs. Huebner and me with a beautiful silk table cover made at the leading local silk factory and entertained us at dinner at the leading Japanese restaurant, Japanese style . . .

Our internal transportation in Japan will approximate between 4,500 and 5,000 miles, of which 2,000 miles will be by air, and the balance by train and auto . . . As yet Japan has only a limited number of airports at distant points from Tokyo, like Fukuoka and Hokkaido. Both the National Railway System and the Japan Air Lines have given us all transportation on a complimentary basis.

Hokkaido, June 15, 1958. Yesterday in Tokyo I met a Press Conference for two hours with 30 representatives of 20 trade newspapers and journals. The meeting was devoted mainly to opinions on various insurance laws recently passed in Japan. In the afternoon, we attended the theater for a Kabuki performance from 4:30 to 8 P.M., including dinner which is served at the theater and while the play is in progress. I enjoyed this performance very much and had the privilege of seeing the actor who plays female roles, prepare his facial appearance and dress . . .

Arriving here in Sapporo on the Island of Hokkaido, a city of 500,000 people, we were met by two small girls dressed most beautifully in Japanese style. They offered two nice flower tokens. A reception committee of life underwriter representatives, as well as from the State Department's Cultural Center in Sapporo, also met us.

At Otaru for two hours I lectured under the auspices of the Otaru Commercial University with 500 students in attendance, and about

150 life underwriters. From 1:30 to 3:00, the University tendered a reception and luncheon (Japanese style) to Mrs. Huebner and me.... I should add that our suite at the Hotel here will be occupied on the 23rd by the Emperor and the Empress of Japan.

Tokyo, June 17, 1958. This morning, by invitation, I visited Prime Minister Kishi, and was informed that I was to receive the Order of the Sacred Treasure (the third class). This afternoon at 3:00, I visited Vice Minister Morinaga (Finance Minister) and in the presence of quite a few people (the Chief of the Insurance Department of Japan, various other officers of the Finance Ministry, Mr. Hirose, Dr. Noguchi, Mrs. Huebner, and insurance men of various associations) Mr. Morinaga presented the Order, which, I was informed, was signed by the Prime Minister, the Head of the Order Division of the Government, and conferred by the Emperor. The symbols of the Order are the decoration, the scroll, and a statement indicating the reason for giving the Order. One of the officers of the Financial Ministry explained that the Order was conferred because of my contribution to the welfare of the Japanese Insurance Industry.

Dr. Noguchi later advised me that the Order has eight grades, and that the third class is rarely given to foreigners, while the second and first classes are largely reserved for high officials of the Government. He told me that Dr. Emory R. Johnson received the same Order as mine 32 years ago for service in the field of transportation. It seems that the Prime Minister does the nominating, the Cabinet gives its approval, and the Emperor signs the Order.

When Dr. Huebner later had the translation of the beautiful scroll he learned that the Emperor actually had conferred the Order five days before. The "Patent of Decoration" read:

The Third Class of the Order of the Sacred Treasure is hereby conferred upon Mr. Solomon S. Huebner, Citizen of the United States of America, by His Majesty the Emperor of Japan.

In witness thereof, the Seal of the State has been affixed to these presents at the Imperial Palace. This Day, the Fourteenth of June of the Thirty-third Year of Showa.

The decoration is a beautiful gold medallion with enameled work and jewels which hangs on a wide blue and white ribbon.

Above, Dr. Huebner holding the decoration of the Order of the Sacred Treasure. *Below,* Dr. Huebner displaying the scroll citation of the Order of the Sacred Treasure. (*Shaw*)

The presentation was a very formal affair. The Japanese gentlemen dressed in cutaway coats and striped trousers, and conducted the ceremony with the great solemnity worthy of the honor it represented.

Manila, June 19, 1958. Mrs. Huebner and I have just arrived at the Philippine Hotel, after a 2,100 mile trip by plane characterized with wonderful cloud effects and other scenery.

On the evening of the 17th, all my closest friends throughout the trip in Japan gave us a family farewell dinner. It was grand and heart-touching. The evening, after dinner, was spent in the singing of American songs, like *Auld Lang Syne*, *My Old Kentucky Home*, etc. On the 18th, all these friends, some 75, came to the airport to see us depart for Manila.

We were met at the Manila airport by some 15 persons, including the representative of the State Department, and the officers of the four insurance associations which I am to address.

Today, the 19th, was a full one. At 10:00 A.M., I visited the Insurance Commissioner, Ceferino Villar. I had a 1½ hour discussion with him and his officers and insurance guests. The main theme was "rebating and what to do about it." At 12:00 there was a luncheon given by the Insular Life F.G.U. Insurance Group at a beautiful Club, called Casino Espanol, and following the meal I spoke by request for 1½ hours on the status of insurance in the science of economics.

Tonight at the Manila Hotel, a dinner is given for Mrs. Huebner and me, jointly sponsored by the Life Insurance Executive Association, 35 in number, and the Manila Fire, Marine and Accident Insurance Association. Another lecture, I know, will be expected. Every day seems to have two lectures, except Saturday and Sunday, June 21 and 22, and the Manila Chapter of the Alumni Association of the University of Pennsylvania wants one of these days.

The Philippines have grown tremendously in population (22,000,000) and Manila is a city of 2,000,000 people. The city has substantially recovered from the war. It is a beautiful city, although very warm. Fortunately, our hotel room and the lecture places are air-cooled.

Manila, June 24, 1958. Since my last letter I have had an opportunity to review my daily notes while in Japan and find the following as regards important events:

Lectures before Insurance Associations	13
Lectures at Universities	7
Lectures at important luncheons and dinners	12
Long presentations for publication:	
Press conferences	2
Radio interview	1
Individual interviews for publication	3
	38

Special events involving considerable time, like considerably-sized luncheons and dinners without a speech, visits to places of national renown, like temples, shrines, imperial palaces, visits to public officials like the Ambassador, the Prime Minister, The Minister of Finance and the Chief of the Insurance Office, and two volcanos still in eruption 32

Our visit to the Philippines is drawing to an end and I enclose a copy of the program. On Thursday, the 19th, I had three addresses, namely an hour and a half round-table discussion at the Insurance Commissioner's office with some 25 guests, a luncheon meeting address at the Insular Life Insurance Group (35 executives) and an address at the evening dinner in our honor by all four of Manila's insurance associations (attended by about 150 with their wives).

On Friday, the 20th, I gave a 2-hour lecture on Life and Health Insurance (with 300 attendance) sponsored by the Life Insurance Executives Association and later a talk at the luncheon meeting of the Life Insurance Executives Association.

On Saturday, Mr. Estrada, Vice President and Treasurer of the F.G.U. Group of Companies showed us the city, and in the evening we were the guests of Mr. M. M. Thomas of the Insurance Company of North America. On Sunday, the 22nd, the Manila Chapter of the University of Pennsylvania Alumni had us in charge from 2:30 P.M. to 5:00 P.M. and motored us to Mt. Tagaytan, a famous volcano.

Our Manila trip included a visit to the Presidential Palace, an exceedingly beautiful structure; a beautiful church built in about 1600; and the four leading cemeteries, viz., the Old Spanish Cemetery, the Modern Philippine Cemetery, the Chinese Cemetery of rare beauty and educational interest, and the Memorial Cemetery for our 17,000 boys who lost their lives during the last war. The Alumni group was not large, but included the Con Cons, father and son, both from the Wharton School. The father attended the Wharton School in 1918–19 and is a member of the Philippine Cabinet . . .

On Monday, June 23rd, from 9:30 to 11:30 A.M. I gave a 2-hour lecture on Fire and Marine Insurance to almost 350 people. I outlined the trends in the non-life insurance industry in the United States. At the noon luncheon meeting, we had an hour of questions and answers. At 8:00 P.M., Dr. Emetero Roa, Sr. gave a dinner in honor of Mrs. Huebner and me at the Sun-Ya Restaurant with 30 top

IL-FGU Insurance Group middle and top management enjoy drinks before luncheon with Dr. Huebner in Manila, 1958.

executives and public officials. It was a real Chinese dinner with ten courses. Dr. Roa asked me to outline life insurance education in the United States because with few exceptions those in attendance could not attend the other lectures.

Today, June 24th, I was scheduled to give a 2-hour lecture on Education and Training of Agents and Insurance Executives (350 in attendance) and a round-table discussion for the luncheon given under the auspices of the Manila Accident and the Manila Marine Insurance Associations. All in all there have been ten lectures or round-table discussions with questions and answers in Manila.

Tonight we leave for Sydney, Australia, at 9:30 P.M., due to arrive on the 25th at 6 P.M.

Dr. Huebner did not mention that the busy June 24, when their plane for the long, long trip to Australia finally took off at midnight, was their golden wedding day. He and Mrs. Huebner had not told their hosts of the anniversary, not wanting to inspire more kindnesses than they were already receiving. However, their showers of mail from the United States assured them that many friends were rejoicing with them in fifty wonderful years of companionship.

In Australia the Huebners were traveling under the guidance of the Life Offices Association of Australasia, and Mr. C. A. Ralph, the president, was their host. They greatly enjoyed the new experience of the Island Continent, which is as large as the United States, with a population of only ten million people, about 60 per cent being concentrated in six main cities. The language there, of course, is English, but the strange inflections made it very difficult to understand for the first day or so, giving Dr. Huebner some embarrassing moments during the question periods following lectures.

Further quotations from letters pick up the story of the Huebner's experiences "down under."

Sydney, June 30, 1958. After a good night's sleep, after a continuous 5,000 mile plane trip, we started our first day (the 26th) in Sydney, the largest city in Australia with a population of 2,000,000. It is a beautiful city, and I know the several auto tours on the program will be interesting and instructive. At noontime, Mrs. Huebner and I were the guests of Mr. Richard Joyce, U.S. Consul, for lunch at the American National Club. Among the guests was Mr. Russ Hauslaib, President of the Club, a student of mine 37 years ago.

On Friday, June 27th, Mrs. Huebner and I were the guests of the Bowater Paper Co., Ltd., on a launch cruise of Sydney Harbor. It seemed to be an endless cruise of a beautiful harbor of enormous size, surrounded by fine residences and cliffs, filled with ships from all corners of the earth, and wonderfully protected from the sea. Some say it is the largest harbor of the world, while others give that distinction to Rio de Janeiro.

On the evening of June 28th, we were the guests of Dr. and Mrs. A. H. Pollard at a private dinner at the Royal Syndey Yacht Squadron, Kirribilli (black tie). The guests were few—only the head executives, with their wives, of life insurance companies operating in Sydney. Dr. Pollard, an actuary, was acting manager of the Mutual Life and Citizens Assurance Company of Sidney during our visit, owing to the absence in England of General Manager A. F. Deer.

At noon, Monday, June 30th, I was the guest of honor at a luncheon given by the Life Offices Association for Australasia, and upon request gave a half-hour address on the "status of insurance in economic science." Following the luncheon meeting, Mrs. Huebner and I were taken to the Sydney Zoo for two hours. We saw more unusual animals* and more species of Birds of Paradise than we shall ever see again. Any foreigner visiting Australia should not fail to see this large and extraordinarily fine and interesting zoological exhibition.

Tonight, I addressed the members of the Insurance Institute of New South Wales at the Mutual Life and Citizens Assurance Company Building, for 1½ hours on "Insurance Education." Two hundred top and junior executives were present, representing all types of insurance. The Chairman said that he was afraid that Australia had long to wait before they could do what we are doing . . . During the meeting a rather touching event occurred. One of the officers in attendance had a copy of my "Property Insurance" book which he found in a Japanese prison camp, where he spent three years as a prisoner. He had asked permission to read it, which was granted. As a result, upon release from prison he entered the insurance busi-

---

* Mrs. Huebner was much taken with the platypus, which has the tail and back feet of a beaver, lays eggs, and nurses its young.

ness, and he wanted the volume autographed as an everlasting token.

Sydney, July 3, 1958. Day before yesterday I addressed two hundred men of the Field Staffs of Member Offices of the Life Offices Association. I spoke on the human life value concept as the basis of life insurance. Following the lecture, Mrs. Huebner and I lunched with the executive officers of the Mutual Life and Citizens Assurance Company, and after the luncheon we were taken on a two-hour sightseeing car tour of the suburbs and the 200 beaches of Sydney . . .

Yesterday two gentlemen representing a group of life companies not recognized by the L.O.A. called on me. They seemed highly impressed by my lecture on "Insurance Education," and wanted help by way of advice for the starting of things in Australia. Thus far, no Australian university gives instruction in insurance along economic lines. . . .

The Vice Chancellor and Principal of Sydney University, Professor H. S. Roberts, invited me to be his guest at a luncheon in the Chancellor's Room on July 2. Present also were five department chairmen and five insurance leaders including Mr. Ralph and Dr. Pollard. We had a long discussion. Chancellor Roberts is about to start a School of Business Administration at the University of Sydney, and it will be the first in Australia. Here will be the chance to introduce insurance in the program of study. The Professor of Economics did not seem to be in opposition. The L.O.A. representatives are favorable, and as I stated before, the non-recognized group of companies seems ready. So it seems historically, as Mr. Ralph said to me, that something real might occur before long. . . .

On the night of July 2, Mrs. Huebner and I were the guests of Mr. and Mrs. M. C. Buttfield at a buffet dinner at the Head Office of the Australian Mutual Provident Society, the largest Australian Life organization (black tie). Mr. Buttfield does not favor our educational procedure, I am advised, believing that the educational effort should be retained within the industry itself (the English idea). But others do not agree with him, I find, and our own view was shared rather liberally. . . .

On July 4, a bit homesick, Dr. and Mrs. Huebner flew to Canberra. There they stayed at the National University guest house. Dr. Huebner had no scheduled lectures, for there were no insurance students, but he conferred with the head of the Australian National University concerning life insurance education along economic lines.

> Melbourne, July 10, 1958. Our visit to Canberra was most pleasant on July 4th and 5th. The National Government is located within a separate district, similar to the D.C. in the U.S. All is still quite new, but the lay-out is such as to promise a wonderful setting for the Federal Government Capital. . . .
>
> The Australian National University is unique. Only 280 are associated with the University as faculty and students; 200 are research professors and 80 are graduate research students. The research departments are medical research, physical research, Pacific studies, and the social sciences, including political science, economics, statistics, economic history, economic theory, law and social philosophy. Applied Economics is not included, and that seems to me a great omission, in a country with so great an economic potential. No School of Business Administration exists as yet in Australia, hence no insurance courses exist as yet. My lectures on education in insurance, and the Human Life Value Concept seem to make considerable converts, and I am happy that everywhere the Vice Chancellors and Economics Professors of the Universities have been in attendance, or have given a special luncheon or dinner.
>
> Our flight to Brisbane, Queensland, over 600 miles, was delightful. Brisbane is tropical and the winter climate delightful. Bananas, pineapples, etc., plus hedges of poinsettias everywhere and other flowers are in great abundance. The people are easy-going and happy.
>
> On July 6th, I had a meeting on insurance with the press reporters for several hours with considerable resulting newspaper publicity. The next day, we had a most enjoyable and instructive 150-mile auto trip to the South Coast of Queensland . . .
>
> On July 8th, I gave a 1½ hour lecture to the Field Staffs of Member Offices of the L.O.A. on the Human Life Value Concept with 250 in attendance. In the evening, I addressed the members of the Insurance Institute of Queensland on "Insurance Education" with 250 attending.

> Wednesday, July 9th, at 7:40 we departed from Brisbane via Sydney by Trans-Australia Airlines for Melbourne, a 1,200 mile trip, and upon arrival at noon were met by representatives of the American Embassy. In the afternoon, I met the insurance press (20 reporters) for about 2 hours of questions and answers. At the same time, Mrs. Huebner met a group of women reporters. She got much more publicity than I. She emphasized two subjects: 1. That education for women is not wasted; and 2. That her dear husband hasn't much use for retirement. In the evening we had a L.O.A. reception in the Banquet Room of the Menzies Hotel with over 100 insurance and university leaders, including the Chancellor of Melbourne University.

The last six days overseas were spent in New Zealand. The Life Offices Association of Australasia planned their trip, and the Life Underwriters Association of New Zealand also cooperated. The Huebners found people of New Zealand very intelligent but generally socialistic in their attitudes. Social legislation is broad and many people feel that emphasis on personal provision for death or sickness is not necessary. Dr. Huebner hammered away at the desirability of supplementing the social program through individual effort. He remembered with considerable satisfaction one newspaper reporter who was at first particularly aggressive in asserting that the government had done all that was necessary for everybody. Dr. Huebner focused his challenges at him. Was he really satisfied to settle for whatever a beneficent government would do for everybody? Had he no ambition to rise above the minimum? Did he have no concern for giving his family more than the common average? In the face of this bombardment of questions the reporter's belligerency weakened and he finally fell back into the crowd with nothing more to say.

The American Ambassador was most cordial and entertained the Huebners and insurance leaders of Wellington. Dr. Huebner gave four major speeches in that city to audiences of several hundred insurance people, and spoke twice also to large groups in Auckland. Following his return to Philadelphia he was delighted to receive a reprint of an article published by a New Zealand actuary expounding his theory of the human life value. He felt that he had planted some seeds that would yield fruit there. Generally, in both Australia and New Zealand, the insurance leaders seem to believe that their educational activities should be kept within the industry, not encouraged in the universities. Even so they have nothing corresponding to the C.L.U., L.U.T.C., or I.I.A. courses. Dr. Huebner hopes that the seeds he planted on this matter will also show life in due time.

The return flight from New Zealand was by way of the Fiji Islands and Hawaii to Los Angeles, thence directly to Philadelphia. Dr. Huebner's summary in his report to the State Department is impressive:

> I thoroughly enjoyed the long and strenuous Japan-Philippines-Australia-New Zealand trip from May 12th to July 30th, with about half of the time in Japan, 22 days in Australia, and 6 days each in Manila and New Zealand. The trip comprised approximately 40,000 miles of travel (37,000 by air), and included 70 main lectures besides press conferences, insurance seminars, and many formal luncheons and dinners, some of them with addresses. Despite the frequent climatic changes we had to undergo on a trip extending far beyond the equator both north and south, Mrs. Huebner and I were fortunate to reach home safe and well, and without experiencing a single day of illness.
>
> Here I should mention my first unforgettable impression, namely, the speed of travel in these modern days. I traveled by air about 105 hours, or less than 4½ days, whereas the old mode of travel would have virtually consumed practically all of the 80 days of the trip, leaving no time for useful work and contact with insurance associations, universities and personal gatherings.

Back at home and in the office again that summer, Dr. Huebner went the extra mile, as is so characteristic of him, in reinforcing the bonds of friendship which had been established with Eastern friends. One of the Japanese insurance officials wrote in a magazine article, "Sometime ago I received, to my great joy, a gracious letter from him informing me that they have at last reached home after a strenuous trip covering nearly forty thousand miles."

CHAPTER TWENTY

Today's Full Calendar

DR. HUEBNER returned from the Orient to find a crowded schedule. One of his first tasks was to prepare his manuscript for a major speech at the National Association of Life Underwriters' annual convention at Dallas, Texas. There in September he was presented to the great crowd assembled for the C.L.U. breakfast session. Hundreds of C.L.U.'s came to the "coffee corral" at 7 A.M., and after their bacon and eggs settled back to listen to the man who was introduced as "the patron saint of the C.L.U. movement." Some of these men had never seen or heard him before. They knew he had labored in promoting the C.L.U. since 1914. They had learned of his recent three months' trip, which the young fellows secretly felt would have exhausted them. Yet here the veteran warrior was, vigorously presenting the challenge to new generations, speaking on the subject, "Where Are We Going C.L.U.-wise in the Next 25 Years?"

Dr. Huebner emphasized the fundamental that "the public comes to recognize a calling as a profession by a two-fold standard, namely (1) the quality of the service performed and (2) by a sufficiently large proportion of the practitioners contacting the public."

At Dallas again he urged that every C.L.U. should interest and motivate each year at least one other life underwriter so

Dr. Huebner congratulates Robert E. Lindwall of Manitowoc, Wisconsin whom he had sponsored during his C.L.U. studies. Dallas, 1958.

that he would get into the C.L.U. study program. He applies this principle to himself, and at Dallas had the pleasure of seeing Robert E. Lindwall of Manitowoc, Wisconsin, receive his C.L.U. Dr. Huebner had been his personal sponsor for ten years. He believes that many C.L.U. candidates need the personal help and encouragement of some friend to keep them on the C.L.U. track. It is admittedly a difficult road to follow for the busy life underwriter.

At the Dallas convention an interesting feature of the C.L.U. conferment exercises was honors shown to the Class of 1933. *The Insurance Field* reported:

> Two fathers, each with two sons who are C.L.U.'s, are members of the C.L.U. class of 25 years ago that received the spotlight of special recognition recently when the American College of Life Underwriters conducted its 31st annual Conferment Exercises.
>
> The class of 1933, the sixth after the American College was founded, consisted originally of 138 men and six women. To all surviving

members whose addresses are known, Dr. S. S. Huebner, president emeritus of the American College, recently wrote a letter inviting them to attend the Conferment and sit at a special table and receive honors.

As might be expected of early C.L.U.'s, almost all members of the class have remained in the life insurance business and made a successful career of it. A few are in educational work associated with life insurance or in insurance journalism. A large number are in home office and field management positions.

Members of the class that received their C.L.U. designations 25 years ago include many who are prominent in the business today. Two are trustees of the American College, and one is past president of the American Society of Chartered Life Underwriters. Several are former directors of the American Society, and quite a number have been active in the affairs of the Society. Many have participated in local and national N.A.L.U. activities.

Of the original class of 144, 29 are deceased and 17 are listed by the College as "address unknown."

Among members of the class of '33 was James Elton Bragg, who was a trustee of the American College at the time of his death, and who for a number of years was chairman of the College's Examination Board. Hardly anyone in C.L.U. history has surpassed the contributions that he made to the world of insurance education and to the C.L.U. program.

Two other members of the class are Trustees of the American College: Charles W. Campbell, vice president of Prudential and prominent in College activities for a number of years; and John O. Todd, president, Todd & Zischke Services, Inc. and special agent in Chicago for Northwestern Mutual Life and a former chairman of the C.L.U. Institute Board as well as the Million Dollar Round Table.

Fred E. LeLaurin, general agent in New Orleans for Aetna Life, accepted Dr. Huebner's invitation to attend and saw his son James V., with Aetna Life in Meridian, Miss., receive his designation. A second son is already a C.L.U.

Dan W. Flickinger, general agent in Indianapolis for John Hancock Mutual Life, a member of the class of '33, also has two sons who have received the designation.

M. Luther Buchanan, with Massachusetts Mutual Life, in Boston, was president of the American Society in 1943–44 and helped build the foundations of the American Society as presently organized.

Among the many other interesting personalities in the 25-year C.L.U. Class is Levi E. Bottens, veteran director of administration for L.U.T.C.

Insurance magazines recently carried the announcement that Julius O. Klein, another member of the class of 1933, has been elected vice president in charge of the Pacific Coast head office of Metropolitan Life.

At the Conferment Exercises, the American College granted the C.L.U. designation to about 635 individuals who have successfully completed their five C.L.U. examinations and met other professional requirements of the American College. Probably about a quarter of these were personally present to stand in a group before Dr. Huebner who administered the professional C.L.U. pledge.

After the Dallas convention Dr. Huebner co-operated in promoting a "Committee of 1000." The purpose was to enroll a thousand C.L.U.'s under a definite pledge to recruit at least one person to C.L.U. study for the year 1958–59. He also engaged in his usual assignment of teaching two C.L.U. Part I classes in the University of Pennsylvania evening school. With these men and women, as always with his Wharton undergraduates, he insists on punctuality in attendance at class. He makes a habit of giving a ten-minute quiz on the current lesson immediately at the beginning of each class session. He realizes that such a plan is not completely popular but assures the students firmly that it is for their own good.

One of the highlights of the fall was the local conferment exercises for the 1958 C.L.U.'s held by the New York City Chapter of the American Society of Chartered Life Underwriters. The ceremony was at luncheon at the Waldorf-Astoria. Under the able leadership of President Margaret Carlsen, the sixty-five new New York C.L.U.'s saw an imposing array of some three hundred guests assembled to do them honor. The head table included officers of New York City life insurance salesmen's organizations, presidents of the C.P.A.'s and C.P.C.U.'s of New York, officers of various kinds of New York insurance educational institutions, officers of the American College and the American Society, the president of the Equitable Life and the chairman of the trustees of the Huebner Foundation. Dr. Henry T. Heald, president of the Ford Foundation, gave the commencement address. Dr. Huebner presented the charge to the graduates using phraseology which has become habitual with him through many such ceremonies over a thirty-year period. In part he said:

> Every Chartered Life Underwriter should conduct himself or herself at all times with honor and dignity, inflexibly avoiding practices that will bring dishonor or reproach on the life underwriting profession or the C.L.U. designation. You should at all times refrain from what might appear as commercializing or misusing the designation, and from an attitude of haughtiness. Be humble—because the more educated a person is, the humbler he should be. Acquisition of knowledge should show, as nothing else can, how much more remains to be acquired. Be industrious and serious in your work, and give generously of your ability, not only to your clients, your fellow underwriters and your company, but also to the improvement of methods, conditions and standards in life underwriting.

Then he led the group as they repeated the solemn C.L.U. pledge with upraised hands.

What flash backs of memories Dr. Huebner must have had as he sat that day in a room which sees the most important ceremonies of New York. Writing Mrs. Carlsen afterward he thanked her for "the grand time I had yesterday visiting the New York Chapter and its large class of new C.L.U.'s." With characteristic humility, he, the one man without whom it could not have happened, concluded: "I wish also to thank you and your associates for the courtesies which were extended to me."

Nineteen hundred and fifty-nine opened as another busy year for a man in retirement. Dr. Huebner was completing a new edition of his *Economics of Life Insurance* and writing two chapters for Dr. Gregg's *Life and Health Insurance Handbook*. He regularly shared staff meetings of the American College and participated in numerous special conferences, such as the five days at Atlantic City working with the C.L.U. Examination Board and another week in Arkansas for the meeting of the Council of Educational Advisers of the American College.

Every few weeks a major speaking engagement took Dr. Huebner away from home. In February he went to Kansas for three lectures for life insurance people and at the University of Kansas. After one talk a little old lady came up to greet him. She acted as though he might know her, but he did not recognize a familiar face. That was not too strange for he had not seen it in over sixty years. He and the visitor had last met when they were graduated together from the Two Rivers High School in Wisconsin in 1898.

In April Dr. Huebner was pleased to go to a famous American city which he had never visited before. The life underwriters of Charleston, South Carolina, invited him to speak to two audiences representing life insurance people from the whole state, as well as bankers, accountants, and other business and professional men. He and Mrs. Huebner, even with their world-wide experiences, found delight in that charming old city with its galleried homes behind high walls and beautiful iron gates. They enjoyed the glories of the spring in the rainbow colors of azaleas and camellias in the famous river gardens nearby.

He was back in Philadelphia in time for a very important ceremony. This was the appointment of Dr. Dan M. McGill to the newly established Frederick H. Ecker Chair of Life Insurance at the University of Pennsylvania. The Metropolitan Life

At the University of Pennsylvania, March 31, 1959. *Left to right*, Frederic W. Ecker, president, Metropolitan Life; Frederick H. Ecker, chairman of the board, Metropolitan Life; Dr. Dan M. McGill, first Ecker Professor, University of Pennsylvania; Dr. S. S. Huebner. (*Jules Schick*)

Insurance Company gave four hundred thousand dollars to provide this first fully endowed chair of insurance in the United States, and probably the first in the world. The Metropolitan had long been a strong supporter of life insurance education through the American College and the Huebner Foundation.

Dr. McGill had been a student of Dr. Huebner's and in accepting his honor he most graciously paid tribute to the "insurance pioneer whose unselfish dedication to insurance education for fifty-five years paved the way for this chair. I refer, of course, to Dr. S. S. Huebner. It was only through his vision and tireless efforts that insurance gained a prominent and respected place in the curricula of higher institutions of learning. More specifically, it was he who developed at the University of Pennsylvania such an eminent insurance faculty that this institution has become the national, if not the international, center of insurance education."

In May Dr. Huebner spoke to some twelve hundred members of the International Insurance Accounting and Statistical Association at their Atlantic City convention. A few days later he had another gratifying experience in being the guest speaker for the Newark, New Jersey Chapter of the American Society of Chartered Life Underwriters when they presented their Distinguished Service Award to the New Jersey Man of the Year. The man honored was John S. Thompson, past president of the Actuarial Society of America, past president and currently vice chairman of the board of the Mutual Benefit Life, and a key man in the development and present operations of the New Jersey Blue Cross Plan. To him as representative of the traditional profession of life insurance—actuarial science, Dr. Huebner was happy to pay honor from the new profession symbolized by the Chartered Life Underwriter.

Another invitation for May had pleased him very much. This was a request to address a Life Insurance Agency Management Association conference on the subject of life insurance and health insurance. He often over the years had referred to health insurance as a natural phase of insurance of the human life value, but past generations of life insurance leaders had not seemed enthusiastic about pushing the idea. Now he was most gratified to have an audience welcoming his opinions. He prepared a paper to deliver, but a temporary illness prevented his going to the meeting—the first time in ten years that health reasons had kept him from fulfilling a speaking engagement. The ideas which he had expected to present developed logically from the essential human life value idea: the wealth of human life, consisting of the dollar value of an individual's talents and abilities and his capacity and determination to use them, is subject to loss through the attacking hazards of accident, sickness, compulsory retirement, weaknesses of old age, and death. Life insurance and health insurance are the complementary protections against loss of that life value. Life insurance and health insurance both serve also as protection against the depletion of an individual's property estate. Life insurance and health insurance both operate as "business interruption insurance" for the family business. The family is dependent upon income, and these forms of insurance will guarantee its continuance.

Life conservation, a matter always of keen interest to Dr. Huebner, logically is a concern too of both types of insurance. Keeping a healthy person healthy is to the advantage of either insurer. Dr. Huebner emphasizes the parallel with property insurance concepts in the new edition of his *Economics of Life Insurance.*

> Prevention of loss in the first instance is real insurance, irrespective of whether life or property values are under consideration. Every working man and woman should be thoroughly examined once each six months, or at least once a year. An inventory of our life status needs to be taken periodically just as we have our buildings and stocks of goods regularly inspected and safeguarded. We should know that probably the majority of untimely deaths occur because some dread disease starts its withering effect unknown to the victim or, if known, is neglected in its initial stages for so long a time that its progress finally passes the point of medical control. Why should we not seek to prolong our working life by nipping in the bud those numerous ailments which are easily checked if discovered in time, but which are sure to kill prematurely if neglected too long?

> Life insurance companies can and should in their way perform the same creative function in the prolongation of the life value that property insurers perform in the field of property values, and they owe the same obligation to policyholders and to society to render this much-needed service. Yet while millions upon millions of dol-

lars are being spent by property insurers in the interest of loss prevention to property, the same service has only fairly been started in the field of life conservation. Here again is another highly creative field for life and health insurance, with tremendous possibilities for good, and with practically all of the opportunity for development in the future.

Formerly the function of property insurance was also regarded primarily as "indemnity" or "risk-bearing," whereas today the emphasis is more and more upon "risk-elimination." The latter function is distinctly gaining in importance as compared with indemnity. With some of the leading types of property insurance, prevention of loss efforts have become the most important insurance activity of all. All property insurers proceed on the theory that loss prevention should always, from both the business and social standpoints, take a prominent place alongside the indemnity function. . . . Practically all types of property insurers—fire, marine, bonding, compensation, steam boiler, credit, title, and the like—are recognizing this special service and their natural fitness and advantage for stamping out as far as possible the causes of loss they are asked to underwrite. Fire insurance companies devote millions of dollars annually to the prevention of loss in the first instance through inspections, general investigations and surveys for recommendatory purposes, experimentation with materials and equipment, educational campaigns along special and general lines, salvage, and so on . . . Marine insurance extends the prevention service to the periodic inspection of hulls, the supervision of packing, the protection and proper stowage of cargo, the safeguarding of passengers and employees, the salvaging of damaged property, and so on. . . .

Measured by magnitude, the human life value of the nation, expressed in dollars is very much greater than the total value of all of the nation's material property. The ratio is about $7 trillion for the human life value as compared with about $700 billion for tangible property values, or about ten to one. . . . The whole subject of the human life value is truly a national welfare subject, highly beneficial to the families that make up the nation. It is deserving of much more thought and missionary zeal than have been bestowed upon the subject thus far.

Dr. Huebner at the ground breaking for the new headquarters of the American College, Bryn Mawr, Pennsylvania, September 21, 1959. Also, *left to right*, Herbert P. Stellwagen, trustee of the American Institute for Property and Liability Underwriters; Robert Dechert, counsel of the American College and American Society; Joseph H. Reese, C.L.U., chairman of the Building Committee.

Looking to the last half of 1959 as this book goes to press, Dr. Huebner sees his calendar already filling with speaking engagements. There are a tour throughout Texas during which ten lectures are scheduled, three addresses in Kansas later in the fall, and various other meetings for life underwriter associations and C.L.U. groups. He has more writing to do and committee responsibilities. He will be one of four speakers for the national seminar on "Life Insurance Today," a new project in continuing education for C.L.U.'s organized jointly by the American College and American Society, which will take place just before the National Association of Life Underwriters convention in September. He will teach his usual two C.L.U. courses at the University of Pennsylvania. He has still the great blessing of being wanted and being useful. He still anticipates adding notches to his gun.

People who are close to Dr. Huebner know that he likes to tabulate activities. The summary of visits and speeches reported in his letters from the Orient indicated that. From the University of Pennsylvania records, the statement has often been made that seventy-five to eighty thousand students have passed through his classes in the day, night, and extension courses.

The question is often asked him: "How many lectures do you suppose you have given?" It was a query he wished he could answer, but as he said he "never got busy" to try to figure it out until this book was in preparation. In 1959 he took his notes and University records and memories and produced some amazing statistics.

During regular university classes at Wharton, at Pennsylvania evening, summer school, and extension sessions, at his C.L.U. classes at Pennsylvania over many years, at his course (including summer school) at Columbia and New York University, at Princeton (for the Navy), and at the University of Pennsylvania College for Women, he figured that he had conducted 18,400 class sessions. His public lectures or addresses to special groups in 280 cities in practically every state in the United States and in 48 foreign cities totaled 4,370.

In some cities he spoke only once; in many, ten to thirty times. In others, like Philadelphia, New York, Chicago, and Atlantic City, he estimated he had lectured to groups, other than in regular university class sessions, well over a hundred times. With such public lectures attendance of two hundred was very common, four hundred to five hundred quite frequent, and occasionally several thousand. In all probability it is conservative to say that he has reached a million people in those lecture audiences in the past fifty-three years. Taking the class sessions and public lectures together there were 22,770 such events in the 19,345 days of 53 years, or more than one a day. Quite a persistent rate of performance!

In reviewing these tabulations, Dr. Huebner mentioned that he had never lectured in Nevada. He often passed through the state in his travels, and he and Mrs. Huebner made a memorable trip to the Hoover Dam while it was in the course of con-

Map in Dr. Huebner's office showing cities where he has lectured. (*Shaw*)

Dr. Huebner with mineral specimens in his study. (*Shaw*)

struction. In addition to being interested in that highest dam in the United States, he was intent upon getting minerals. In the great earth-moving and blasting operations many interesting things turned up. Some of the workmen were alert to their finds and Dr. Huebner was able to get from them some fine Scotch agates and rare jasper specimens. On the same trip they saw Death Valley where he picked up a piece of talc which long served as a paper weight on his desk. They also went to the multimillion-dollar mansion in a remote canyon on the edge of Death Valley where they met the legendary Death Valley Scotty with his red necktie and five-gallon hat. They marveled at the profane old miner's rambling Spanish "castle," miles from civilization with its pipe organ and two grand pianos in the midst of priceless antiques.

Looking back over the course of his life Dr. Huebner offered a summary and an appraisal. He felt that he had lived up to his own standard of doing what he could to help himself, or to

First recipients of the 25-year C.L.U. Teacher Award, September 23, 1959. *Left to right,* George S. Buck, C.L.U., of Seattle; Dr. Huebner; Albert J. Schick, C.L.U., of Newark, New Jersey.

accomplish what he considered an important objective. "Lots of people just sit there," he said.

He saw the need for insurance as a subject for collegiate study along economic lines. He took steps to get it established, first in the University of Pennsylvania, then in other American schools of higher education, and now he is still promoting the idea in foreign countries.

He found that his first academic treatment of the subject did not appeal to the students. He worked out a track which provided a basic philosophy for life underwriting and took life insurance into the area of profits and business, beyond the realm of just philanthropy.

He discovered that college teaching which he loved did not pay enough to meet his family needs. He took to the lecture platform, which solved that problem and at the same time promoted other causes to which he was devoted.

Dr. Emory R. Johnson told him early in his career that necessary textbooks did not exist for work which needed to be done. He wrote many and inspired the writing of even more.

He felt, as a professor of insurance, the scorn of his non-department associates for his field of work. He dedicated himself to making insurance a profession in which competent workers might be proud of their calling.

Wherever he was, he made himself felt.

Since 1937, Dr. and Mr. Huebner have made their home in the comfortable house they built in Merion Station, a close suburb of Philadelphia. It is the place where William Penn and his Welsh Quakers made their first settlement. The "Station" in the borough name suggests the Pennsylvania Main Line, and it is in that neighborhood. However, its real significance was discovered by the Huebners in Australia. There they saw no "farm" or "ranch," but everywhere a "station," the word carried by emigrating Britons "down under" as well as to the new world of America.

The Huebner house is squarely built of gray native stone. It has white-framed, many-paned windows and a broad white front door with a delicate fan light and shining brass eagle knocker. Shading the front walk a tall ginkgo tree calls to mind far places and distant ages.

Within the house, Dr. and Mrs. Huebner are surrounded by souvenirs of their rich life together. There are photographs of grandchildren: Stephen, a sophomore at Princeton, Bernard and Elizabeth in high school. There is a lovely oil landscape painted by daughter-in-law Betty. They have many little bronzes from the Orient, including a Buddha-like figure of an old man with a scraggly beard sitting cross-legged with an antelope beside him, which is the Chinese symbol of insurance. On built-in shelves and deep window sills are Wedgewood pieces, rare lavender Chinese porcelains, and black pottery made by María the Potter of San Ildefonso in the American

Dr. Huebner's most recent studio photograph. (*Bachrach*)

Southwest. A gold cabinet holds Mexican dolls and tiny Alaska totem poles. On the walls are many woven Japanese pictures, and an embroidered one showing a restless sea. The ocean picture has special meaning because as a young couple the Huebners often admired a seascape which they were too poor to own. This cherished picture of a similar scene was a gift to

Dr. Huebner from the Tokyo University of Commerce many years later and somehow seems the fulfillment of an old dream. In a position of special honor hangs the beautiful Japanese scroll of the Third Order of the Sacred Treasure, flanked on either side by the jeweled medallion of the Order and the medallion of the Insurance Hall of Fame.

Two walls of Dr. Huebner's study display, in specially built cases, hundreds of geological specimens from all parts of the world. A lump of sulphur as big as two fists came from Sicily and is much finer than Louisiana sulphur. When Dr. Huebner read in the newspaper that a shipload was arriving in Philadelphia, he met the boat at the dock to buy this prized specimen. A little rough piece of emerald is a faulty fragment of a stone from which a jeweler had taken a nearly perfect gem worth thousands of dollars. One cabinet contains only agates—a

Dr. and Mrs. Huebner in the study. (*Huebner*)

superb collection of polished stones, green and gray, cream and white, rose, brown and yellow.

Over the fireplace mantle in the study hangs the John Newton Russell Award plaque, together with the Phi Beta Kappa Associates membership scroll and the testimonial given at his retirement by the Insurance Society of the University of Pennsylvania. The Ph.D. diploma from the University of Pennsylvania is in this room too, and a drawing of the seal of the Huebner Foundation, the laminated plaque of the C.L.U. key and pledge, a Malacca cane from Mr. Hirose of Japan, the pen, given him by Admiral Benson, with which the Marine Insurance Syndicates Agreements were signed, and many other treasures rich in associations.

In the midst of these mementos are two sturdy dark oak rocking chairs. There, Dr. and Mrs. Huebner sit together, reading, talking, or just rocking contentedly, thinking how a teacher with a purpose can serve his generation.

Dr. Huebner's Positions, Degrees, Awards, and Other Honors

Dr. Huebner's Present Positions with Date of First Appointment

President Emeritus, American College of Life Underwriters, September 1, 1952.

Member of the Executive Committee of the American College of Life Underwriters throughout the history of the College, 1927.

Life Trustee, American College of Life Underwriters, 1938.

Member of the Examination Board of the American College of Life Underwriters, 1944.

Honorary Chairman, Governing Committee of the David McCahan Foundation (American College of Life Underwriters), 1955.

Member of the Board of Directors of the American Society of Chartered Life Underwriters, 1948.

Chairman, Board of Trustees, American Institute for Property and Liability Underwriters, Inc., 1942 (date of origin).

Life Trustee, American Institute for Property and Liability Underwriters, Inc., 1956.

Honorary Chairman, Administrative Board, S. S. Huebner Foundation for Insurance Education, 1941.

Member of the Pension Research Council, University of Pennsylvania, 1952.

Emeritus Professor of Insurance, University of Pennsylvania, July 1, 1953.

Member of the First International Insurance Conference, 1957.

Member of the Commission on Insurance Terminology, American Association of University Teachers of Insurance, 1959.

Public lecturer on insurance subjects throughout the United States and internationally, author of many current insurance articles and teacher of two C.L.U. classes at the University of Pennsylvania.

Dr. Huebner's Past Positions with Dates of Responsibility

Harrison Fellow in Economics, University of Pennsylvania, 1903–4.

Instructor in Insurance, University of Pennsylvania, 1904–6.

Assistant Professor of Insurance, University of Pennsylvania, 1906–8.

Professor of Insurance, University of Pennsylvania, 1908–53.

Chairman, Insurance Department (first Chairman of the Department), University of Pennsylvania, 1913–52.

Special Lecturer (Insurance) at New York University, 1917.

Special Lecturer (Insurance) at Columbia University, 1915–19.

Dean of The American College of Life Underwriters (first Dean), 1927–34.

President of The American College of Life Underwriters (third President), 1934–52.

Chairman, Executive Committee, The American College of Life Underwriters, 1934–52.

Chairman, Insurance Committee of the National Conference on Street and Highway Safety, 1924.

Member, Advisory Insurance Committee, United States Chamber of Commerce, 1924–30.

Member, Committee on Insurance and Fire Prevention of the Philadelphia Chamber of Commerce, 1925–51.

Member, Committee on Insurance and Pensions of the American Association of University Professors, 1924–40.

Educational adviser to the Massachusetts Mutual Life Insurance Company, 1930–34.

Member, Educational Council of the University of Pennsylvania, 1942–46.

Chairman of the Committee on Professional Standards in Life and Property Insurance, American Association of University Teachers of Insurance, which had charge of the preliminary negotiations leading to the American Institute for Property and Liability Underwriters, Inc., 1941–42.

Chairman of the Advisory Committee appointed at first meeting held by the leading organizations in property and casualty insurance to take charge of the consideration of the advisability of adopting a professional program of education comparable to the C.L.U. movement in life insurance, May 16, 1942.

Expert to the Congressional Committee on the Merchant Marine of the House of Representatives in charge of the shipping investigation, 1912–16, which led to the passage of the United States Shipping Act of 1916 and the creation of the United States Shipping Board.

Special expert in insurance to the United States Shipping Board and the Congressional Committee on the Merchant Marine, in charge of the marine insurance investigation, 1918–23, which led to the creation of the American Hull Marine Insurance Syndicates and the passage of the Model Marine Insurance Law of March 4, 1922.

Special expert in insurance to the United States Shipping Board, 1926–27, 1929–30, 1933–34.

President (the first), American Association of University Teachers of Insurance, 1933 and 1934.

Member, Committee on the Shipping Board Bureau of the Business Advisory and Planning Committee of the Department of Commerce, 1934.

Member, War Department's Advisory Committee on Insurance, 1941–45.

Special expert in insurance to the Civil Aeronautics Board, 1943–45.

Dr. Huebner's Degrees, Awards, and Other Special Honors

Valedictorian of Graduating Class, Two Rivers High School, Wisconsin, 1898.

University of Wisconsin
- Joint debating honors, 1901 and 1903.
- Phi Beta Kappa, 1902.
- B.L. degree, 1902.
- Scholarship in Economics, 1902.
- M.L. degree, 1903.

University of Pennsylvania
- Harrison Fellowship in Economics, 1903.
- Ph.D. degree, 1905.

Beta Gamma Sigma, 1916.
Pi Gamma Mu, 1925.
Sc.D. degree, 1931. (Honorary)

Fellow of the Insurance Institute of America, 1925.

National Institute of Social Sciences, election to, 1925.

Oriental lecture trip, as exchange professor to Japan, China, Manchuria, Korea, The Philippines, and Hong Kong, 1927.

American Philosophical Society, election to, 1930.

Fellow of the Casualty Actuarial Society, 1932.

President's Cup Award of the Philadelphia Life Underwriters Association (first recipient), 1937.

S. S. Huebner Foundation for Insurance Education (created in his honor by the life insurance industry), 1941.

John Newton Russell National Award (first recipient), National Association of Life Underwriters, 1942.

Phi Beta Kappa Associates, election to, 1947.

University of Pennsylvania Alumni Award of Merit, 1948.

Portrait by Alice Kent Stoddard contributed by the Chartered Life Underwriters of the United States, and located in the headquarters of the American College of Life Underwriters, 1950.

Insurance Society of New York, honorary member, 1952.

John Hancock Mutual Life Insurance Company, testimonial citation, 1952.

Insurance Forum of San Francisco, first honorary member, 1953.

The Japanese Society of Insurance Science, honorary member, 1953.

Annual Alumni Award of the University of Pennsylvania Club of Suburban New Jersey, 1953.

Northwestern Mutual Life Insurance Company, testimonial citation, 1953.

Portrait by Alfred Jonniaux contributed by the graduates of the Wharton School specializing in insurance, and located in the headquarters of the S. S. Huebner Foundation for Insurance Education, University of Pennsylvania, 1953.

Insurance Company Education Directors' Society, honorary member, 1954.

Honorary Texan, commissioned by the Governor of Texas, 1955.

Fiftieth Anniversary of Insurance Education, as a tribute with citation signed by the Governor of Wisconsin, the President of the University of Wisconsin, the President of the Wisconsin Association of Life Underwriters, and the President of the American Society of Chartered Life Underwriters, Milwaukee, Wisconsin, May 27, 1955.

Benjamin Franklin Cup Award (first recipient), University of Pennsylvania Club of New York City, 1956.

Insurance Hall of Fame, Griffith Foundation for Insurance Education, Ohio State University, election to (first living recipient of Hall of Fame election), 1957.

International Insurance Lecture Trip, under the auspices of the United States Department of State, to Japan, The Philippines, Australia, and New Zealand, 1958.

The Third Class of the Order of the Sacred Treasure, conferred by the Emperor of Japan, June 14, 1958.

25-Year C.L.U. Teacher Award (inscribed silver Philadelphia bowl), awarded September 23, 1959.

Bibliography of Publications by and about Dr. Huebner

Listings in the various divisions are generally chronologically by date of publication since this has value in a biographical study.

Books Authored by Dr. Huebner

Property Insurance. New York: 1st and 2d revised ed., D. Appleton and Co., 1911, 421 pp., and 1922, 601 pp.; 3d revised ed., D. Appleton-Century Co., 1938, 682 pp.

College textbook.

Steamship Agreements and Affiliations in the American Foreign and Domestic Trade. Washington, D.C.: U.S. Government Printing Office, 1914, 500 pp.

United States Government report prepared in connection with the Congressional Shipping Investigation.

The Stock Exchange Business. New York: Doubleday, Page and Co., 1918, 98 pp.

A course of study with references, published for the Investment Bankers Association of America and the Association of Stock Exchange Firms.

Life Insurance. New York: 1st and 2d ed., D. Appleton and Co., 1915, 482 pp., and 1923, 496 pp.; 3d ed., D. Appleton-Century Company, 1935, 692 pp.; 4th ed., Appleton-Century-Crofts, Inc., 1950, 599 pp.

College textbook.

Report on Legislative Obstructions to the Development of Marine Insurance in the United States. Washington, D.C.: U.S. Government Printing Office, 1920, 100 pp.

United States Government report prepared in connection with the Congressional marine insurance investigation.

Report on the Status of Marine Insurance in the United States. Washington, D.C.: U.S. Government Printing Office, 1920, 100 pp.

United States Government report prepared for the Committee on the Merchant Marine and Fisheries of the House of Representatives.

Marine Insurance. New York: D. Appleton-Century Co., 1920, 265 pp.

Textbook.

The Stock Market. New York: D. Appleton-Century Co., 1922, 496 pp.; 2d ed., 1934, 590 pp.

College textbook.

The Economics of Life Insurance. Human Life Values: Their Financial Organization, Management, and Liquidation. New York: 1st ed., D. Appleton and Co., 1927, 219 pp.; revised and enlarged 2d ed., D. Appleton-Century Co., 1944, 272 pp.; revised 3d ed., Appleton-Century-Crofts, Inc., 1959, 244 pp.

College textbook.

Life Insurance as Investment. Joint authorship with David McCahan. New York: D. Appleton and Co., 1933, 291 pp.

College textbook.

Property Insurance. Joint authorship with Kenneth Black, Jr. New York: Appleton-Century-Crofts, Inc., 1957, 568 pp.

College textbook.

Life Insurance. Joint authorship with Kenneth Black, Jr. New York: Appleton-Century-Crofts, Inc., 1958, 582 pp.

College textbook.

Volumes Edited by Dr. Huebner

In the *Annals of the American Academy of Political and Social Science.*

Insurance. Vol. 26 (September, 1905), 431 pp.

Stocks and the Stock Market. Vol. 35 (May, 1910), 264 pp.

American Produce Exchange Markets. Vol. 38 (September, 1911), 351 pp.

Government Regulation of Water Transportation. Vol. 55 (September, 1914), 306 pp.

Modern Insurance Problems. Vol. 70 (March, 1917), 347 pp.

Bonds and the Bond Market. Vol. 88 (March, 1920), 223 pp.

Modern Insurance Tendencies. Vol. 130 (March, 1927), 238 pp.

Organized Commodity Markets. Vol. 155, Part I (May, 1931), 244 pp.

Modern Insurance Developments. Vol. 161 (May, 1932), 284 pp.

In the Appleton Series, *Life Insurance, Its Economic and Social Relations.* New York: D. Appleton and Co.

HUEBNER, S. S. *Economics of Life Insurance*, 1927, 219 pp.

HUEBNER, S. S., and MCCAHAN, DAVID. *Life Insurance as Investment*, 1933, 291 pp.

HUTTINGER, E. PAUL. *The Law of Salesmanship*, 1927, 250 pp.

LOMAN, HARRY J. *Life Insurance in Relation to Taxation*, 1928, 257 pp.

MADDEN, JAMES L. *Wills, Trusts and Estates*, 1927, 258 pp.

SCULLY, C. ALISON and GANSE, FRANKLIN W. *Business Life Insurance Trusts*, 1930, 277 pp.

STEVENSON, JOHN A. *Education and Philanthropy*, 1927, 190 pp.

WOODS, EDWARD A. *The Sociology of Life Insurance*, 1928, 331 pp.

Other

Special Diplomatic and Consular Reports Dealing with Methods and Practices of Steamship Lines Engaged in the Foreign Carrying Trade of the United States. Washington, D.C.: U.S. Government Printing Office, 1913, 324 pp.

Edited for the Congressional Committee on the Merchant Marine and Fisheries.

Articles, Speeches and Booklets Authored by Dr. Huebner

American College of Life Underwriters (publications)

The American College of Life Underwriters: Its Aims and Standards. Booklet written by Dr. Huebner as dean of the College. Undated, 11 pp.

The Professional Concept in Life Underwriting. Booklet. 1952, revised 1956, 8 pp.

"Expanding Harvests." Conferment address delivered at the joint dinner of the American College of Life Underwriters and the American Society of Chartered Life Underwriters, Cleveland, Ohio; August 26, 1953. Published in a booklet, *Educational Progress in Life Underwriting*, 1953, pp. 21–39.

The Economics of Health Insurance. Booklet. 1956, revised 1958, 13 pp.

"Discussion of Implications to Life Insurance of John Sloan Dickey's Lecture on 'The American Design: E. Pluribus Unum, but

Still Many.' " Dr. Dickey's lecture was the first David McCahan lecture given under the auspices of the David McCahan Foundation of The American College of Life Underwriters. The lecture and discussion were published together in booklet form, 1957, 7 pp.

"Where Are We Going C.L.U.-wise in the Next Twenty-five Years?" Address delivered before the American Society of Chartered Life Underwriters, Dallas, Texas; September 10, 1958. Published by the College in a booklet, *A World We've Never Seen*, 8 pp.

Annals of the American Academy of Political and Social Science

"The Distribution of Stock Holdings in American Railways," Vol. 22 (November, 1903), pp. 63–78.

This article won the award of the Harrison Fellowship in Economics at the University of Pennsylvania.

"The Main Features of the Present Foreign Trade of the United Kingdom," Vol. 23 (January, 1904), pp. 84–104.

"The Relation of the Government in Germany to the Promotion of Commerce," Vol. 24 (November, 1904), pp. 95–109.

"Development and Present Status of Marine Insurance in the United States," Vol. 26 (September, 1905), pp. 241–72.

"Policy Contracts in Marine Insurance," Vol. 26 (September, 1905), pp. 273–99.

"Federal Supervision and Regulation of Insurance," Vol. 26 (November, 1905), pp. 69–95.

"The Study of Insurance in American Universities," Vol. 28 (July, 1906), pp. 82–100.

"Bibliography on Securities and Stock Exchanges," Vol. 35 (May, 1910), pp. 217–32.

"The Scope and Function of the Stock Market," Vol. 35 (May, 1910), pp. 1–23.

"The Functions of Produce Exchanges," Vol. 38 (September, 1911), pp. 1–35.

"Steamship Line Agreements and Affiliations in the American Foreign and Domestic Trade," Vol. 55 (September, 1914), pp. 75–111.

"Introduction" in Bruce D. Mudgett's *The Total Disability Provision in American Life Insurance Contracts*, Vol. 59 (Supplement to May, 1915), 4 pp.

"The American Security Market during the War," Vol. 68 (November, 1916), pp. 93–107.

"Life Insurance in Its Relation to Thrift," Vol. 87 (January, 1920), pp. 183–89.

"Foreword" in *Bonds and the Bond Market.* Vol. 88 (March, 1920), pp. 1–3.

This foreword emphasizes the potential estate assured through life insurance vs. other investments for the mass of families.

"American Transportation Insurance Facilities in Foreign Countries," Vol. 127 (September, 1926), pp. 181–85.

"Foreword" in *Modern Insurance Tendencies.* Vol. 130 (March, 1927), pp. v–vii.

"Insurance Instruction in American Universities and Colleges," Vol. 130 (March, 1927), pp. 213–19.

"Insurance in China," Vol. 152 (November, 1930), pp. 105–8.

"The Insurance Service of Commodity Exchanges," Vol. 155 (May, 1931), pp. 1–6.

"The Investment Objectives of Life Insurance," Vol. 161 (May, 1932), pp. 14–19.

"Insurance Instruction in American Universities and Colleges," prepared jointly with David McCahan, Vol. 161 (May, 1932), pp. 163–77.

Journal of American Insurance

"Marine Insurance as It Affects Shipping and Commerce," Vol. 2, No. 4 (April, 1925), pp. 5, 6, 24.

"The Brussels Rules—as Viewed from the Underwriter's Standpoint," Vol. 2, No. 8 (August, 1925), pp. 5, 6, 25.

"The Services of Insurance," Vol. 2, No. 9 (September, 1925), pp. 5, 6, 35.

"The Family as a Business from an Insurance Standpoint," Vol. 2, No. 10 (October, 1925), pp. 5, 6, 24.

"Life Insurance as Property Insurance," Vol. 3, No. 1 (January, 1926), pp. 11, 12, 28.

"Multiple Line Insurance: Pros and Cons concerning the Desirability of Individual Companies Carrying Diversified Risks," Vol. 3, No. 2 (February, 1926), pp. 11, 12, 15.

"Economics of Automobile Insurance," Vol. 3, No. 4 (April, 1926), pp. 7, 8, 28.

National Association of Life Underwriters: *Proceedings* of annual conventions (identified by number and year), *Life Association News* (*News*), and booklets.

"Life Insurance Education." Address at Cincinnati, September 15, 1914, when theme of convention was "Education," 25th *Proceedings*, 1914, pp. 66–80.

"The Human Value in Business Compared with the Property Value." Address at Los Angeles, 35th *Proceedings*, 1924, pp. 17–40.

This speech was the first public promulgation of the human life value concept. It was distributed widely in booklet form by the Association.

Outline of Collegiate Courses in the Functions, Principles and Practices of Life Insurance. Booklet, 1926, 36 pp.

The Extent and Importance of the Monetary Value of Human Life. Booklet, 1926, 20 pp.

How Life Insurance Benefits the Premium Payer. Booklet, 1927, 28 pp.

"The Value of Life Insurance to the Policyholder Himself," 39th *Proceedings*, 1928, pp. 25–30.

"The American College of Life Underwriters," 39th *Proceedings*, 1928, pp. 95–98.

"The American College of Life Underwriters," 40th *Proceedings*, 1929, pp. 162–72.

"The Financial Value of the Chartered Life Underwriter Course of Study," 41st *Proceedings*, 1930, pp. 158–68.

"The Conserving Influence of the C.L.U. Program upon Life Underwriting," 42d *Proceedings*, 1931, pp. 130–36.

The Dependable Solvency of Annuities. Booklet, 1932, 15 pp.

"The Economics of Annuities from the Selling Point of View," 43d *Proceedings*, 1932, pp. 32–40. Distributed also as a booklet by the Association.

"Elevation of Life Insurance Educationally with the Public," 43d *Proceedings*, 1932, pp. 136–45.

"What the C.L.U. Program Means to the Institution of Life Insurance," 44th *Proceedings*, 1933, pp. 97–108.

"A Look Ahead in Insurance Education," *News*, Vol. 42, No. 7 (March, 1948), 2 pp.

"The 'Endless Golden Chain' in Life Insurance," *News*, Vol. 48, No. 11 (November, 1953), 2 pp.

"Economics of Accident and Health Insurance," *News*, Vol. 49, No. 5 (May, 1954), pp. 33–41.

University of Pennsylvania (publications)

Life Insurance and Annuities for University Bequests. Booklet written with David McCahan, published by the Executive Committee on Bequests. Undated, 22 pp.

"Life Insurance as an Economic Force in the Community." Lecture in the free public lecture course of the University of Pennsylvania, 1915–1916, 17 pp.

"The Science of Business." Commencement address, June 18, 1924. Published in the *Proceedings*, Vol. 24, No. 40 (June 21, 1924), pp. 61–68.

"Ideals in Business." Commencement address, Evening School of Accounts and Finance. *The Lantern* (November, 1925), pp. 7–10.

"The Services of Life Insurance Salesmen to the Community," *The Lantern* (March, 1926), 2 pp.

"Wharton Influence on Insurance in the Orient," *Pennsylvania Gazette*, Vol. 26, No. 17 (February, 1928), pp. 425–27.

"A University Viewpoint of the Field of Life Insurance Underwriting," *University of Pennsylvania Placement Review*, Vol. 3, No. 3 (August, 1931), pp. 12–14.

"Can the Individual Hedge through the Security Market?" Address before the Seventh Annual Wharton Institute. Published by the University of Pennsylvania Club of New York in *Proceedings of Conference on Debt, Taxation and Inflation*, held in New York City, May 8 and 9, 1936 for the alumni and faculty of the Wharton School of Finance and Commerce, pp. 22–32.

"Life Insurance as a Financial Basis for a College Education," *University of Pennsylvania Placement Review*, Vol. 9, No. 2 (Summer, 1937), pp. 11–15.

"Student Loans Supported by Life Insurance," *University of Pennsylvania Placement Review*, Vol. 9, No. 3 (Autumn, 1937), pp. 15–17.

"The American Security Market in the Event of Another World War," *General Magazine and Historical Chronicle*, Vol. 42, No. 1 (October, 1939), pp. 63–68.

Other

"Inheritance Taxes in the United States." Article republished with permission from the *Quarterly Journal of Economics* (October,

1904) in Charles J. Bullock's *Selected Readings in Public Finance*, chap. 16, pp. 373–95. Boston: Ginn and Co., 1906.

"Review of Insurance Legislation." In the *Review of Legislation* published by the New York State Education Department. 1905, pp. 283–95; 1906, pp. 217–32; and 1907–8, pp. 311–34.

"State Supervision and Regulation of Fire Insurance Companies." Article published in *The Year Book* of the Fire Insurance Society of Philadelphia. September, 1906, 21 pp.

"Taxation of Life and Fire Insurance Companies." Address delivered before the First National Conference of the National Tax Association, Columbus, Ohio, November, 1907. Published in the Association's *Proceedings*, 1908, pp. 595–604.

"The Security Market." Annual articles in the *American Year Book*. New York: Appleton, 1910–1919, 1925–1951.

"Taxation of Inheritances." Address delivered before the International Tax Association, Toronto, Canada, October, 1908. Published in the Association's *Proceedings*, 1909, pp. 195–205.

"Life Insurance Education." Address delivered before the annual convention of the Fidelity Mutual Life Insurance Company, Philadelphia. Published in the *Fidelity Field Man*, Vol. 5, No. 7 (July, 1916), pp. 10–14.

"Life Insurance and the War," *The Scientific Monthly*, Vol. 4, No. 4 (April, 1917), pp. 342–54.

"Rise and Decline of American Marine Insurance." Address before the 8th Annual Meeting of the Chamber of Commerce of the United States, April 27, 1920. *Minutes*, pp. 255–65, available in manuscript at the Chamber library.

"Theft and Pilferage in the Export and Import Trade," *Bulletin of the Pan-American Union* (March, 1922), pp. 220–27.

"Life Insurance Savings." Address delivered before the Philadelphia Sales Congress, March 23, 1923. Printed and distributed by the Fidelity Mutual Life Insurance Company, Philadelphia, 4 pp.

"Savings, Investments and Life Insurance for Dentists." Address before the Academy of Stomatology of Philadelphia, December 19, 1922. *Dental Cosmos*, Vol. 65 (April, 1923), pp. 405–12.

"Vision in Insurance." Address delivered at the 11th Annual Convention of the Insurance Federation of Pennsylvania, May 21, 1924. Published by the Federation, 10 pp.

"The Importance of Human Life Values in Business Compared with Property Values," *The Research & Review News*, Vol. 4, No. 8 (August, 1924), pp. 14–17.

"The Scientific Treatment of Life Values Through Life Insurance." Address delivered before the 75th anniversary meeting of the National Life Insurance Company, Montpelier, Vermont, August 27, 1925. Published by the National Life Insurance Co., 21 pp.

"The Monetary Value of Human Life." Address before the New England life insurance sales congress of the Boston Association of Life Underwriters, March 26, 1926. Published in the *Insurance-Age Journal* (April 1, 1926), pp. 8–13.

"Everyday Application of the Life Value Idea," *Manager's Magazine*, Vol. 2, No. 2 (April, 1927), pp. 3–6.

"Versicherungs-Unterricht Auf Den Hochschulen Der Vereinigten Staaten Von Amerika," *Zeitschrift fur die gesamte Versicherungs-Wissenschaf*, Band 30, Heft 1, 1928.

"Insurance and Trusts." Address delivered before the 13th Annual Convention and published in the *Proceedings of the Financial Advertisers Association* (September, 1928), pp. 95–106.

"Significant Indications of Insurance Tendencies of the Future," *The Weekly Underwriter and The Insurance Press* (May 25, 1929), 70th anniversary issue, pp. 9, 124, 125.

"A New Vision in Salesmanship." Address delivered before the 23d Annual Convention of the Association of Life Insurance Presidents, December 13, 1929, published in the *Proceedings*, pp. 190–94.

"Business Risks and Their Insurance." Address delivered before the American Management Association, published by the Association as *Financial Management Series: No. 35*. New York, 1930, 24 pp.

"An Educational Program in Property and Casualty Insurance—The Professional Concept of Insurance." Address published in *Proceedings of the 35th Annual Convention of the National Association of Mutual Companies, August, 1930*, pp. 77–80. (See pp. 161–63 for copy of the resolution approving professional education as suggested.)

"Unemployment Insurance." Address published in the *Proceedings of the American Philosophical Society*, Vol. 71, No. 2 (1932), pp. 49–72.

"Life Insurance. The Great Financial Emergency Safeguard." Address at the Policyholders' Luncheon of the Philadelphia Association of Life Underwriters on Life Insurance Day, January 21, 1932. Published by the Association, 31 pp.

"The Inherent Solvency of Legal Reserve Life Insurance." Address published in *Proceedings of the 1932 Annual Conference of the Life Office Management Association*, September, 1932, pp. 120–32.

The Dependable Security of Legal Reserve Life Insurance as a Depository Institution. Booklet published by the Financial Independence Committee, Hartford, Connecticut, 1933, 16 pp.

"Economic Functions of the Stock Market as a Business Agency and the Proposed National Securities Exchange Act of 1934." Address published in *Proceedings of the American Philosophical Society*, Vol. 74, No. 1 (1934), pp. 77–92.

"Survey of Fire Insurance Situation in the Philadelphia School System." Report to Philadelphia Board of Education, December, 1934. This report was duplicated in large numbers and used in many cities of the United States.

Outline of Collegiate Course on the Economic Services, Principles and Practices of Organized Stock Exchange Markets. Booklet outlining subject matter and bibliography for a fifteen-week survey course. Philadelphia: John C. Winston Company, 1935, 39 pp..

Survey of Stock Exchange Markets as a Subject of Instruction in American Universities and Colleges. Booklet reporting a study undertaken at the suggestion of the New York Stock Exchange. Philadelphia: John C. Winston Company, undated (prepared in 1935), 28 pp.

"C.L.U. Movement: Its Growth and Place in Underwriting," *Life Insurance Selling*, Vol. 10, No. 3 (March, 1935), 5 pp.

"Life Insurance: Yesterday, Today, Tomorrow." Address made during Life Insurance Week, May 16, 1935, before the annual policyholders' luncheon of the Philadelphia Association of Life Underwriters. Published by various trade journals, including *Provident Notes* issued by the Provident Mutual Life Insurance Company, June 25, 1935, 3 pp.

"Risk and Insurance," chap. 14, pp. 345–86, in Walter E. Spahr's *Economic Principles and Problems*, Vol. I, 3d ed. New York: Farrar and Rinehart, Inc., 1936.

"Outstanding Factors Affecting the Life Insurance Branch Manager and General Agent Today," *Manager's Magazine*, Vol. 11, No. 1 (January-February, 1936), pp. 2–5.

"New Insurance Needs of Business." Address delivered at the Chamber of Commerce of the United States Annual Meeting, April 29, 1936, which included discussion of a program for the establishment of an American College of Property and Casualty Underwriters. Recorded in the 24th annual meeting *Minutes*, pp. 374–78, available in manuscript at the Chamber library.

"Growth of the C.L.U. Movement and Its Future," *Life Insurance Selling*, Vol. 11, No. 3 (March, 1936), 5 pp.

"A Professional Standard Based Upon a Professional Designation." Address published in the *Insurance Broker-Age*, official publication of the Insurance Brokers Association of New York, Vol. 4, No. 6 (June, 1936), 2 pp.

"The American College of Life Underwriters—Completion of the Pioneering Decade—Beginning of the Decade of Expansion," *Life Insurance Selling*, Vol. 12, No. 5 (May, 1937), 5 pp.

"What the C.L.U. Program Has Done for Life Underwriters," *Rough Notes* (September, 1936), pp. 11–12.

"Human Life Value of the Veterinarian and How to Treat It." Address before the American Veterinary Medical Association, July 7, 1938, New York City. Published in the *Proceedings* of the Association.

"Stocks and Bonds." Annual article on this subject in the *Encyclopedia Britannica Book of the Year*. Chicago: 1938–51.

"Educational Progress in Life Underwriting." Conferment address delivered before the Fourteenth Conferment of the American College of Life Underwriters. Published by the American Society of Chartered Life Underwriters, Philadelphia, 1941, 19 pp.

"Proposed American College of Property and Casualty Underwriters," *Casualty and Surety Journal*, Vol. 2, No. 8 (October, 1941), pp. 50–59.

"Historical Background of the American Institute for Property and Liability Underwriters, Inc.," *Proceedings of the American Association of University Teachers of Insurance*, Vol. 9, No. 1 (March, 1942), 24 pp.

"The Future of Insurance." Address before the 30th Annual Meeting of the Chamber of Commerce of the United States, April 28, 1942. Recorded in the *Minutes*, pp. 281–89, available in manuscript at the Chamber library.

The Need for Collegiate Instruction in Insurance. Booklet published by The American Society of Chartered Life Underwriters, Philadelphia, 1943, 27 pp.

"A Report of Progress of the American Institute for Property and Liability Underwriters, Inc.," *Proceedings of the American Association of University Teachers of Insurance*, Vol. 10, No. 1 (March, 1943), 14 pp.

"Report on the First Year of Operations of the American Institute for Property and Liability Underwriters, Inc.," *Proceedings of the American Association of University Teachers of Insurance*, Vol. 11, No. 1 (March, 1944), 7 pp.

"The Economic Outlook for the Coming Decade and the Part Life Insurance will Play," *United States Review*, Vol. 153, No. 13 (September 23, 1944), 3 pp.

"Report on the Second Year of Operations of the American Institute for Property and Liability Underwriters, Inc.," *Proceedings of the American Association of University Teachers of Insurance*, Vol. 12, No. 1 (March, 1945), pp. 92–98.

"New Horizons in Life Insurance," *Journal of the American Society of Chartered Life Underwriters*, Vol. 1, No. 1 (September, 1946), pp. 5–14.

"Stocks and Bonds—1937–1946," *Ten Eventful Years*, Vol. 4, pp. 165–73. Chicago: Encyclopedia Britannica, 1947.

"The American College: Some Aspects of Its Operational History." Article prepared jointly by S. S. Huebner and David McCahan. *Journal of the American Society of Chartered Life Underwriters*, Vol. 1, No. 3 (March, 1947), pp. 201–16.

"A Look Ahead." Address delivered before the 12th Annual Meeting of the American Association of University Teachers of Insurance, December 29, 1947. Published in *Journal of the American Association of University Teachers of Insurance*, Vol. 15, No. 1 (March, 1948), pp. 72–83.

"A Half Century of Insurance Progress." Address before the Hemispheric Insurance Conference in New York. Published by the *West-East Insurance Monitor*, Vol. 2, No. 1 (February, 1948), pp. 1–4.

"The Life Underwriter of the Future—He Will Be a Professional Man and Educator, a Community Leader." Address before the C.L.U. Luncheon of the Annual Convention of the Pennsylvania Association of Life Underwriters, May 20, 1948. Published in condensed form in *United States Review*, Vol. 160, No. 22 (May 29, 1948), pp. 28–41.

"The Contribution of the American College of Life Underwriters to the Life Insurance Institution." Address delivered before the Million Dollar Round Table, French Lick Springs, Indiana, September 20, 1948, and published in the *Proceedings.*

"Emory Richard Johnson (1864–1950)." A memorial including a bibliography of Dr. Johnson's works. Published in the *American Philosophical Society Year Book 1950* (January 1, 1950–December 31, 1950), pp. 304–9.

"Professional Progress in Insurance Education." Address prepared for the Insurance Lecture Series, sponsored by the School of Business Administration of the University of Connecticut under a grant from the New York Life Insurance Company. Printed as a pamphlet by the School, Spring, 1954, 23 pp.

The Economic Importance of Non-cancellable, Guaranteed Renewable Accident and Health Insurance. Booklet prepared for and published by the Southwest Indemnity and Life Insurance Company, Dallas, Texas, 1954, 7 pp.

"The American College of Life Underwriters." Paper presented to the Fifth Hemispheric Insurance Conference, Rio de Janeiro, August, 1954, 6 pp. (Spanish and Portuguese manuscript translations available in the library of the Insurance Society of New York.)

"American Institute for Property and Liability Underwriters." Paper presented to the Fifth Hemispheric Insurance Conference, Rio de Janeiro, August, 1954, 7 pp. (Spanish and Portuguese manuscript translations available in the library of the Insurance Society of New York.)

"Development of Insurance Education in the Universities and Colleges of the United States." Paper presented to Fifth Hemispheric Insurance Conference, Rio de Janeiro, August, 1954, 7 pp. (English manuscript and Spanish and Portuguese manuscript translations available in the library of the Insurance Society of New York.)

"Conserving the Human Life Value." Address delivered October 8, 1954, before the Third Biennial Insurance Institute sponsored by the University of Nebraska and the Insurance Federation of Nebraska. Published in *Best's Insurance News*, Vol. 55, No. 8 (December, 1954), pp. 17, 18, 53–57.

"What a C.L.U. Should Know about A & H," *Life Insurance Courant*, Vol. 60, No. 9 (September, 1955), pp. 52–54; Vol. 60, No. 10 (October, 1955), pp. 55–57.

"Education—The Great Ally of the Life Underwriter." Address delivered before the Convention and Sales Congress of the Wisconsin State Association of Life Underwriters. Published by the *Spectator* in pamphlet form, January, 1956, 8 pp.

"Insurance and Dollar Value of Human Life." Address before the University of Pennsylvania Club of New York at the time of the Benjamin Franklin Cup award to Dr. Huebner. Published in the Annual Policyholders Number of the *Weekly Underwriter*, Vol. 174, No. 19 (May 12, 1956), 2 pp.

"The Manager's Obligations," *Manager's Magazine*, Vol. 31, No. 4 (July, 1956), 3 pp.

"Life Insurance and Education," *Insurance World 1957—Life, Accident, and Sickness*. New Haven: Yale University, 1957, 2 pp.

"The Human Life Value in our Economy and Its Proper Protection." Address before the New York Chapter, American Society of Chartered Life Underwriters at its Ninth Annual Estate Planners Day. Published in the *Proceedings* of the New York Chapter, April 24, 1957, 6 pp.

"Future Patterns in Life Insurance Distribution—An Educator's View," *Journal of Insurance*, Vol. 24, No. 3 (December, 1957), pp. 9–20.

"Environment for Private Insurance in the United States." Address before the International Insurance Conference, May, 1957, to be published in the conference *Proceedings*.

"The Human Life Value Concept." Address delivered before the Home Office Life Underwriters Association, and published in the Association's *Proceedings*, Vol. 34 (May, 1958), pp. 12–30.

"Human Life Values—The Concept," chap. 1, pp. 3–10, in *Life and Health Insurance Handbook* by Davis W. Gregg. Homewood, Ill.: Richard D. Irwin, Inc., 1959.

"Human Life Values—Scientific Use of Life and Health Insurance," chap. 2, pp. 11–20, in *Life and Health Insurance Handbook* by Davis W. Gregg. Homewood, Ill.: Richard D. Irwin, Inc., 1959.

"Insurance." Address before the Insurance Accounting and Statistical Association May 18, 1959, referring to life, property and casualty insurance. Published in the 1959 *Proceedings* of the Association, pp. 9–18.

"A Modern Look at the Economics of Life Insurance." Address at the first National C.L.U. Seminar, Philadelphia, September 21, 1959. Published in *The Journal of the American Society of Chartered Life Underwriters*, Vol. 13, No. 4 (Fall, 1959), pp. 301–13.

Dictionaries for Which Dr. Huebner Served as Special Editorial Consultant in the Field of Insurance

The American College Dictionary. New York: Random House, Inc., 1947.

Webster's New International Dictionary. 2d ed., Unabridged. Springfield, Mass.: G. and C. Merriam Company, 1934.

Publications Referring Extensively to Dr. Huebner

HAZARD, WILLIS HATFIELD. "Professor Huebner's 'Economics of Life Insurance,' Including an Appreciation of the Series of Technical Books of Which It Is the Foundation Member," *The Standard* (May 26, 1928), 3 pp.

The Wharton School: Its First Fifty Years, 1881–1931. Printed for the Wharton School, University of Pennsylvania, 1931. Citation of S. S. Huebner for honorary degree of Doctor of Science, pp. 54, 55, and other references.

WOODS, LAWRENCE W., JR. *The First Decade, 1927–1937: A Brief History of the American College of Life Underwriters.* Philadelphia: The National Chapter of Chartered Life Underwriters, 1937.

GATES, THOMAS S. (president of the University of Pennsylvania). "Education, Insurance and Research," an address delivered at the 32d Annual Convention of the Association of Life Insurance Presidents, New York, December 1, 1938. Published in the *General Magazine* of the University of Pennsylvania, Vol. 41, No. 3, pp. 324–32.

"Dr. S. S. Huebner Serves Twenty-five Years in University Insurance Department." Testimonial commemorating the establishment of the Insurance Department of the Wharton School at the University of Pennsylvania. *The Daily Pennsylvanian*, February 22, 1938.

MCCAHAN, DAVID. "Solomon Stephen Huebner—World's Foremost Insurance Educator." Biographical article profusely illustrated with personal photographs. *Life Association News*, Vol. 34, No. 11 (July, 1940), pp. 965–69.

———. "Solomon Stephen Huebner—Down Through the Years." A ten-page tribute to Dr. Huebner included in the program of the testimonial dinner in his honor, Philadelphia, September 26, 1940.

COOPERATING COMMITTEE. *Announcement* of the S. S. Huebner Foundation for Insurance Education, 1941.

"Citation for S. S. Huebner." In connection with the Alumni Award of Merit, January 19, 1946. *Pennsylvania Gazette*, Vol. 44, No. 7 (March, 1946).

CRAIG, WALTER A. "The American College," *Journal of the American Society of Chartered Life Underwriters*, Vol. 1, No. 3 (March, 1947), pp. 189, 190.

CLARK, ERNEST J., SR. "The American College: Its Founding," *Journal of the American Society of Chartered Life Underwriters*, Vol. 1, No. 3 (March, 1947).

"The Next Big Step for Wharton." Brochure published by the University of Pennsylvania Development Fund in behalf of The Wharton School, 1949, 28 pp. Frontispiece photograph of Dr. Huebner and personal references.

TEAF, E. ADRIAN. "The Society of Chartered Property and Casualty Underwriters—September 2, 1943 to June 11, 1948," *Annals of the Society of Chartered Property and Casualty Underwriters*, Vol. 1, No. 1 (March, 1949), pp. 5–20.

"Mr. Wharton School." Article in the publication of the University of Pennsylvania Evening School, *The Lantern*, Vol. 31, No. 2 (December, 1951), 3 pp.

The Huebner Issue of the *Journal of the American Society of Chartered Life Underwriters*, Vol. 6, No. 3 (June, 1952). Prefatory tribute by the editors, tribute by President Harold E. Stassen of the University of Pennsylvania, articles by former students of Dr. Huebner, and "A Collection of Huebnerian Philosophy of Life and Life Insurance" selected by Dr. David McCahan and Dr. Davis W. Gregg.

HILL, GRANT L. "A Tribute to Dr. S. S. Huebner," a statement made during the program of the annual meeting of the Life Insurance Agency Management Association, November, 1952, and printed in the *Proceedings* with Dr. Huebner's response, pp. 5–15.

"It's Readjustment, Not Retirement for Doctor Solomon S. Huebner," *Philadelphia Sunday Bulletin*, June 7, 1953.

"Dr. Huebner's Commencement," *The Spectator*, Vol. 161 (September, 1953), pp. 22–23.

John Hancock Mutual Life Insurance Company full page advertisement tribute to Dr. Huebner. *The Insurance Salesman*, August, 1955, cover page.

"Salute to C.L.U.'s," *The Insurance Salesman*, editorial (August, 1955), p. 30.

CARROLL, JAMES A. "An Exclusive Interview with Dr. Huebner," *Manager's Magazine*, Vol. 3, No. 1 (January-February, 1958), pp. 3–4.

"The Record Interviews Dr. Huebner," *Prudential Record*, April, 1958, pp. 8–12.

HUEBNER, JOHN M. Introduction of Dr. Huebner as speaker before the Home Office Life Underwriters Association, published in the *Proceedings*, Vol. 34 (May, 1958), pp. 10–11.

Insurance Review of Tokyo and Osaka, Japan. Three special issues devoted to Dr. Huebner and his 1958 visit to Japan, presenting verbatim interviews with Dr. Huebner and articles by many authors. Vol. 10, No. 5 (May, 1958), Vol. 10, No. 8 (July, 1958), Vol. 10, No. 11 (September, 1958).

SUMNER, EDWIN F. W. (resident actuary, The Colonial Mutual Life Assurance Society, Limited, Wellington, New Zealand). "The Human Life Value Concept—and Life Assurance," 1958, 4 pp.

"Family An Economic Institution," *Eastern Underwriter Gold Book*, Vol. 60, No. 40 (October 2, 1959), p. 74.

Biographical Publications Presenting Extensive Reference to Dr. Huebner

(Dates refer to editions showing the latest references.)

Cyclopedia of Insurance in the United States. New York: Index Publishing Company, 1958.

Directory of American Scholars. 2d ed. Lancaster, Pa.: Science Press, 1951.

International Who's Who. London: Europa Publications Ltd., 1958.

Who Knows—and What. Chicago: A. N. Marquis Co., 1949.

Who's Who in America. Chicago: A. N. Marquis Co., 1958–59.

Who's Who in American Education. Nashville: Who's Who in American Education, Inc., 1947–48.

Who's Who in the East. Chicago: A. N. Marquis Co., 1948.

Who's Who in Pennsylvania. Chicago: A. N. Marquis Co., 1939.

World Biography. Bethpage, N.Y.: Institute for Research in Biography, 1954.

Volumes Dedicated to Dr. Huebner

KULP, C. A. Casualty Insurance. New York: Ronald Press Co., 1928, 1947, 1956.

RIEGEL, ROBERT, and LOMAN, HARRY J. *Insurance Principles and Practices.* New York: Prentice-Hall Inc., 1921.

WOODS, EDWARD A. *America's Human Wealth.* New York: F. S. Crofts and Company, 1927.

The Author's Bibliography

As noted in the foreword, the greatest part of the material for this book came from personal interviews with Dr. and Mrs. Huebner, members of their family, and associates of Dr. Huebner at the University and in the insurance industry.

Background material, statistical information, and facts of chronology came from a variety of sources. Minutes of the American College of Life Underwriters, unpublished records of the National Association of Life Underwriters, the files of *The Eastern Underwriter* from 1914 to date, and catalogs and records of the University of Pennsylvania and of the University of Wisconsin were used extensively.

Since the book was written for the general reader, source references throughout the text seemed undesirable. However, for interested students, annotations are provided for all printed material quoted directly.

The following list presents the major works of reference used as well as those from which verbatim quotations were taken.

ALLEN, FREDERICK LEWIS. *Since Yesterday*. New York: Harper and Brothers, 1940.

AMERICAN ASSOCIATION OF UNIVERSITY TEACHERS OF INSURANCE. *Proceedings*, Vol. 1, 9, 10, 11.

AMERICAN INSTITUTE FOR PROPERTY AND LIABILITY UNDERWRITERS. *Announcement. C.P.C.U.—Education Program—Professional Examinations*. Philadelphia, 1957–58.

AMERICAN SOCIETY OF CHARTERED LIFE UNDERWRITERS. "C.L.U. Diploma Presentation" section from *A Manual for Chapters*. Philadelphia. (Undated)

ARNOLD, THURMAN. "The Crash—and What It Meant," in *The Aspirin Age* (ed. ISABEL LEIGHTON). New York: Simon and Schuster, 1949.

ASSOCIATION OF LIFE INSURANCE PRESIDENTS. *Proceedings of the Twenty-third Annual Convention*. New York, 1929.

BROGAN, DENIS W. *The Era of Franklin D. Roosevelt*. New Haven: Yale University Press, 1950.

CHEYNEY, EDWARD POTTS. *History of the University of Pennsylvania 1740–1940*. Philadelphia: University of Pennsylvania Press, 1940.

CLARK, ERNEST J. "The Founding of the American College of Life Underwriters," *Journal of the American Society of Chartered Life Underwriters*, Vol. 1, No. 3 (March, 1947).

CLARK, PAUL F. Manuscript article, not yet published, 1959.

COMMITTEE OF THE ASSOCIATION OF LIFE AGENCY OFFICERS FOR THE AMERICAN COLLEGE OF LIFE UNDERWRITERS. *Report* (October, 1937).

CURTI, MERLE, and CARSTENSEN, VERNON. *The University of Wisconsin*, Vol. 1. Madison: University of Wisconsin Press, 1949.

FEDERAL WRITERS' PROJECT. *Wisconsin. A Guide to the Badger State.* New York: Duell, Sloan and Pearce, 1941.

FRANKLIN, BENJAMIN. *Autobiography*. New York: Heritage Press, 1951.

GROSS, MASON. *Rhodes of Africa.* New York: Frederick A. Praeger, 1957.

GRUENBERG, FREDERICK P. "Wharton School and its Middle Westerners," *The General Magazine and Historical Chronicle*, Vol. 57, Nos. 3 and 4 (Spring-Summer, 1955).

HAZARD, WILLIS HATFIELD. "Professor Huebner's 'Economics of Life Insurance,' Including an Appreciation of the Series of Technical Books of Which It Is the Foundation Member," *The Standard*, Vol. 102, No. 21 (May 26, 1928).

HENDRICK, BURTON J. *Story of Life Insurance.* New York: McClure, Phillips and Co., 1907.

HERRING, HUBERT. *Good Neighbors—Argentina, Brazil, Chile and Seventeen Other Countries.* New Haven: Yale University Press, 1941.

HODGE, FREDERICK WEBB (ed.). *Handbook of American Indians.* Bureau of American Ethnology, Bulletin 30, Part 2 N-Z. Washington, D.C.: U.S. Government Printing Office, 1910.

HOME OFFICE LIFE UNDERWRITERS ASSOCIATION. *Proceedings*, Vol. 39. Worcester, Mass.: Commonwealth Press, 1958.

HUEBNER, GROVER G., and KRAMER, ROLAND L. *Foreign Trade: Principles and Practices.* New York: D. Appleton-Century Co., 1935.

HUEBNER, SOLOMON S. *The Economics of Life Insurance.* 3d ed. New York: Appleton-Century-Crofts, Inc., 1959.

———. *Life Insurance: A Textbook.* 1st ed. New York: D. Appleton and Company, 1915.

———. *Marine Insurance.* New York: D. Appleton-Century Co., 1920.

———. *Report on Steamship Agreements and Affiliations in the American Foreign and Domestic Trade*, Vol. 4 in the *Proceedings of the Committee on the Merchant Marine and Fisheries in the Investigation of Shipping Conditions under H. Res. 587*. Washington, D.C.: U.S. Government Printing Office, 1914.

———. "Theft and Pilferage in the Export and Import Trade," *Bulletin of the Pan-American Union* (March, 1922), pp. 220–27.

———. "Historical Background of the American Institute for Property and Liability Underwriters, Inc.," *Proceedings of the American Association of University Teachers of Insurance*, Vol. 9, No. 1 (March, 1942).

———. "Report on the First Year of Operations of the American Institute for Property and Liability Underwriters, Inc.," *Proceedings of the American Association of University Teachers of Insurance*, Vol. 11, No. 1 (March, 1944).

———. "A Report of Progress of the American Institute for Property and Liability Underwriters, Inc.," *Proceedings of the American Association of University Teachers of Insurance*, Vol. 10, No. 1 (March, 1943).

———. *The Stock Market*. New York: D. Appleton and Co., 1922.

———. (ed.). "Bonds and the Bond Market," *Annals of the American Academy of Political and Social Science*, Vol. 88 (March, 1920).

THE S. S. HUEBNER FOUNDATION FOR INSURANCE EDUCATION. *Announcement*. Philadelphia, 1941.

HUNT, HEROLD C. *Education in Family Finance: the First Ten Years*. New York: National Committee for Education in Family Finance, 1959.

HURLEY, EDWARD N. *The Bridge to France*. Philadelphia: J. B. Lippincott Co., 1927.

Insurance Field, December 12, 1958.

Insurance Lecture Series, Spring 1954. Storrs, Conn.: School of Business Administration, University of Connecticut, 1954.

Insurance Review (Japanese), Vol. 10, Nos. 5, 8, 11. (May, July, September, 1958).

JOHNSON, EMORY R. *The Wharton School. Its First Fifty Years, 1881–1931*. Philadelphia: Privately printed for the Wharton School, 1931.

JOHNSON, EMORY R.; HUEBNER, GROVER G., and WILSON, G. LLOYD. *Transportation: Economic Principles and Practices*. New York: D. Appleton-Century Co., Inc., 1940.

Journal of the American Society of Chartered Life Underwriters, Vol. 1 (March, 1947), Vol. 6 (June, 1952).

Journal of Insurance, Vol. 24 (December, 1957).

KELSEY, R. WILFRED. "Report of the Division of Education in Family Finance," *Annual Meeting and Staff Reports*. New York: Institute of Life Insurance, 1958.

"Kossuth, Louis." *Encyclopedia Americana*, Vol. 16. New York: Americana Corp., 1946.

LEEMING, JOSEPH. *Ships and Cargoes*. Garden City: Doubleday, Page & Co., 1926.

MACLEAN, JOSEPH B. *Life Insurance*. 6th ed. New York: McGraw-Hill Book Co., Inc., 1951.

MASON, GREGORY. *Columbus Came Late*. New York: Century Company, 1931.

MCCAHAN, DAVID. "Solomon Stephen Huebner . . . Down Through the Years." Biographical sketch in dinner program in honor of Dr. Huebner, Philadelphia, September 26, 1940.

———. (ed.). *Life Insurance Trends at Mid-Century*. Philadelphia: University of Pennsylvania Press, 1950.

MCCAHAN, DAVID, and GREGG, D. W. "A Collection of Huebnerian Philosophy," *Journal of the American Society of Chartered Life Underwriters*, Vol. 6 (June, 1952).

MCDOWELL, CARL E., and GIBBS, HELEN M. *Ocean Transportation*. New York: McGraw-Hill Book Co., Inc., 1954.

MCGILL, DAN M. *Fundamentals of Private Pensions*. Homewood, Ill.: Richard D. Irwin, Inc., 1955.

MEHR, ROBERT I., and OSLER, ROBERT W. *Modern Life Insurance*. New York: Macmillan Co., 1949.

MUTUAL BENEFIT LIFE INSURANCE COMPANY. *The Pelican*, Vol. 18 (1920), Vol. 19 (1921).

NATIONAL ASSOCIATION OF LIFE UNDERWRITERS. *Proceedings*. New York: 1914–1935.

ROOSEVELT, THEODORE. *American Problems*. New York: Charles Scribner's Sons, 1926.

SCOYEN, EIVIND T., and TAYLOR, FRANK L. *The Rainbow Canyons*. Stanford, Calif.: Stanford University Press, 1931.

SMITH, DARRELL H. and BETTERS, PAUL V. *The United States Shipping Board. Its History, Activities and Organization*. Service Monographs of the United States Government No. 63. Washington, D.C.: Brookings Institute, 1931.

STALSON, J. OWEN. *Marketing Life Insurance*. Cambridge, Mass.: Harvard University Press, 1942.

STASSEN, HAROLD E. "Dr. Solomon S. Huebner," *Journal of the American Society of Chartered Life Underwriters*, Vol. 6 (June, 1952).

Statement on Life Insurance, filed with the Temporary National Economic Committee, August, 1940, by 151 companies representing 60 per cent of the assets of American life insurance. Copy in the files of the Mutual Benefit Life Insurance Company.

STONE, MILDRED F. *A Short History of Life Insurance*. Indianapolis: The Insurance Research and Review Service, 1947.

Testimonial Dinner to Dr. Solomon Stephen Huebner at Bellevue-Stratford Hotel, September 26, 1940. Contemporary verbatim report in manuscript.

TURNER, FREDERICK JACKSON. *The Early Writings of Frederick Jackson Turner*. Madison: University of Wisconsin Press, 1938.

WARD, WILLIAM R. *Down the Years*. Newark, N.J.: Privately printed by The Mutual Benefit Life Insurance Company, 1932.

WINTER, WILLIAM D. *Marine Insurance: Its Principles and Practice*. New York: McGraw-Hill Book Co., 1929.

WOODS, LAWRENCE C., JR. *The First Decade*. Philadelphia: The National Chapter—Chartered Life Underwriters, 1937.

Author's Annotations

(Sources as Listed in the Complete Bibliography)

Chapter 3. P. 38*n*. F. J. Turner, *Early Writings*, p. 199.

Chapter 4. P. 46. E. R. Johnson, *Wharton School*, pp. 11 and 12.
P. 47. E. P. Cheyney, *History*, p. 289.
P. 48. *Ibid.*, p. 289.
P. 50. *Ibid.*, pp. 289, 290.
P. 58. Theodore Roosevelt, *American Problems*, p. 418.

Chapter 6. P. 74. David McCahan, "Solomon Stephen Huebner."
P. 81. E. R. Johnson, *Wharton School*, p. 31.
P. 90. *Ibid.*, pp. 36, 37.
P. 91. *Ibid.*, pp. 54, 55.

Chapter 7. P. 97. S. S. Huebner, *The Stock Market*, pp. 53, 57.
P. 100. Letter to the author, August 12, 1959.
P. 103. Editorial, *The Pelican*, Vol. 19, p. 321.
S. S. Huebner, *Economics of Life Insurance*, p. 198.

Chapter 8. P. 106. S. S. Huebner, *Steamship Agreements*, p. 9.
P. 109. *Ibid.*, p. 21.
Ibid., p. 41.
P. 110. *Ibid.*, p. 48.
Pp. 110–12. *Ibid.*, pp. 49–51.
P. 115. E. N. Hurley, *Bridge to France*, pp. 75, 76.
P. 117. S. S. Huebner, *Marine Insurance*, p. 203.
P. 119. *Ibid.*, p. 255.
P. 121. *The Eastern Underwriter*, April 29, 1921, pp. 16, 17.

Chapter 9. Pp. 127–31. S. S. Huebner, *25th Proceedings—N.A.-L.U.*, pp. 67–80.
P. 132. E. J. Clark, *26th Proceedings—N.A.L.U.*, p. 170.
P. 134. S. S. Huebner, *Life Insurance*, p. 428.
P. 137. *The Eastern Underwriter*, February 21, 1919, p. 12.
Ibid., March 19, 1920, p. 12.

P. 138. *Ibid.*, April 2, 1920, p. 25.
Ibid., May 7, 1920, p. 26.
P. 139. *Ibid.*, p. 12.
Ibid., March 5, 1920, p. 11.
Pp. 140–44. S. S. Huebner, *The Pelican*, Vol. 18, pp. 354, 388, 389.

Chapter 10. P. 145. S. S. Huebner, *Life Insurance*, p. 13.
Pp. 146–50. S. S. Huebner, *35th Proceedings—N.A.-L.U.*, pp. 17–40.

Chapter 11. P. 155. E. J. Clark, "The Founding of the American College," p. 195.
P. 157. *Ibid.*, pp. 198, 199.
Pp. 159–61. W. H. Hazard, "Professor Huebner's 'Economics of Life Insurance,'" pp. 987, 988.
Pp. 162–63. E. A. Woods, *38th Proceedings—N.A.L.U.*, pp. 362, 363, 365–67.
Pp. 167–69. S. S. Huebner, *39th Proceedings—N.A.-L.U.*, pp. 95–97.
P. 169. J. S. Myrick, *Ibid.*, p. 12.
P. 170. L. C. Woods, *The First Decade*, pp. 14, 15.

Chapter 12. P. 192. Committee of Life Agency Officers, *Report*, p. 1.
Ibid., pp. 3–8.

Chapter 13. P. 195. Testimonial dinner report, p. 1.
P. 196. *Ibid.*, p. 8.
P. 198. *Ibid.*, pp. 17, 18.
Pp. 199–201. *Ibid.*, pp. 22, 23.
P. 201. *The Eastern Underwriter*, October 4, 1940, p. 19.
P. 203–5. S. S. Huebner Foundation, *Announcement*, pp. 3–6.

Chapter 14. Pp. 211, 212. S. S. Huebner, "A Report of Progress," p. 2.
P. 214. *Ibid.*, pp. 6, 7.
P. 215. S. S. Huebner, "Report on First Year of Operations," p. 3.
P. 218. S. S. Huebner, *Life Insurance*, p. 16.
S. S. Huebner, *25th Proceedings—N.A.L.U.*, p. 73.
S. S. Huebner, Verbal statement to the author.

Chapter 15. P. 235. D. M. McGill, *Fundamentals of Private Pension Plans*, p. vi.

P. 236. H. E. Stassen, "Dr. Solomon S. Huebner," p. 199.

Pp. 236–38. David McCahan and D. W. Gregg, "A Collection of Huebnerian Philosophy," pp. 202–13.

Pp. 239, 240. G. L. Hill's autographed manuscript in Dr. Huebner's files.

Pp. 241, 242. *The Eastern Underwriter*, September 12, 1952, p. 2.

Chapter 16. P. 252. S. S. Huebner, *Economics*, p. 19.

P. 255. S. S. Huebner, *Bonds and the Bond Market*, p. 1.

Chapter 17. P. 262. Edward Mellor, C.L.U., letter to the author, December 17, 1958.

P. 264. Helen Millett, letter to the author, January 9, 1959.

Chapter 18. P. 281. S. S. Huebner, "Professional Progress in Insurance Education," pp. 1–3.

P. 282. Roy Hofheinz manuscript in Dr. Huebner's files.

P. 285. Framed scroll in Dr. Huebner's study.

P. 288. Manuscript in Dr. Huebner's files.

P. 292. *The Eastern Underwriter*, September 27, 1957, p. 23.

Pp. 293–96. S. S. Huebner, "Future Patterns of Life Insurance Distribution," pp. 9–20.

Chapter 19. P. 300. J. M. Huebner, *Proceedings of the Home Office Life Underwriters Association*, Vol. 39, pp. 10, 11.

P. 301. S. S. Huebner, *Proceedings of the Home Office Life Underwriters Association*, Vol. 39, p. 12.

Pp. 301–5. *Ibid.*, pp. 27–29.

P. 306. Y. Kunizaki, *Insurance Review*, September, 1958, p. 7.

P. 307. C. Ono, *Insurance Review*, September, 1958, p. 10.

P. 308. H. Itami, *Insurance Review*, September, 1958, p. 13.

Pp. 309–20. From the files of Dr. Gregg.
P. 320. Translation in Dr. Huebner's files.
Pp. 322–29. From the files of Dr. Gregg.
P. 330. Copy in Dr. Huebner's files.

Chapter 20. Pp. 333–35. *Insurance Field*, December 12, 1958, p. 16.
P. 336. "C.L.U. Diploma Presentation," p. 16. Quotation supplied by Mrs. Carlsen.
P. 338. Dr. Gregg in letter to American College and Society Trustees, April 13, 1959.
Pp. 340, 341. S. S. Huebner, *Economics of Life Insurance*, pp. 229–31.

Index

I

This book has been set on the Linotype in 12 point and 10 point Bodoni Book, leaded 2 points. Chapter numbers are in 10 point Caledonia Bold; chapter titles are in 24 point Dom Casual. The size of the type page is 24 by 42 picas.